Beginning VB 2008 Databases

From Novice to Professional

Vidya Vrat Agarwal and
James Huddleston

Apress®

Beginning VB 2008 Databases: From Novice to Professional

Copyright © 2008 by Vidya Vrat Agarwal and James Huddleston

ISBN-13 (pbk): 978-1-59059-947-1

ISBN-10 (pbk): 1-59059-947-0

ISBN-13 (electronic): 978-1-4302-0560-9

ISBN-10 (electronic): 1-4302-0560-1

Printed and bound in the United States of America 9 8 7 6 5 4 3 2 1

Lead Editor: Dominic Shakeshaft
Technical Reviewer: Fabio Claudio Ferracchiati
Editorial Board: Clay Andres, Steve Anglin, Ewan Buckingham, Tony Campbell, Gary Cornell,
    Jonathan Gennick, Matthew Moodie, Joseph Ottinger, Jeffrey Pepper, Frank Pohlmann,
    Ben Renow-Clarke, Dominic Shakeshaft, Matt Wade, Tom Welsh
Senior Project Manager: Sofia Marchant
Copy Editor: Liz Welch
Associate Production Director: Kari Brooks-Copony
Senior Production Editor: Laura Cheu
Compositor: Linda Weidemann, Wolf Creek Press
Proofreader: Nancy Sixsmith
Indexer: Broccoli Information Management
Artist: April Milne
Cover Designer: Kurt Krames
Manufacturing Director: Tom Debolski

Distributed to the book trade worldwide by Springer-Verlag New York, Inc., 233 Spring Street, 6th Floor, New York, NY 10013. Phone 1-800-SPRINGER, fax 201-348-4505, e-mail orders-ny@springer-sbm.com, or visit http://www.springeronline.com.

For information on translations, please contact Apress directly at 2855 Telegraph Avenue, Suite 600, Berkeley, CA 94705. Phone 510-549-5930, fax 510-549-5939, e-mail info@apress.com, or visit http://www.apress.com.

Apress and friends of ED books may be purchased in bulk for academic, corporate, or promotional use. eBook versions and licenses are also available for most titles. For more information, reference our Special Bulk Sales–eBook Licensing web page at http://www.apress.com/info/bulksales.

To my sweet little daughter (Pearly) and beloved wife (Rupali).

You are precious in my eyes,
and honored, and I love you.

—Vidya Vrat Agarwal

Contents at a Glance

Contents

About the Authors

 **VIDYA VRAT AGARWAL**, is a Microsoft .NET Purist and an MCT, MCPD, MCTS, MCSD.NET, MCAD.NET, and MCSD. He works with Lionbridge Technologies and his business card reads *Subject Matter Expert (SME)*. He is also a lifetime member of the Computer Society of India (CSI). He started working on Microsoft .NET with its beta release. Vidya has been involved in software development, evangelism, consultation, corporate training, and T3 programs on Microsoft .NET for various employers and corporate clients. You can read his articles at www.ProgrammersHeaven.com, and he also reviews the .NET Preparation Kits available at www.ucertify.com. He has contributed as technical reviewer to many books published by Apress; he is also the author of another Apress book titled *Beginning C# 2008 Databases: From Novice to Professional*.

Vidya lives with his beloved wife Rupali and lovely daughter Vamika ("Pearly"). He believes that nothing will turn into a reality without them. He is the follower of the concept "No pain, no gain," and believes that his wife is his greatest strength. He is a bibliophile; when he is not working on technical stuff, he likes to spend time with his family and also likes reading spiritual and occult science books. Vidya blogs at http://dotnetpassion.blogspot.com.

JAMES HUDDLESTON has worked with computers since 1974, specializing in database design and development since 1980. He has a bachelor's degree in Latin and Greek from the University of Pennsylvania and a juris doctor degree from the University of Pittsburgh. A technical reviewer of dozens of computer books, including *Beginning C# Objects: From Concepts to Code* (Apress, 2004), he finds databases an endlessly fascinating area of work and almost as intellectually rewarding as his hobby: translating Homer's *Iliad* and *Odyssey* from the original Greek.

About the Technical Reviewer

FABIO CLAUDIO FERRACCHIATI is a senior consultant and a senior analyst/developer using Microsoft technologies. He works for Brain Force (www.brainforce.com) in its Italian branch (www.brainforce.it). He is a Microsoft Certified Solution Developer for .NET, a Microsoft Certified Application Developer for .NET, and a Microsoft Certified Professional, as well as a prolific author and technical reviewer. Over the past ten years he's written articles for Italian and international magazines and coauthored more than ten books on a variety of computer topics. You can read his LINQ blog at www.ferracchiati.com.

Acknowledgments

Though my name appears on the cover page of the book, I am not alone in achieving this. There are many people who have been directly, or indirectly, associated with me throughout my journey of writing this book. Let me have this opportunity to thank them all one by one.

Thanks to the Apress team I have worked with directly. To Sofia Marchant, the project manager: thanks, Sofia, for all your patience and support throughout this book. Thanks to Dominic Shakeshaft, my editor, who has reviewed my work. Thanks to Liz Welch, the copy editor; she has been so helpful in finding the errors that could have easily been missed by anyone but that would have made a huge impact if not corrected. Thanks to Laura Cheu from the production team for giving me an opportunity to look at the final chapters that were the result of her hard work. I would also like to thank all those people from Apress with whom I have not interacted but who are associated with this book, such as graphic artists, printers, and so forth. Thank you, guys.

Thanks to my technical reviewer, Fabio Claudio Ferracchiati, for his thorough review of the script and for testing the code. He has been so objective in finding any issues and helping me to come up with something even better.

Thanks to my parents and my parent in-law for always wishing the best for me and having unbreakable faith in me.

Finally, my heartfelt thanks to those two who have been with me throughout this one-year-long journey when I was only focused on book authoring; they are the integral part of my life: my wife Rupali and my two-and-a-half-year-old daughter Vamika (Pearly)—many thanks to you both for all the support you have shown by staying awake those late nights to keep me company so I wouldn't feel sleepy and for giving me a peaceful environment in which to concentrate—and of course, for those many cups of tea with sweet smiles as well. Thanks for sacrificing all those weekends until I reached the end of the book and for always motivating and supporting me to complete the chapters and meet the deadlines. My sweet little daughter, I remember all those moments when you were so desperate to play with me but I could not look up from my laptop screen, and you have also been such a darling doll, like your mom, to leave with a smile. Thanks for everything, especially for being in my life. I would not have achieved anything without you; thanks for being my inspiration and strength. I owe a lot of time, much more love to you, my angels, and I love you.

Also, big, big thanks to the great God and my late grandparents for showering their blessings on me. I promise to be the best kid of yours.

Introduction

As most of the real-world applications interact with the data stored in relational databases, so every VB programmer needs to know how to access data. This book specifically covers how to interact with SQL Server 2005 databases using VB 2008. This book also covers LINQ and ADO.NET 3.5, the most exciting features of .NET Framework 3.5. The chapters that focus on the database concepts will help you understand the database concepts as if you'd learned them from a pure database concepts book. I have also covered many new features of T-SQL that SQL Server 2005 has brought in.

The book has been written in such a way that it will be easily understood by beginners and professionals alike. If you want to learn Visual Studio 2008 to build database applications, then this is the right book for you. It will not only walk you through all the concepts that an application developer may have to use, but will also explain what each piece of code you will write does.

The chapters in this book are organized in such a manner that you will build a strong foundation before moving on to the next higher-level chapter.

Who This Book Is For

If you are an application developer who likes to interact with databases using C#, then this book is for you—it covers programming SQL Server 2005 using VB 2008.

This book does not require or even assume that you have a sound knowledge of VB 2005, SQL Server 2000, and database concepts. I have written this book in such a way that, even if you don't have any of that background, you can pick up this book and learn. I have covered all the fundamentals that other books assume a reader must have before moving on with the chapters. This book is a must for any application developer who wants to interact with databases using VB 2008 and development tools.

What This Book Covers

This book covers Visual Studio 2008, SQL Server 2005, VB 2008, LINQ, and ADO .NET 3.5. All these tools and technologies are explained using various concepts and code examples. I have also tried to map the type of applications used in this book with the demand of real-life applications, so that you can utilize the concepts that you will learn throughout this book in your professional life.

How This Book Is Organized

This book is organized in such a way that the reader will find all the necessary concepts in the previous chapter before moving on to the next chapter. I have also taken care to avoid including references to the chapters that I will cover in the latter part of the book, so readers can concentrate on that chapter completely rather than switching their focus among the chapters to cover the concepts.

The concepts explained in each chapter have been explained with code examples under the section "Try It Out," followed by another section, "How It Works," which will help you understand each code statement and its purpose.

How to Download the Sample Code

All the source code is available in the Source Code/Download section at www.apress.com.

Contacting the Author

You can reach Vidya Vrat Agarwal at Vidya_mct@yahoo.com or visit his blog at http://dotnetpassion.blogspot.com.

CHAPTER 1

■■■

Getting Your Tools

This book is designed to help you learn how to access databases with VB 2008, previously known as VB 9.0 and VB Orcas. The development tools used throughout this book are Microsoft Visual Studio 2008 (code-named Visual Studio Orcas) and Microsoft SQL Server 2005 Express Edition, both of which work with Microsoft .NET Framework version 3.5. This latest version of .NET also provides extensive support for Language Integrated Query (LINQ), and because it is an extension of the .NET Framework 3.0 (previously known as WinFX), it supports NET 3.0 features such as Windows Presentation Foundation (WPF), Windows Communication Foundation (WCF), and Windows Workflow Foundation (WF).

Microsoft Visual Studio 2008, the latest version of Visual Studio, provides functionality for building WPF, WCF, WF, and LINQ applications by using VB 2008 or other .NET languages. Visual Studio 2008 targets multiple .NET Framework versions by allowing you to build and maintain applications for .NET 2.0 and .NET 3.0 in addition to its native and default support for .NET 3.5.

Note Code names are interesting things. For example, the .NET common language runtime (CLR) was code-named Lightning because it was another milestone for Microsoft after its best-selling technology Visual Basic, which has been around since 1991 and was code-named Thunder.

Visual Studio products have a specific code-name methodology based on some cities in and islands of the United States. Orcas is one of the San Juan islands, located north of Seattle.

SQL Server 2005 is one of the most advanced relational database management systems (RDBMSs) available. An exciting feature of SQL Server 2005 is the integration of the .NET CLR into the SQL Server 2005 database engine, making it possible to implement database objects using managed code written in a .NET language such as Visual C# .NET or Visual Basic .NET. Besides this, SQL Server 2005 comes with multiple services such as analysis services, data transformation services, reporting services, notification services, and Service Broker. SQL Server 2005 offers one common environment, named SQL Server Management Studio, for both database developers and database administrators (DBAs).

■**Note** If you ever worked with SQL Server 2000, you'll recall there are two separate interfaces named SQL Server Query Analyzer and SQL Server Enterprise Manager (the latter also known as Microsoft Management Console, or MMC), which are specifically designed for database developers and database administrators, respectively.

SQL Server 2005 Express Edition is the relational database subset of SQL Server 2005 that provides virtually all the online transaction processing (OLTP) capabilities of SQL Server 2005, supports databases up to 4GB in size (and up to 32,767 databases per SQL Server Express, or SSE, instance), and can handle hundreds of concurrent users. SSE doesn't include SQL Server's data warehousing and Integration Services components. It also doesn't include business intelligence components for online analytical processing (OLAP) and data mining, because they're based on SQL Server's Analysis Services server, which is completely distinct from its relational database engine.

SQL Server 2005 Express Edition is also completely distinct from its predecessor, Microsoft SQL Server Desktop Engine (MSDE), which was a subset of SQL Server 2000. MSDE databases cannot be used with SSE, but they can be upgraded to SSE databases.

Now that you know a little about these development tools, we'll show you how to obtain and install them and the sample databases you'll need to work through this book. In this chapter, we'll cover the following:

- Obtaining Visual Studio 2008

- Installing SQL Server Management Studio Express

- Installing the Northwind sample database

- Installing the AdventureWorks sample database

Obtaining Visual Studio 2008

As mentioned previously, working through the examples in this book requires Visual Studio 2008 to be installed on your PC. To find information about Visual Studio 2008 and where to get the setup CDS and so forth, go to `http://msdn.microsoft.com/vstudio`.

You can also directly download the installer ISO image files from the MSDN Subscriptions site (`http://msdn.microsoft.com`). Access the downloadable setup files by clicking the Visual Studio link in the Developer Center, and then extract the downloaded file and run `Setup.exe`.

If you have a setup DVD or CDs of Visual Studio 2008, just put the DVD or CD into your PC's disk drive and complete the setup by following the instructions, making sure that you have enough disk space on your C drive.

Installing SQL Server Management Studio Express

To install SQL Server Management Studio Express for the purpose of working through the examples in this book, follow these steps:

1. Go to `http://www.microsoft.com/downloads` and in the search text box enter **SQL Server Management Studio**.

2. In the returned results, you should see a link at the top titled Microsoft SQL Server Management Studio Express. Click this link to go to the download page.

3. On the download page, click the Download button to download the SQL Server Management Studio Express installer file `SQLServer2005_SSMSEE.msi`.

4. Save this file to a location on your host PC (such as on the desktop). When the download of the file is complete, click Close.

5. Run the `SQLServer2005_SSMSEE.msi` setup file to start the installation process. The Welcome window shown in Figure 1-1 will appear. Click Next.

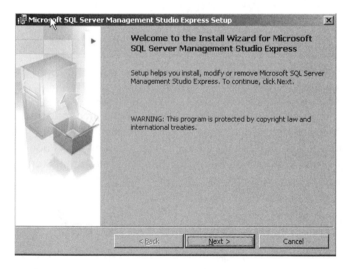

Figure 1-1. *Welcome window for installing SQL Server Management Studio Express*

6. When the License Agreement window appears, click the I Agree radio button, and then click the now-enabled Next button.

7. Fill out the registration information on the next screen by providing your name and company details.

8. When the Feature Selection window appears, click Next.

9. In the Ready to Install the Program window, click Install to begin installation. You will see a progress bar that indicates the status of the installation (see Figure 1-2).

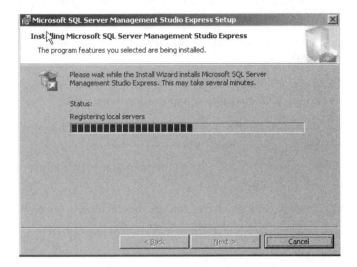

Figure 1-2. *SQL Server Management Studio Express installation in progress*

10. When the Completing the SQL Server Management Setup window appears, click the Finish button.

Because SQL Server Management Studio Express comes without a preconfigured database, you need to download and configure databases to be used inside SQL Server Management Studio Express to follow the examples in this book. The next section talks about installing and configuring the first of two databases in SQL Server Management Studio Express, Northwind.

Installing the Northwind Sample Database

Next, you will download the Northwind sample database to be used with SQL Server Management Studio Express.

Installing the Northwind Creation Script

To install the script that creates the Northwind sample database, follow these steps:

1. Go to http://www.microsoft.com/downloads and in the search text box enter **sample database**.

2. In the returned results, you should see a link near the top titled "NorthWind and pubs Sample Databases for SQL Server 2000." Click this link to go to the download page.

3. Click the Download button to download SQL2000SampleDb.msi, and click Save in the dialog box that appears.

4. Specify your installation location (such as the desktop) and click Save. When the download is complete, click Close.

5. Run the SQL2000SampleDb.msi file to start the installation process. The Welcome window shown in Figure 1-3 will appear. Click Next.

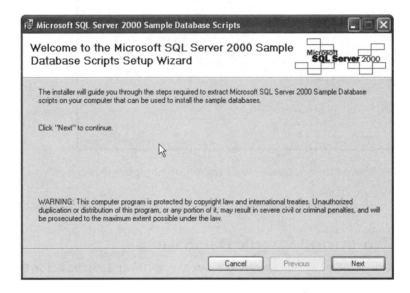

Figure 1-3. *Northwind installation scripts Setup Wizard Welcome window*

6. When the License Agreement window appears, click the I Agree radio button, and then click the now-enabled Next button.

7. When the Choose Installation Options window appears, click Next.

8. When the Confirm Installation window appears, click Next.

9. A progress window briefly appears, followed by the Installation Complete window (see Figure 1-4). Click Close.

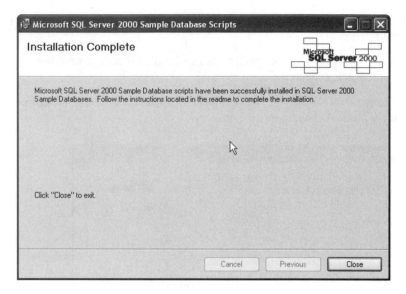

Figure 1-4. *Northwind installation scripts Installation Complete window*

The installation files have been extracted to C:\SQL Server 2000 Sample Databases.

Creating the Northwind Sample Database

You need to run a Transact-SQL (T-SQL) script to create the Northwind database. You'll do that with the SQL Server command-line utility sqlcmd.

To create the Northwind sample database, follow these steps:

1. Open a command prompt, and then go to the C:\ SQL Server 2000 Sample Databases directory, which contains the instnwnd.sql file.

2. Enter the following command, making sure to use -S, not -s:

```
sqlcmd -S .\sqlexpress -i instnwnd.sql
```

This should produce the output shown in Figure 1-5.

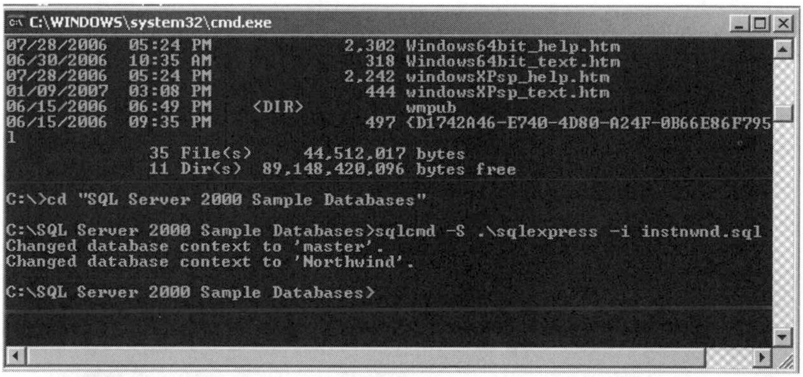

Figure 1-5. *Creating the Northwind database*

This command executes the sqlcmd program, invoking it with two options. The first option, -S .\sqlexpress, tells sqlcmd to connect to the SQLEXPRESS instance of SQL Server Express on the local machine (represented by .). The second option, -i <instnwnd.sql>, tells sqlcmd to read the file instnwnd.sql and execute the T-SQL in it.

■**Tip** Visual Studio 2008 comes with an SSE instance, so sqlcmd can connect to SSE. A Windows service named MSSQL$SQLEXPRESS gets created during the installation of SSE, and it should automatically start, so the SQLEXPRESS instance should already be running. If sqlcmd complains that it can't connect, you can start the service from a command prompt with the command net start mssql$sqlexpress.

To make sure the Northwind sample database has been created successfully, try accessing it. You'll use sqlcmd interactively.

1. At the command prompt, enter the following command, which runs sqlcmd and connects to the SQLEXPRESS instance (see Figure 1-6):

```
sqlcmd -S .\sqlexpress
```

Figure 1-6. *Connecting to SQLEXPRESS with* sqlcmd

2. At the sqlcmd prompt (1>), enter the following T-SQL:

```
use northwind
select count(*) from employees
go
```

The first two lines are T-SQL statements: USE specifies the database to query, and SELECT asks for the number of rows in the Employees table. GO is not a T-SQL statement but a sqlcmd command that signals the end of the T-SQL statements to process. The result, that there are nine rows in Employees, is shown in Figure 1-7.

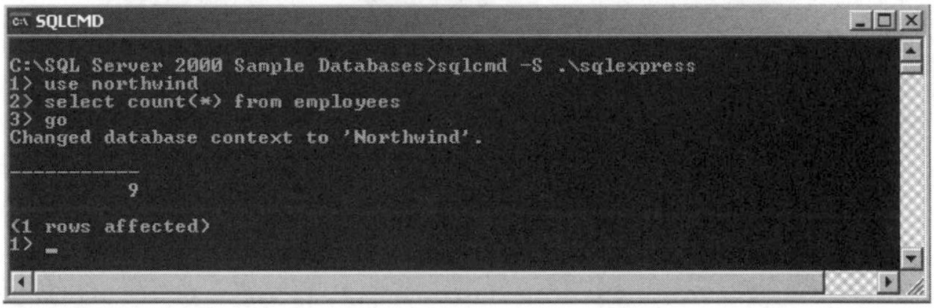

Figure 1-7. *Running a simple query against the Northwind database*

3. Enter the sqlcmd command quit to exit sqlcmd (see Figure 1-8).

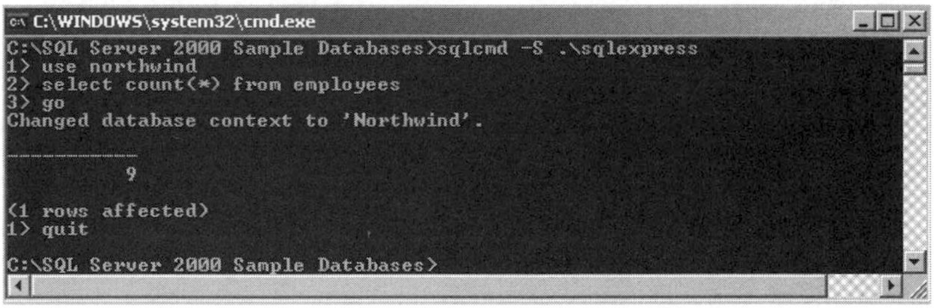

Figure 1-8. *Exiting* sqlcmd

■**Note** We don't cover sqlcmd further, since we submit SQL with SQL Server Management Studio Express from this point on, but we recommend you play with it. It's the latest command-line tool for SQL Server, superseding the earlier osql and isql tools, and it's still a very valuable tool for database administrators and programmers.

Installing the AdventureWorks Sample Database

For the purposes of this book, you also must install the AdventureWorks database for SQL Server 2005. This database, which contains data for a fictitious cycling company, is a totally new one specially designed and developed for SQL Server 2005 only. To start, you first install the AdventureWorks creation script, and then you create the database.

Installing the AdventureWorks Creation Script

To install the creation script for the AdventureWorks sample database, follow these steps:

1. Navigate to the following URL: `www.codeplex.com/MSFTDBProdSamples/Release/ProjectReleases.aspx?ReleaseId=5705`.

2. On the displayed page under the Files section, click `AdventureWorksDB.msi`. Accept the license when prompted.

3. In the dialog box that opens, click Save, specify your install folder (such as the host machine's desktop), and click Save.

4. When the download is complete, click Close.

5. Now run the `AdventureWorksDB.msi` file to start the installation process. A message box will be followed by the Welcome window (see Figure 1-9). Click Next.

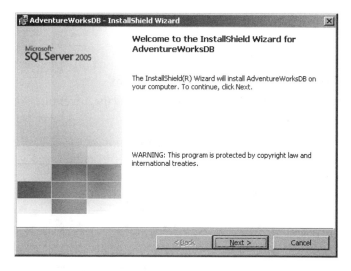

Figure 1-9. *AdventureWorks InstallShield Wizard Welcome window*

6. When the License Agreement window appears, click the I Accept radio button, and then click the now-enabled Next button.

7. When the Destination Folder window appears, click Next.

8. When the Ready to Install the Program window appears, click Install.

9. A progress window briefly appears, followed by the InstallShield Wizard Completed window (see Figure 1-10). Click Finish.

Figure 1-10. *AdventureWorks database installation is complete.*

The installation files have been extracted to `C:\Program Files\Microsoft SQL Server\`
`MSSQL.1\MSSQL\Data`.

Creating the AdventureWorks Sample Database

You need to access SQL Server Management Studio Express to create the AdventureWorks database. To do so, follow these steps:

1. Open SQL Server Management Studio Express, and in the Connect to Server dialog box, ensure that *<YOUR_SERVER_NAME>* is shown as the server name (see Figure 1-11). Click Connect.

■**Note** The server name we use throughout this book is ORCASBETA2_VSTS. You may choose to use some other server on your PC.

---

2. SQL Server Management Studio Express will open as shown in Figure 1-12. Right-click the Databases node in Object Explorer (located on the left side), and click Attach in the context menu.

Figure 1-11. *Connecting to the server*

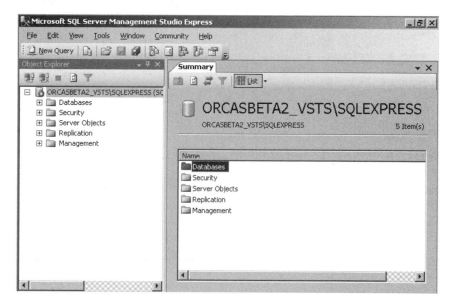

Figure 1-12. *SQL Server Management Studio Express*

3. In the Attach Database window, click Add.

4. In the Locate Database Files window, select the file AdventureWorks_Data.mdf and click OK. The Attach Database window will now have the AdventureWorks_Data.mdf and AdventureWorks_Log.ldf files mapped; these are required for AdventureWorks to be attached (see Figure 1-13). Click OK.

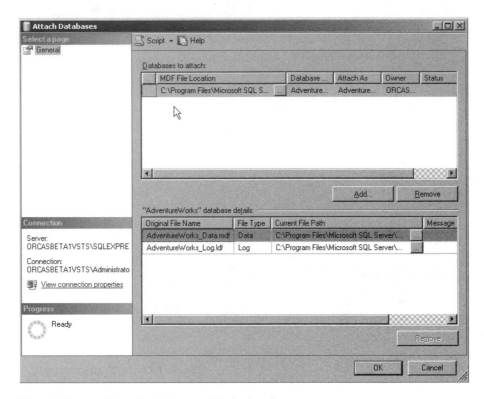

Figure 1-13. *Attaching the AdventureWorks database*

5. Expand the Databases node, and you will see that the AdventureWorks database has been successfully added to this node, as shown in Figure 1-14.

■**Note** Also notice that the Northwind database is available in Object Explorer as well, since you installed it earlier.

Now you have all the basic tools you require to move ahead and work through the examples in this book.

Close SQL Server Management Studio Express, and delete the SQLServer2005_SSMSEE.msi, SQL2000SampleDb.msi, and AdventureWorksDB.msi files from the desktop or your specified location.

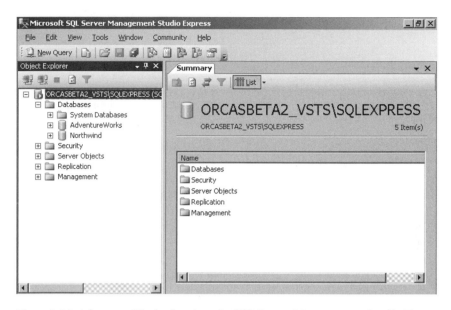

Figure 1-14. *AdventureWorks database in SQL Server Management Studio Express*

Summary

In this chapter, you learned to install Visual Studio 2008, SQL Server Management Studio Express, and the sample Northwind and AdventureWorks databases. You used `sqlcmd` to create and query the Northwind database from a SQLExpress instance. You also used SQL Server Management Studio Express to attach the AdventureWorks database in SQL Server 2005.

Now that you have your tools, it's time to get acquainted with them.

■ ■ ■

CHAPTER 2

Getting to Know Your Tools

Now that you've installed the tools you'll use in this book, we'll show you just enough about them so you can use them easily to do the things you need to do the rest of the way. We'll focus on Visual Studio 2008 and SQL Server Management Studio Express (SSMSE).

In this chapter, we'll cover the following:

- Understanding how versions of Microsoft .NET Framework work in the green bit and red bit assembly model

- Using Microsoft Visual Studio 2008

- Using SQL Server Management Studio Express

Microsoft .NET Framework Versions and the Green Bit and Red Bit Assembly Model

As mentioned in Chapter 1, Visual Studio 2008 supports various .NET Framework versions. To ensure this compatibility, Visual Studio 2008 comes installed with .NET 2.0 and .NET 3.0 along with .NET 3.5. Navigate to C:\WINDOWS\Microsoft.NET\Framework, and you will see individual folders for each .NET Framework version installed, as shown in Figure 2-1.

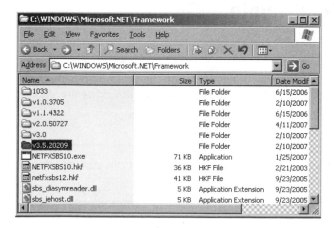

Figure 2-1. *.NET Framework versions installed in Visual Studio 2008*

Having the various .NET Framework versions on a given Visual Studio 2008 system could also be achieved by installing one .NET Framework version on top of another version—for example, .NET 3.0 installed atop .NET 2.0, and then .NET 3.5 installed atop .NET 3.0.

.NET Framework 3.5 holds *green bit assemblies*, which are additional assemblies that can be installed above other existing .NET Framework assemblies without affecting them. For example, installing .NET 3.0 on a .NET 2.0 system does not affect the .NET 2.0 assemblies. In a similar manner, .NET 3.5 assemblies do not affect either .NET 2.0 or 3.0 if you install .NET 3.5 on top of them. See the list of green bit assemblies in Figure 2-2.

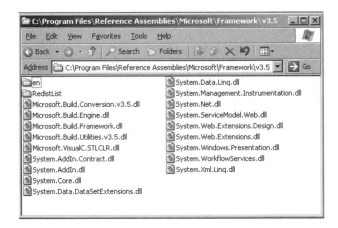

Figure 2-2. *.NET 3.5 green bit assemblies*

Red bit assemblies are the assemblies that ship as either part of the platform or part of a development tool. For example, Windows Vista ships WPF, WCF, and so forth, and Visual Studio 2008 ships .NET 2.0. In addition, assemblies delivered as service packs, hot fixes, or updates are also considered to be red bit assemblies.

Using Microsoft Visual Studio 2008

Now it's time for you to familiarize yourself with the workings of Visual Studio 2008. Follow these steps:

1. Select Start ➤ Programs ➤ Microsoft Visual Studio 2008 and then click Microsoft Visual Studio 2008. You will see a splash screen for Visual Studio 2008, followed by the start page (see Figure 2-3).

■**Note** The first time you load Visual Studio 2008, it may take a little longer to get to the start page than it will eventually, as some initial configurations need to be performed.

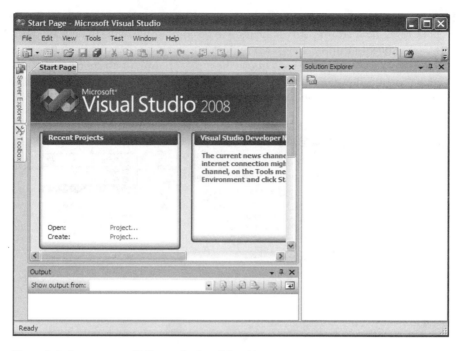

Figure 2-3. *Start page of Microsoft Visual Studio 2008*

2. To take a look at the project templates, click File ➤ New ➤ Project. This opens the New Project window, shown in Figure 2-4, where you will see all the project templates you can use with Visual Basic.

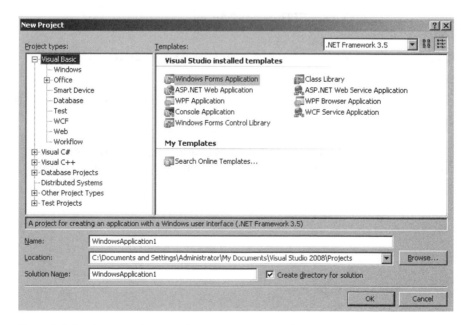

Figure 2-4. *Project templates in the New Project window*

3. While selecting your desired project template, you can also choose the .NET Framework version you want your application to be compatible with. To develop .NET 2.0– or 3.0–specific applications in Visual Studio 2008, you have to explicitly define the .NET Framework version before you choose the project template. To specify a .NET version, click the drop-down list button just below the title bar and on the right side of the New Project window, as you see in Figure 2-5.

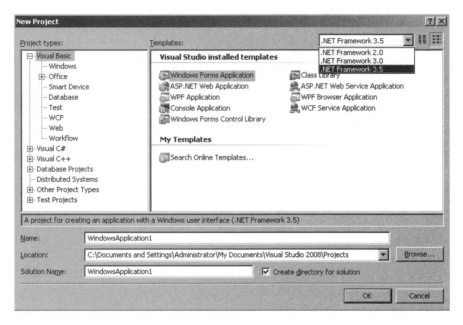

Figure 2-5. *Choosing the .NET Framework version*

Try It Out: Creating a Simple Console Application Project Using Visual Studio 2008

In this example, you'll create a simple Console Application project in Visual Studio 2008:

1. Open Visual Studio 2008 if it's not already open.

2. Click File ➤ New ➤ Project, and select Visual Basic language's Console Application template. In the Name text box of the selected project template, type **FirstApp** (see Figure 2-6) and click OK.

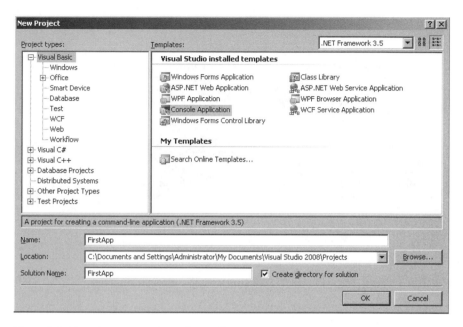

Figure 2-6. *Creating a new Console Application project*

3. Now replace the code of Module1.vb with the code in Listing 2-1.

Listing 2-1. *Replacement Code for* Module1.vb

```
Imports System
Imports System.Linq
Imports System.Collections.Generic
Imports System.Text


    Namespace FirstApp
        Class Program
            Shared Sub Main(ByVal args() As String)
                Console.WriteLine("Welcome to VB 9.0")
                Console.ReadLine()
            End Sub
        End Class
    End Namespace
```

4. Run the application by pressing Ctrl+F5. Your results should appear as shown in Figure 2-7.

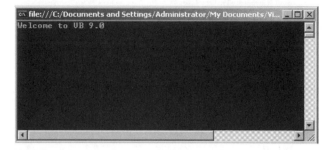

Figure 2-7. *Output of your simple Console Application project*

How It Works

Let's take a look at how the code works, starting with the `using` directives:

```
Imports System
Imports System.Linq
Imports System.Collections.Generic
Imports System.Text
```

The references to `System.Linq`, `System.Collections.Generic`, and `System.Text` are actually not needed in this small program, since you don't explicitly use any of their members, but it's a good habit to always include them, as they are by default part of `Program.cs`.

The following specifies the string to be printed on the console:

```
Console.WriteLine("Welcome to VB 9.0");
```

The following method specifies that output will be shown to you until you press the Enter key:

```
Console.ReadLine();
```

Go ahead and close the Visual Studio environment. Next, we'll get you acquainted with SQL Server Management Studio Express.

Using SQL Server Management Studio Express

SQL Server Management Studio Express is the GUI interface for SQL Server 2005. It combines the features of two earlier SQL Server GUI tools, Enterprise Manager (also known as Microsoft Management Console) and Query Analyzer, to make database administration and T-SQL development possible from a single interface. We use it in the examples in this book primarily to submit T-SQL, but here we'll discuss briefly its Object Explorer feature, which lets you view database objects.

Let's take a quick tour of SSMSE:

1. To open SSMSE, click Start ➤ Programs ➤ Microsoft SQL Server 2005 ➤ SQL Server Management Studio to bring up the window shown in Figure 2-8. Click Connect.

Figure 2-8. *Connecting to SQL Server*

2. A window containing Object Explorer and the Summary tab will appear, and you should be connected to your SQL Server instance named ORCASBETA2_VSTS\ SQLEXPRESS (see Figure 2-9). The top node in Object Explorer should be your SQL Server instance, and the Summary tabbed pane should display folder icons for the five other nodes in Object Explorer. Expand the Databases node in Object Explorer.

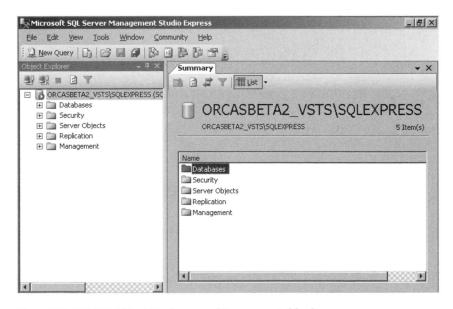

Figure 2-9. *SSMSE Object Explorer and Summary tabbed pane*

3. Expand the System Databases node, and your screen should resemble that shown in Figure 2-10. As you can see, SSMS has four system databases:

- The *master* database is the main controlling database, and it records all the global information that is required for the SQL Server instance.

- The *model* database works as a template for new databases to be created; in other words, settings of the model database will be applied to all user-created databases.

- The *msdb* database is used by SQL Server Agent for scheduling jobs and alerts.

- The *tempdb* database holds temporary tables and other temporary database objects, either generated automatically by SQL Server or created explicitly by you. The temporary database is re-created each time the SQL Server instance is started, so objects in it do not persist after SQL Server is shut down.

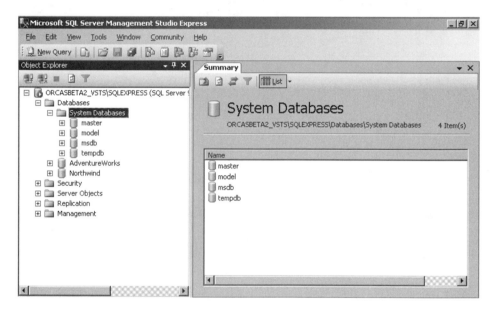

Figure 2-10. *System databases*

4. Click the AdventureWorks node in Object Explorer, and then click New Query to bring up a new SQL edit window, as shown in Figure 2-11. As mentioned in Chapter 1, AdventureWorks is a new sample database introduced for the first time with SQL Server 2005.

5. To see a listing of the tables residing inside AdventureWorks, type the query **select name from sysobjects where xtype='U'** and click the Execute button. The table names will appear in the Results tab (see Figure 2-11). If you navigate to the Messages tab, you will see the message "70 row(s) affected," which means that the AdventureWorks database consists of 70 tables.

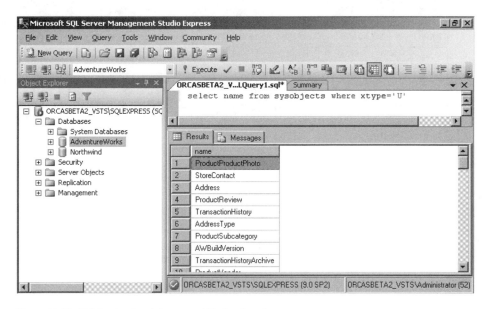

Figure 2-11. *Tables in the AdventureWorks database*

6. Click File ➤ Disconnect Object Explorer.

7. Click the Northwind node in Object Explorer, and then click New Query. To see the table names residing inside Northwind, type the query **select name from sysobjects where xtype='U'** and click the Execute button. A listing of tables in the database will appear in the Results tab (see Figure 2-12). If you navigate to the Messages tab, you will see the message "13 row(s) affected," which means that the Northwind database consists of 13 tables.

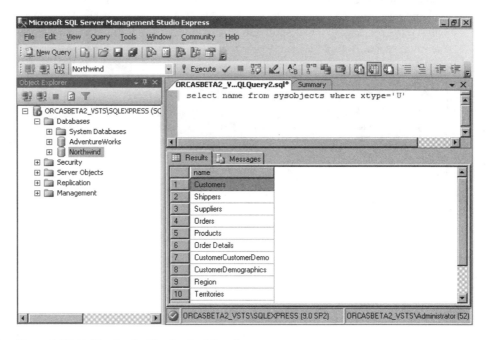

Figure 2-12. *Tables in the Northwind database*

8. Click File ➤ Disconnect Object Explorer, and then close SQL Server Management Studio Express.

Summary

In this chapter, we covered just enough about Visual Studio 2008 and SQL Server Management Studio to get you familiar with the kinds of things you'll do with these tools later in this book. Besides these tools, we also covered a bit about multiple .NET Framework versions on a single system.

Now that your tools are installed and configured, you can start learning how to do database programming by learning the basics of T-SQL.

CHAPTER 3

■■■

Getting to Know Relational Databases

Now that you have gotten to know the tools you'll use in this book, we'll step back a bit to give you a brief introduction to the important concepts of the PC database world before diving into the examples.

In this chapter, we'll cover the following:

- What is a database?

- Choosing between a spreadsheet and a database

- Why use a database?

- Benefits of using a relational database management system

- Comparing desktop and server RDBMS systems

- The database life cycle

- Mapping cardinalities

- Understanding keys

- Understanding data integrity

- Normalization concepts

- Drawbacks of normalization

What Is a Database?

In very simple terms, a *database* is a collection of structured information. Databases are designed specifically to manage large bodies of information, and they store data in an organized and structured manner that makes it easy for users to manage and retrieve that data when required.

A *database management system* (DBMS) is a software program that enables users to create and maintain databases. A DBMS also allows users to write queries for an individual database to perform required actions like retrieving data, modifying data, deleting data, and so forth.

DBMSs support *tables* (a.k.a. *relations* or *entities*) to store data in *rows* (a.k.a. *records* or *tuples*) and *columns* (a.k.a. *fields* or *attributes*), similar to how data appears in a spreadsheet application.

A *relational database management system*, or RDBMS, is a type of DBMS that stores information in the form of related tables. RDBMS is based on the *relational model*.

Choosing Between a Spreadsheet and a Database

If databases are much like spreadsheets, why do people still use database applications? A database is designed to perform the following actions in an easier and more productive manner than a spreadsheet application would require:

- Retrieve all records that match particular criteria.

- Update or modify a complete set of records at one time.

- Extract values from records distributed among multiple tables.

Why Use a Database?

Following are some of the reasons we use databases:

- *Compactness*: Databases help in maintaining large amounts of data, and thus completely replace voluminous paper files.

- *Speed*: Searches for a particular piece of data or information in a database are much faster than sorting through piles of paper.

- *Less drudgery*: Maintaining files by hand is dull work; using a database completely eliminates such maintenance.

- *Currency*: Database systems can easily be updated and so provide accurate information all the time and on demand.

Benefits of Using a Relational Database Management System

RDBMSs offer various benefits by controlling the following:

- *Redundancy*: RDBMSs prevent having multiple duplicate copies of the same data, which takes up disk space unnecessarily.

- *Inconsistency*: Each redundant set of data may no longer agree with other sets of the same data. When an RDBMS removes redundancy, inconsistency cannot occur.

- *Data integrity*: Data values stored in the database must satisfy certain types of consistency constraints. (We'll discuss this benefit in more detail in the section "Understanding Data Integrity" later in this chapter.)

- *Data atomicity*: In event of a failure, data is restored to the consistent state it existed in prior to the failure. For example, fund transfer activity must be atomic. (We cover the fund transfer activity and atomicity in more detail in Chapter 8.)

- *Access anomalies*: RDBMSs prevent more than one user from updating the same data simultaneously; such concurrent updates may result in inconsistent data.

- *Data security*: Not every user of the database system should be able to access all the data. Security refers to the protection of data against any unauthorized access.

- *Transaction processing*: A transaction is a sequence of database operations that represents a logical unit of work. In RDBMSs, a transaction either commits all the changes or rolls back all the actions performed until the point at which failure occurred.

- *Recovery*: Recovery features ensure that data is reorganized into a consistent state after a transaction fails.

- *Storage management*: RDBMSs provide a mechanism for data storage management. The internal schema defines how data should be stored.

Comparing Desktop and Server RDBMS Systems

In the industry today, we mainly work with two types of databases: desktop databases and server databases. Here, we'll give you a brief look at each of them.

Desktop Databases

Desktop databases are designed to serve a limited number of users and run on desktop PCs, and they offer a less-expensive solution wherever a database is required. Chances are you have worked with a desktop database program—Microsoft SQL Server Express, Microsoft Access, Microsoft FoxPro, FileMaker Pro, Paradox, and Lotus represent a wide range of desktop database solutions.

Desktop databases differ from server databases in the following ways:

- *Less expensive*: Most desktop solutions are available for just a few hundred dollars. In fact, if you own a licensed version of Microsoft Office Professional, you're already a licensed owner of Microsoft Access, which is one of the most commonly and widely used desktop database programs around.

- *User friendly*: Desktop databases are quite user friendly and easy to work with, as they do not require complex SQL queries to perform database operations (although some desktop databases also support SQL syntax if you would like to code). Desktop databases generally offer an easy-to-use graphical user interface.

Server Databases

Server databases are specifically designed to serve multiple users at a time and offer features that allow you to manage large amounts of data very efficiently by serving multiple user requests simultaneously. Well-known examples of server databases include Microsoft SQL Server, Oracle, Sybase, and DB2.

Here are some other characteristics that differentiate server databases from their desktop counterparts:

- *Flexibility*: Server databases are designed to be very flexible to support multiple platforms, respond to requests coming from multiple database users, and perform any database management task with optimum speed.

- *Availability*: Server databases are intended for enterprises, and so they need to be available 24/7. To be available all the time, server databases come with some high-availability features, such as mirroring and log shipping.

- *Performance*: Server databases usually have huge hardware support, and so servers running these databases have large amounts of RAM and multiple CPUs, and this is why server databases support rich infrastructure and give optimum performance.

- *Scalability*: This property allows a server database to expand its ability to process and store records even if it has grown tremendously.

The Database Life Cycle

The database life cycle defines the complete process from conception to implementation. The entire development and implementation process of this cycle can be divided into small phases; only after the completion of each phase can you move on to the next phase, and this is the way you build your database block by block.

Before getting into the development of any system, you need to have strong a life-cycle model to follow. The model must have all the phases defined in proper sequence, which will help the development team to build the system with fewer problems and full functionality as expected.

The database life cycle consists of the following stages, from the basic steps involved in designing a global schema of the database-to-database implementation and maintenance:

- *Requirement analysis*: Requirements need to be determined before you can begin design and implementation. The requirements can be gathered by interviewing both the producer and the user of the data; this process helps in creating a formal requirement specification.

- *Logical design*: After requirement gathering, data and relationships need to be defined using a conceptual data modeling technique such as an entity relationship (ER) diagram.

- *Physical design*: Once the logical design is in place, the next step is to produce the physical structure for the database. The physical design phase involves table creation and selection of indexes.

- *Database implementation*: Once the design is completed, the database can be created through implementation of formal schema using the data definition language (DDL) of the RDBMS.

- *Data modification*: Data modification language (DML) can be used to query and update the database as well as set up indexes and establish constraints such as referential integrity.

- *Database monitoring*: As the database begins operation, monitoring indicates whether performance requirements are being met; if they are not, modifications should be made to improve database performance. Thus the database life cycle continues with monitoring, redesign, and modification.

Mapping Cardinalities

Tables are the fundamental components of a relational database. In fact, both data and relationships are stored simply as data in tables.

Tables are composed of rows and columns. Each column represents a piece of information.

Mapping cardinalities, or *cardinality ratios*, express the number of entities to which another entity can be associated via a relationship set. *Cardinality* refers to the uniqueness of data values contained in a particular column of a database table. The term *relational database* refers to the fact that different tables quite often contain related data. For example, one sales rep in a company may take many orders, which were placed by many customers. The products ordered may come from different suppliers, and chances are that each supplier can supply more than one product. All of these relationships exist in almost every database and can be classified as follows:

One-to-One (1:1)   For each row in Table A, there is at most only one related row in Table B, and vice versa. This relationship is typically used to separate data by frequency of use to optimally organize data physically. For example, one department can have only one department head.

One-to-Many (1:M)   For each row in Table A, there can be zero or more related rows in Table B, but for each row in Table B, there is at most one row in Table A. This is the most common relationship. An example of a one-to-many relationship of tables in Northwind is shown in Figure 3-1. Note the Customers table has a CustomerID field as the *primary key* (indicated by the key symbol on the left), which has a relation with the CustomerID field of the Orders table; CustomerID is considered a *foreign key* in the Orders table. The link shown between the Customers and Orders tables indicates a one-to-many relationship, as many orders can belong to one customer. Here, Customers is referred to as the *parent* table, and Orders is the *child* table in the relationship.

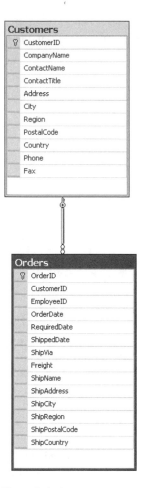

Figure 3-1. *A one-to-many relationship*

Many-to-Many (M:M)   For each row in Table A, there are zero or more related rows in Table B, and vice versa. Many-to-many relationships are not so easy to achieve, and they require a special technique to implement them. This relationship is actually implemented in a one-many-one format, so it requires a third table (often referred to as a *junction table*) to be introduced in between that serves as the path between the related tables.

This is a very common relationship. An example from Northwind is shown in Figure 3-2: an order can have many products and a product can belong to many orders. The Order Details table not only represents the M:M relationship, but also contains data about each particular order-product combination.

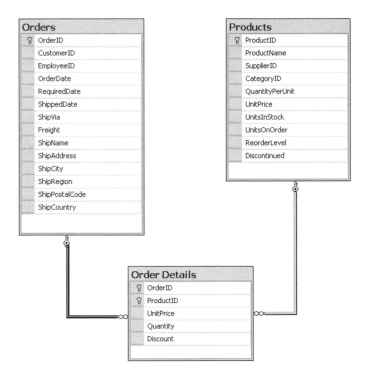

Figure 3-2. *A many-to-many relationship*

■**Note** Though relationships among tables are extremely important, the term *relational database* has nothing to do with them. Relational databases are (to varying extents) based on the *relational model of data* invented by Dr. Edgar F. Codd at IBM in the 1970s. Codd based his model on the mathematical (set-theoretic) concept of a *relation*. Relations are sets of tuples that can be manipulated with a well-defined and well-behaved set of mathematical operations—in fact, two sets: *relational algebra* and *relational calculus*. You don't have to know or understand the mathematics to work with relational databases, but if you hear it said that a database is relational because it "relates data," you'll know that whoever said it doesn't understand relational databases.

Understanding Keys

The key, the whole key, and nothing but the key, so help me Codd.

Relationships are represented by data in tables. To establish a relationship between two tables, you need to have data in one table that enables you to find related rows in another table. That's where *keys* come in, and RDBMSs mainly work with two types of keys, as mentioned earlier: primary keys and foreign keys.

A key is one or more columns of a relation that is used to identify a row.

Primary Keys

A primary key is an attribute (column) or combination of attributes (columns) whose values uniquely identify records in an entity.

Before you choose a primary key for an entity, an attribute must have the following properties:

- Each record of the entity must have a not-null value.

- The value must be unique for each record entered into the entity.

- The values must not change or become null during the life of each entity instance.

- There can be only one primary key defined for an entity.

Besides helping in uniquely identifying a record, the primary key also helps in searching records as an index automatically gets generated as you assign a primary key to an attribute.

An entity will have more than one attribute that can serve as a primary key. Any key or minimum set of keys that could be a primary key is called a *candidate key*. Once candidate keys are identified, choose one, and only one, primary key for each entity.

Sometimes it requires more than one attribute to uniquely identify an entity. A *primary key* that consists of more than one attribute is known as a *composite key*. There can be only one *primary key* in an entity, but a *composite key* can have multiple attributes (i.e., a *primary key* will be defined only once, but it can have up to 16 attributes). The primary key represents the parent entity. Primary keys are usually defined with the IDENTITY property, which allows insertion of an auto-incremented integer value into the table when you insert a row into the table.

Foreign Keys

A foreign key is an attribute that completes a relationship by identifying the parent entity. Foreign keys provide a method for maintaining integrity in the data (called *referential integrity*) and for navigating between different instances of an entity. Every relationship in the model must be supported by a foreign key. For example, in Figure 3-1 earlier, the Customers and Orders tables have a primary key and foreign key relationship, where the Orders table's CustomerID field is the foreign key having a reference to the CustomerID field, which is the primary key of the Customers table.

Understanding Data Integrity

Data integrity means that data values in a database are correct and consistent. There are two aspects to data integrity: *entity integrity* and *referential integrity*.

Entity Integrity

We mentioned previously in "Primary Keys" that no part of a primary key can be null. This is to guarantee that primary key values exist for all rows. The requirement that primary key values exist and that they are unique is known as *entity integrity* (EI). The DBMS enforces *entity integrity* by not allowing operations (INSERT, UPDATE) to produce an invalid primary key. Any operation that creates a duplicate primary key or one containing nulls is rejected. That is, to establish entity integrity, you need to define primary keys so the DBMS can enforce their uniqueness.

Referential Integrity

Once a relationship is defined between tables with foreign keys, the key data must be managed to maintain the correct relationships, that is, to enforce *referential integrity* (RI). RI requires that all foreign key values in a child table either match primary key values in a parent table or (if permitted) be null. This is also known as satisfying a *foreign key constraint*.

Normalization Concepts

Normalization is a technique for avoiding potential update anomalies, basically by minimizing redundant data in a logical database design. Normalized designs are in a sense "better" designs because they (ideally) keep each data item in only one place. Normalized database designs usually reduce update processing costs but can make query processing more complicated. These trade-offs must be carefully evaluated in terms of the required performance profile of a database. Often, a database design needs to be *denormalized* to adequately meet operational needs.

Normalizing a logical database design involves a set of formal processes to separate the data into multiple, related tables. The result of each process is referred to as a *normal form*. Five normal forms have been identified in theory, but most of the time third normal form (3NF) is as far as you need to go in practice. To be in 3NF, a *relation* (the formal term for what SQL calls a table and the precise concept on which the mathematical theory of normalization rests) must already be in second normal form (2NF), and 2NF requires a relation to be in first normal form (1NF). Let's look briefly at what these normal forms mean.

First Normal Form (1NF)   In first normal form, all column values are *scalar*; in other words, they have a single value that can't be further decomposed in terms of the data model. For example, although individual characters of a string can be accessed through a procedure that decomposes the string, only the full string is accessible *by name* in SQL, so, as far as the data model is concerned, they aren't part of the model. Likewise, for a Managers table with a manager column and a column containing a list of employees in Employees table who work for a given manager, the manager and the list would be accessible by name, but the individual employees in the list wouldn't be. All relations—and SQL tables—are by definition in 1NF since the lowest level of accessibility (known as the table's *granularity*) is the column level, and column values are scalars in SQL.

Second Normal Form (2NF)   Second normal form requires that *attributes* (the formal term for SQL columns) that aren't parts of keys be *functionally dependent* on a key that uniquely identifies them. Functional dependence basically means that for a given key value, only one value exists in a table for a column or set of columns. For example, if a table contained employees and their titles, and more than one employee could have the same title (very likely), a key that uniquely identified employees wouldn't uniquely identify titles, so the titles wouldn't be functionally dependent on a key of the table. To put the table into 2NF, you'd create a separate table for titles—with its own unique key—and replace the title in the original table with a foreign key to the new table. Note how this reduces data redundancy. The titles themselves now appear only once in the database. Only their keys appear in other tables, and key data isn't considered redundant (though, of course, it requires columns in other tables and data storage).

Third Normal Form (3NF)   Third normal form extends the concept of functional dependence to *full functional dependence*. Essentially, this means that all nonkey columns in a table are uniquely identified by the whole, not just part of, the primary key. For example, if you revised the hypothetical 1NF Managers-Employees table to have three columns (ManagerName, EmployeeId, and EmployeeName) instead of two, and you defined the composite primary key as ManagerName + EmployeeId, the table would be in 2NF (since EmployeeName, the nonkey column, is dependent on the primary key), but it wouldn't be in 3NF (since EmployeeName is uniquely identified by part of the primary key defined as column named EmployeeId). Creating a separate table for employees and removing EmployeeName from Managers-Employees would put the table into 3NF. Note that even though this table is now normalized to 3NF, the database design is still not as normalized as it should be. Creating another table for managers using an ID shorter than the manager's name, though not required for normalization here, is definitely a better approach and is probably advisable for a real-world database.

Drawbacks of Normalization

Database design is an art more than a technology, and applying normalization wisely is always important. On the other hand, normalization inherently increases the number of tables and therefore the number of operations (called *joins*) required to retrieve data. Because data is not in one table, queries that have a complex join can slow things down. This can cost in the form of CPU usage: the more complex the queries, the more CPU time is required.

Denormalizing one or more tables, by intentionally providing redundant data to reduce the number or complexity of joins to get quicker query response times, may be necessary. With either normalization or denormalization, the goal is to control redundancy so that the database design adequately (and ideally, optimally) supports the actual use of the database.

Summary

This chapter has described basic database concepts. You also learned about desktop and server databases, the stages of the database life cycle, and the types of keys and how they define relationships. You also looked at normalization forms for designing a better database.

In the next chapter, you'll start working with database queries.

CHAPTER 4

■ ■ ■

Writing Database Queries

In this chapter, you will learn about coding queries in SQL Server 2005. SQL Server uses T-SQL as its language, and it has a wide variety of functions and constructs for querying. You will also be exploring new T-SQL features of SQL Server 2005 in this chapter. You will see how to use SQL Server Management Studio Express (SSMSE) and the AdventureWorks and Northwind databases to submit queries.

In this chapter, we'll cover the following:

- Comparing QBE and SQL

- SQL Server Management Studio Express

- Beginning with queries

- Common table expressions

- GROUP BY clause

- PIVOT operator

- ROW_NUMBER() function

- PARTITION BY clause

- Pattern matching

- Aggregate functions

- DATETIME functions

- Joins

Comparing QBE and SQL

Two main languages have emerged for RDBMSs—QBE and SQL.

Query by Example (QBE) is an alternative, graphical-based, point-and-click way of querying a database. QBE was invented by Moshé M. Zloof at IBM Research during the mid-1970s, in parallel to the development of SQL. It differs from SQL in that it has a graphical user interface that allows users to write queries by creating example tables on the screen. QBE is especially suited for queries that are not too complex and can be expressed in terms of a few tables.

QBE was developed at IBM and is therefore an IBM trademark, but a number of other companies also deal with query interfaces like QBE. Some systems, such as Microsoft Access, have been influenced by QBE and have partial support for form-based queries.

Structured Query Language (SQL) is the standard relational database query language. In the 1970s, a group at IBM's San Jose Research Center (now the Almaden Research Center) developed a database system named *System R* based on Codd's model. To manipulate and retrieve data stored in System R, a language called *Structured English Query Language* (SEQUEL) was designed. Donald D. Chamberlin and Raymond F. Boyce at IBM were the authors of the SEQUEL language design. The acronym SEQUEL was later condensed to SQL. SQL was adopted as a standard by the American National Standards Institute (ANSI) in 1986 and then ratified by the International Organization for Standardization (ISO) in 1987; this SQL standard was published as SQL 86, also known as SQL 1. Since then, the SQL standards have gone through many revisions. After SQL 86, there was SQL 89 (which included a minor revision); SQL 92, also known as SQL 2 (which was a major revision); and then SQL 99, also known as SQL 3 (which added object-oriented features that together represent the origination of the concept of ORDBMSs, or object relational database management systems).

Each database vendor offers its own implementation of SQL that conforms at some level to the standard but typically extends it. T-SQL does just that, and some of the SQL used in this book may not work if you try it with a database server other than SQL Server.

■**Tip** Relational database terminology is often confusing. For example, neither the meaning nor the pronunciation of SQL is crystal clear. IBM invented the language back in the 1970s and called it SEQUEL, changing it shortly thereafter to Structured Query Language SQL to avoid conflict with another vendor's product. SEQUEL and SQL were both pronounced "sequel." When the ISO/ANSI standard was adopted, it referred to the language simply as "database language SQL" and was silent on whether this was an acronym and how it should be pronounced. Today, two pronunciations are used. In the Microsoft and Oracle worlds (as well as many others), it's pronounced "sequel." In the DB2 and MySQL worlds (among others), it's pronounced "ess cue ell." We'll follow the most reasonable practice. We're working in a Microsoft environment, so we'll go with "sequel" as the pronunciation of SQL.

Beginning with Queries

A *query* is a technique to extract information from a database. You need a query window into which to type your query and run it so data can be retrieved from the database.

Note Many of the examples from this point forward require you to work in SSMSE. Refer to "Using SQL Server Management Studio Express" in Chapter 2 for instructions if you need to refresh your memory on how to connect to SSMSE.

Try It Out: Running a Simple Query

1. Open SSMSE, expand the Databases node, and select the AdventureWorks database.

2. Click the New Query button in the top-left corner of the window, as shown in Figure 4-1, and then enter the following query:

```
Select * from Sales.SalesReason
```

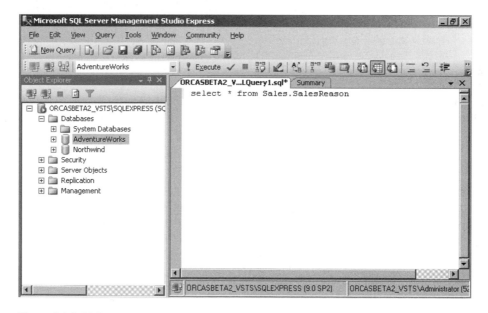

Figure 4-1. *Writing a query*

3. Click Execute (or press F5 or select Query ➤ Execute), and you should see the output shown in the Results window as in Figure 4-2.

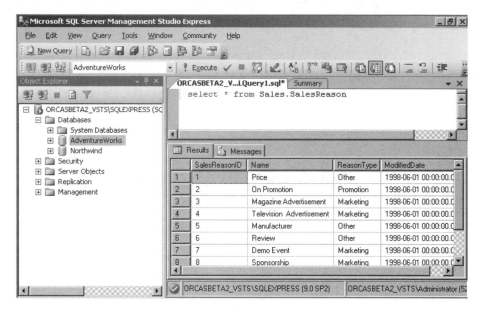

Figure 4-2. *Query Results window*

How It Works

Here, you use the asterisk (*) with the SELECT statement. The asterisk indicates that all the columns from the specified table should be retrieved.

Common Table Expressions

Common table expressions (CTEs) are new to SQL Server 2005. A CTE is a named temporary result set that will be used by the FROM clause of a SELECT query. You then use the result set in any SELECT, INSERT, UPDATE, or DELETE query defined within the same scope as the CTE.

The main advantage CTEs provide you is that the queries with derived tables become simpler, as traditional T-SQL constructs used to work with derived tables usually require a separate definition for the derived data (such as a temporary table). Using a CTE to define the derived table makes it easier to see the definition of the derived table with the code that uses it.

A CTE consists of three main elements:

- Name of the CTE followed by the WITH keyword

- The column list (optional)

- The query that will appear within parentheses, ( ), after the AS keyword

Try It Out: Creating a CTE

To create a CTE, enter the following query into SSMSE and execute it. You should see the results shown in Figure 4-3.

```
WITH TopSales (SalesPersonID,TerritoryID,NumberOfSales)
AS
(
      SELECT SalesPersonID,TerritoryID, Count(*)
      FROM Sales.SalesOrderHeader
      GROUP BY SalesPersonID, TerritoryID
)
      SELECT * FROM TopSales
      WHERE SalesPersonID IS NOT NULL
      ORDER BY NumberOfSales DESC
```

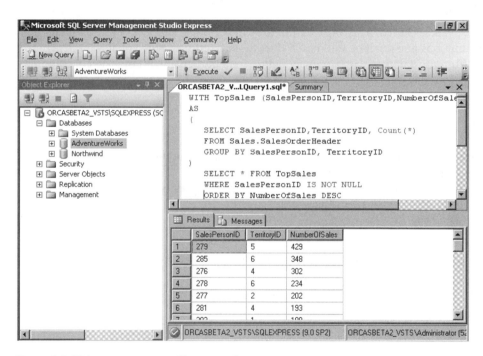

Figure 4-3. *Using a common table expression*

How It Works

The CTE definition line in which you specify the CTE name and column list:

```
WITH TopSales (SalesPersonID,TerritoryID,NumberOfSales)
```

consists of three columns, which means that this SELECT statement:

```
SELECT SalesPersonID,TerritoryID, Count(*)
```

will also have three columns, and the individual column specified in the SELECT list will map to the columns specified inside the CTE definition.

By running the CTE, you will see the SalesPersonID, TerritoryID, and NumberOfSales made in that particular territory by a particular salesperson.

GROUP BY Clause

The GROUP BY clause is used to organize output rows into groups. The SELECT list can include aggregate functions and produce summary values for each group. Often you'll want to generate reports from the database with summary figures for a particular column or set of columns. For example, you may want to find out the total quantity of each card type that expires in a specific year from the Sales.CreditCard table.

Try It Out: Using the GROUP BY Clause

The Sales.CreditCard table contains the details of credit cards. You need to total the cards of a specific type that will be expiring in a particular year.

Open a New Query window in SSMSE. Enter the following query and click Execute. You should see the results shown in Figure 4-4.

```
Use AdventureWorks
Go
  Select CardType, ExpYear,count(CardType) AS 'Total Cards'
  from Sales.CreditCard
  Where ExpYear in (2008,2009)
  group by ExpYear,CardType
  order by CardType,ExpYear
```

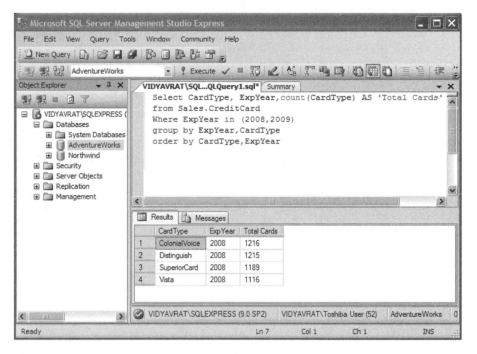

Figure 4-4. *Using* GROUP BY *to aggregate values*

How It Works

You specify three columns and use the COUNT function to count the total number of cards listed in the CardType column of the CreditCard table:

```
Select CardType, ExpYear,count(CardType) AS 'Total Cards'
from Sales.CreditCard
```

Then you specify the WHERE condition, and the GROUP BY and ORDER BY clauses. The WHERE condition ensures that the cards listed will be those that will expire in either 2008 or 2009:

```
Where ExpYear in (2008,2009)
```

The GROUP BY clause enforces that the results be displayed in the form of groups for the ExpYear and CardType columns:

```
group by ExpYear,CardType
```

The ORDER BY clause ensures that the result shown will be organized in proper sequential order based on CardType and ExpYear:

```
order by CardType,ExpYear
```

PIVOT Operator

A common scenario where PIVOT can be useful is when you want to generate cross-tabulation reports to summarize data. The PIVOT operator can rotate rows to columns. For example, suppose you want to query the Sales.CreditCard table in the AdventureWorks database to determine the number of credit cards of a particular type that will be expiring in specified year.

If you look at the query for GROUP BY mentioned in the previous section and shown earlier in Figure 4-4, the years 2008 and 2009 have also been passed to the WHERE clause, but they are displayed only as part of the record and get repeated for each type of card separately, which has increased the number of rows to eight. PIVOT achieves the same goal by producing a concise and easy-to-understand report format.

Try It Out: Using the PIVOT Operator

The Sales.CreditCard table contains the details for customers' credit cards. You need to total the cards of a specific type that will be expiring in a particular year.

Open a New Query window in SSMSE. Enter the following query and click Execute. You should see the results shown in Figure 4-5.

```
Use AdventureWorks
Go
select CardType ,[2008] as Year2008,[2009] as Year2009
from
(
select CardType,ExpYear
from Sales.CreditCard
)piv  Pivot
(
count(ExpYear) for ExpYear in ([2008],[2009])
)as carddetail
order by CardType
```

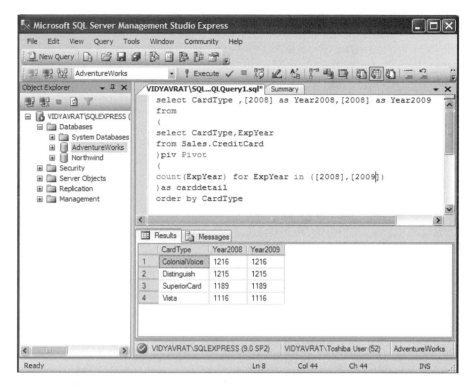

Figure 4-5. *Using the* PIVOT *operator to summarize data*

How It Works

You begin with the SELECT list and specify the columns and their aliases as you want them to appear in the result set:

```
select CardType ,[2008] as Year2008,[2009] as Year2009
from
```

Then you specify the SELECT statement for the table with column names from which you will be retrieving data, and you also assign a PIVOT operator to the SELECT statement:

```
select CardType,ExpYear
from Sales.CreditCard
) piv  Pivot
```

Now you need to count the cards of particular type for the years 2008 and 2009 as specified in this statement:

```
(
count(ExpYear) for ExpYear in ([2008],[2009])
)as carddetail
```

The ORDER BY clause will arrange the credit card names listed under CardType column in the asscending order by the type of card:

```
order by CardType
```

ROW_NUMBER() Function

SQL Server 2005 has introduced the ROW_NUMBER() function for ranking: it returns a unique, sequential number for each row of the returned result set.

Try It Out: Using the ROW_NUMBER() Function

To see how ROW_NUMBER() works, open a New Query window in SSMSE. Enter the following query and click Execute. You should see the results shown in Figure 4-6.

```
select SalesPersonID, Bonus,
ROW_NUMBER() over (order by SalesPersonID) as [RowCount]
from Sales.SalesPerson
```

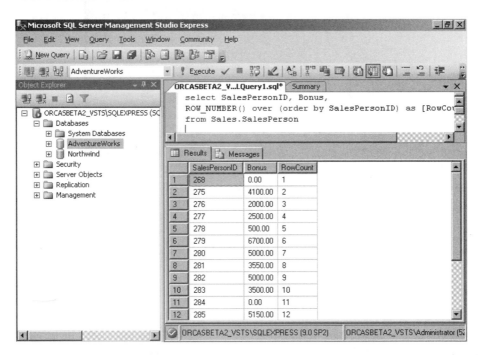

Figure 4-6. *Using the* ROW_NUMBER() *function*

How It Works

You specify the following as part of the SELECT statement:

```
ROW_NUMBER() over (order by SalesPersonID) as [RowCount]
```

Here, you use the ROW_NUMBER() function over the SalesPersonID column and show the row number count in a column titled RowCount. The RowCount column name appears in the square brackets ([ ]) here because RowCount is a keyword in SQL Server and so can't be used directly; if you try to do so, you will get an error.

PARTITION BY Clause

The PARTITION BY clause can be used to divide the result set into partitions to which the ROW_NUMBER() function is applied. The application of the ROW_NUMBER() function with the PARTITION BY clause returns a sequential number for each row within a partition of a result set, starting at 1 for the first row in each partition.

Try It Out: Using the PARTITION BY Clause

To see how PARTITION BY works, open a New Query window in SSMSE. Enter the following query and click Execute. You should see the results shown in Figure 4-7.

```
select CustomerID, TerritoryID ,
Row_Number() over (Partition by TerritoryID
order by CustomerID) as [RowCount]
from Sales.Customer
Where TerritoryID in (1,2) AND
CustomerID Between 1 and 75
```

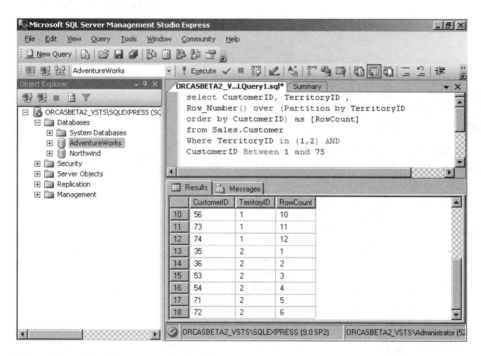

Figure 4-7. *Using the* PARTITION BY *clause*

Notice that the RowCount column lists sequential numbers starting at one for each row of the result set, and this numbering restarts as TerritoryID changes. If you look at the result shown in Figure 4-7, you will see that the RowCount column displays numbering from 1 to 12 for all those territories that have TerritoryID value 1. The numbering restarts for the TerritoryID 2.

How It Works

You specify the following as part of the SELECT statement:

```
Row_Number() over (Partition by TerritoryID
order by CustomerID) as [RowCount]
```

The ROW_NUMBER() function implemented with OVER and PARTITION BY helps to divide the result set into the partition for individual territories as specified in the WHERE clause shown here:

```
Where TerritoryID in (1, 2)
```

Pattern Matching

Pattern matching is a technique that determines whether a character string matches a specified pattern. A pattern can be created by using a combination of regular characters and wildcard characters. During pattern matching, regular characters must exactly match as specified in the character string. LIKE and NOT LIKE (negation) are the operators used for pattern matching. Remember that pattern matching is case sensitive. SQL Server supports the following wildcard characters for pattern matching:

- *% (percent mark)*: This wildcard represents zero to many characters. For example, WHERE title LIKE '%VB 2008%' finds all book titles containing the text "VB 2008," regardless of where in the title that text occurs—at the beginning, middle, or end. In this case, book titles such as "VB 2008: An Introduction," "Accelerated VB 2008," and "Beginning VB 2008 Databases" will be listed.

- *_ (underscore)*: A single underscore represents any single character. By using this wildcard character, you can be specific in your search about the character length of the data you seek. For example, WHERE au_fname LIKE '_ean' finds all the first names that consist of four letters and that end with "ean" (Dean, Sean, and so on). WHERE au_fname LIKE 'a___n' finds all the first names that begin with "a" and end with "n" and have any other three characters in between, such as allan, amman, aryan, and so on.

- *[ ] (square brackets)*: These specify any single character within the specified range, such as [a-f], or set, such as [abcdef] or even [adf]. For example, WHERE au_lname LIKE '[C-K]arsen' finds author last names ending with "arsen" and starting with any single character between "C" and "K," such as Carsen, Darsen, Larsen, Karsen, and so on.

- *[^] (square brackets and caret)*: These specify any single character not within the specified range, such as [^a-f], or set, such as [^abcdef]. For example, WHERE au_lname LIKE 'de[^l]%' retrieves all author last names starting with "de," but the following letter cannot be "l."

Try It Out: Using the % Character

To see how the % wildcard character works, open a New Query window in SSMSE. Enter the following query and click Execute. You should see the results shown in Figure 4-8.

```
select Title + ' ' + FirstName + ' ' + LastName
as "Person Name"
from Person.Contact
where FirstName like 'A%' and Title is not null
```

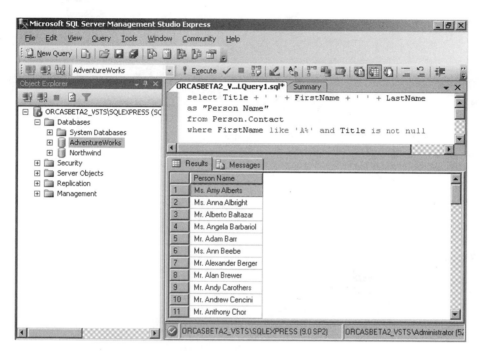

Figure 4-8. *Using the* LIKE *operator with* %

How It Works

You concatenate the three columns Title, FirstName, and LastName into one column titled "Person Name" using the + operator as follows:

```
select Title + ' ' + FirstName + ' ' + LastName
as "Person Name"
```

You specify the WHERE clause with a pattern using the LIKE operator to list all people whose first name begins with the letter "A" and consists of any number of letters. You also specify the condition that the null values from the Title column should not be listed:

```
where FirstName like 'A%' and Title is not null
```

Try It Out: Using the _ (Underscore) Character

To see how the _ wildcard character works, open a New Query window in SSMSE. Enter the following query and click Execute. You should see the results shown in Figure 4-9.

```
select Title + ' ' + FirstName + ' ' + LastName
as "Person Name"
from Person.Contact
where FirstName like 'B____a' and Title is not null
```

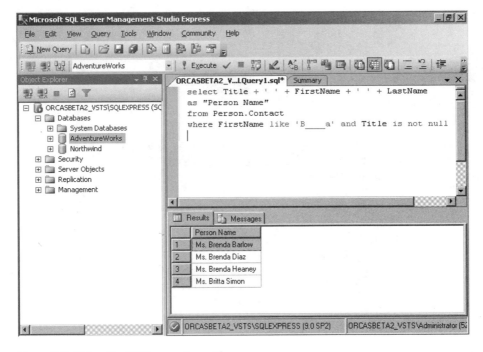

Figure 4-9. *Using the* LIKE *operator with* _

How It Works

You concatenate the three columns Title, FirstName, and LastName into one column titled "Person Name" using the + operator.

```
select Title + ' ' + FirstName + ' ' + LastName
as "Person Name"
```

You specify the WHERE clause with a pattern using the LIKE operator to list all people whose first name consists of a total six characters. As per the WHERE clause, FirstName must begin with "B" and end with "a" and have any four letters in between. You also specify the condition that the null values should not be listed from the Title column:

```
where FirstName like 'B____a' and Title is not null
```

Try It Out: Using the [ ] (Square Bracket) Characters

To see how the [ ] characters work in pattern matching, open a New Query window in SSMSE. Enter the following query and click Execute. You should see the results shown in Figure 4-10.

```
select Title + ' ' + FirstName + ' ' + LastName
as "Person Name"
from Person.Contact
where FirstName like '[A-I]__' and Title is not null
```

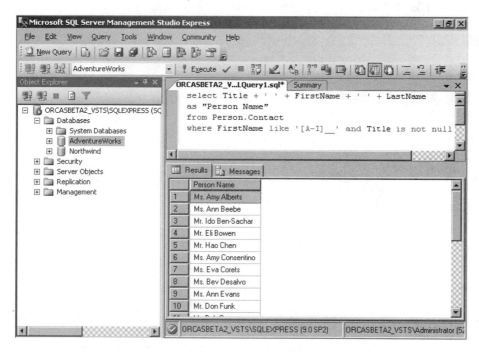

Figure 4-10. *Using the* LIKE *operator with* [ ]

How It Works

You concatenate the three columns Title, FirstName, and LastName into one column titled "Person Name" using the + operator:

```
select Title + ' ' + FirstName + ' ' + LastName
as "Person Name"
```

You specify the WHERE clause with a pattern using the LIKE operator to list all people whose first name consists of a total of three characters. As per the WHERE clause, FirstName must begin with a letter that falls in the range between "A" and "I" and must end with any other two letters. You also specify the condition that null values should not be listed from the Title column:

```
where FirstName like '[A-I]__' and Title is not null
```

Try It Out: Using the [^] (Square Bracket and Caret) Characters

To see how the [^] characters work in pattern matching, open a New Query window in SSMSE. Enter the following query and click Execute. You should see the results shown in Figure 4-11.

```
select Title + ' ' + FirstName + ' ' + LastName
as "Person Name"
from Person.Contact
where FirstName like '_[^I][a]__' and Title is not null
```

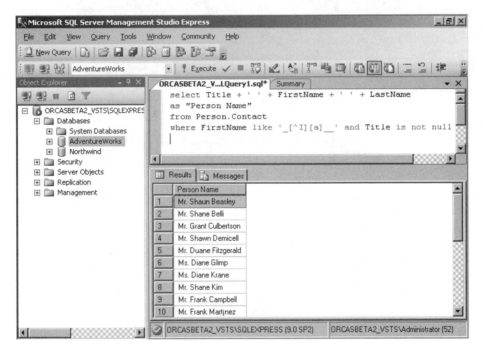

Figure 4-11. *Using the* LIKE *operator with* [^]

How It Works

You concatenate the three columns Title, FirstName, and LastName into one column titled "Person Name" using the + operator:

```
select Title + ' ' + FirstName + ' ' + LastName
as "Person Name"
```

You specify the WHERE clause with a pattern using the LIKE operator to list all people whose first name consists of a total five characters. As per the WHERE clause, FirstName may begin with any two letters except for "I," followed by "a," and then any other two letters. You also specify the condition that null values should not be listed from the Title column:

```
where FirstName like '_[^I][a]__' and Title is not null
```

Aggregate Functions

SQL has several built-in functions that aggregate the values of a column. Aggregate functions are applied on sets of rows and return a single value. For example, you can use aggregate functions to calculate the average unit price of orders placed. You can find the order with the lowest price or the most expensive. MIN, MAX, SUM, AVG, and COUNT are frequently used in aggregate functions.

Try It Out: Using the MIN, MAX, SUM, and AVG Functions

Let's find the minimum, maximum, sum, and average of the unit price (UnitPrice) of each sales order (SalesOrderID) from the SalesOrderDetail table.

Open a New Query window in SSMSE. Enter the following query and click Execute. You should see the results shown in Figure 4-12.

```
select SalesOrderID,min(UnitPrice)as "Min",
max(UnitPrice) as "Max",Sum(UnitPrice) as "Sum",
Avg(UnitPrice)as "Avg"
from Sales.SalesOrderDetail
where SalesOrderID between 43659 and 43663
group by SalesOrderID
```

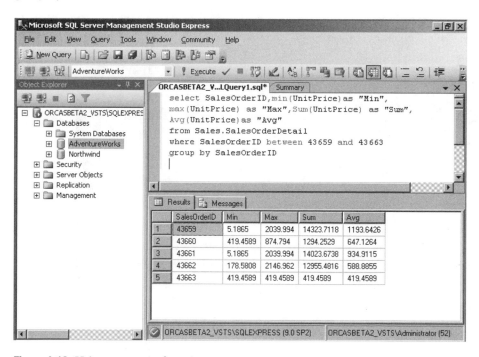

Figure 4-12. *Using aggregate functions*

How It Works

You use the MIN and MAX functions to find the minimum and maximum values, the SUM function to calculate the total value, and the AVG function to calculate the average value:

```
min(UnitPrice) as "Min",
max(UnitPrice) as "Max",
Sum(UnitPrice) as "Sum",
Avg(UnitPrice)as "Avg"
```

Since you want the results listed by SalesOrderID, you use the GROUP BY clause. From the result set, you see that order 1 had a minimum unit price of 5.1865, a maximum unit price of 2039.994, a total unit price of 14323.7118, and an average unit price of 1193.6426.

Try It Out: Using the COUNT Function

Let's find the count of records from the Person.Contact table.

Open a New Query window in SSMSE. Enter the following query and click Execute. You should see the results shown in Figure 4-13.

```
Select count(*) as "Total Records" from Person.Contact
Select count(Title)as "Not Null Titles" from Person.Contact
```

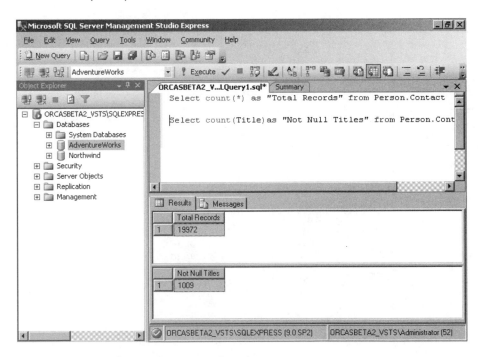

Figure 4-13. *Using the* COUNT *aggregate function*

How It Works

The COUNT function has different behaviors depending on the parameter passed to the function. If you try COUNT(*), the query will return you the number of total records available in the table as shown in the topmost results: table Person.Contact contains a total of 19,972 records.

If you pass a column name to the COUNT function, it will return the total number of records again, but it will ignore all those rows that contain null values for that column. In the second query, you are querying the same table, which has listed 19,972 records, but as your second query applies to the Title column, it returns only 1,009 records, because this time it has ignored all null values.

DATETIME Functions

Although the SQL standard defines a DATETIME data type and its components, YEAR, MONTH, DAY, HOUR, MINUTE, and SECOND, it doesn't dictate how a DBMS makes this data available. Each DBMS offers functions that extract parts of DATETIMEs. Let's look at some examples of T-SQL DATETIME functions.

Try It Out: Using T-SQL Date and Time Functions

Let's practice with T-SQL date and time functions.

Open a New Query window in SSMSE (the database context does not affect this query). Enter the following query and click Execute. You should see the results shown in Figure 4-14.

```
select
current_timestamp'standard datetime',
getdate()'Transact-SQL datetime',
datepart(year, getdate())'datepart year',
year(getdate())'year function',
datepart(hour, getdate())'hour'
```

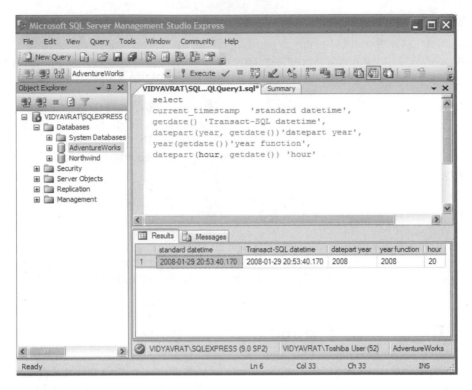

Figure 4-14. *Using date and time functions*

How It Works

You use a nonstandard version of a query, omitting the FROM clause, to display the current date and time and individual parts of them. The first two columns in the SELECT list give the complete date and time:

```
current_timestamp 'standard datetime',
getdate()  'Transact-SQL datetime',
```

The first line uses the CURRENT_TIMESTAMP value function of standard SQL; the second uses the GETDATE function of T-SQL. They're equivalent in effect, both returning the complete current date and time.

The next two lines each provide the current year. The first uses the T-SQL DATEPART function; the second uses the T-SQL YEAR function. Both take a DATETIME argument and return the integer year. The DATEPART function's first argument specifies what part of a DATETIME to extract. Note that T-SQL doesn't provide a date specifier for extracting a complete date, and it doesn't have a separate DATE function:

```
datepart(year, getdate()) 'datepart year',
year(getdate()) 'year function',
```

The final line gets the current hour. The T-SQL DATEPART function must be used here since no HOUR function is analogous to the YEAR function. Note that T-SQL doesn't provide a time specifier for extracting a complete time, and it doesn't have a separate TIME function:

```
datepart(hour, getdate()) 'hour'
```

You can format dates and times and alternative functions for extracting and converting them in various ways. Dates and times can also be added and subtracted and incremented and decremented. How this is done is DBMS-specific, though all DBMSs comply to a reasonable extent with the SQL standard in how they do it. Whatever DBMS you use, you'll find that dates and times are the most complicated data types to employ. But in all cases you'll find that functions (sometimes a richer set of them than in T-SQL) are the basic tools for working with dates and times.

Tip When providing date and time input, character string values are typically expected; for example, 6/28/2004 would be the appropriate way to specify the value for a column holding the current date from the example. However, DBMSs store dates and times in system-specific encodings. When you use date and time data, read the SQL manual for your database carefully to see how to best handle it.

Joins

Most queries require information from more than one table. A *join* is a relational operation that produces a table by retrieving data from two (not necessarily distinct) tables and matching their rows according to a *join specification*.

Different types of joins exist, which you'll look at individually, but keep in mind that every join is a *binary* operation—that is, one table is joined to another, which may be the same table since tables can be joined to themselves. The join operation is a rich and somewhat complex topic. The next sections will cover the basics.

For the join examples, we are using the all-time favorite database, Northwind. To connect with Northwind, perform the following steps in SSMSE:

1. Select File ➤ Disconnect Object Explorer, close all open windows, and click the No button if prompted to save changes to items.

2. Again, click File ➤ Connect Object Explorer. In the Connect to Server dialog box, select *<ServerName>*\SQLEXPRESS as the server name and then click Connect.

3. In Object Explorer, select the Northwind database.

Inner Joins

An inner join is the most frequently used join. It returns only rows that satisfy the join specification. Although in theory any relational operator (such as > or <) can be used in the join specification, the equality operator (=) is almost always used. Joins using the equality operator are called *natural joins*.

The basic syntax for an inner join is as follows:

```
select
    <select list>
from
    left-table INNER JOIN right-table
    ON
    <join specification>
```

Notice that INNER JOIN is a binary operation, so it has two operands, left-table and right-table, which may be base tables or anything that can be queried (for example, a table produced by a subquery or by another join). The ON keyword begins the join specification, which can contain anything that could be used in a WHERE clause.

Try It Out: Writing an Inner Join

Let's retrieve a list of orders, the IDs of the customers who placed them, and the last name of the employees who took them.

Open a New Query window in SSMSE (remember to make Northwind your query context). Enter the following query and click Execute. You should see the results shown in Figure 4-15.

```
select
    orders.orderid,
    orders.customerid,
    employees.lastname
from
    orders inner join employees
    on
    orders.employeeid = employees.employeeid
```

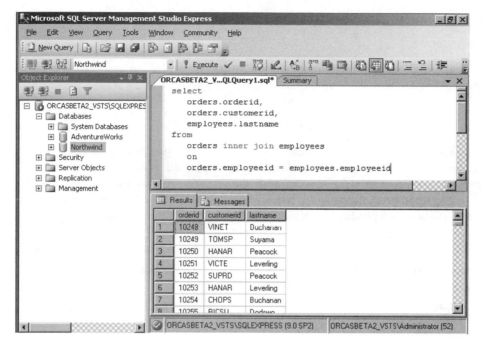

Figure 4-15. *Using* INNER JOIN

How It Works

Let's start with the SELECT list:

```
select
    orders.orderid,
    orders.customerid,
    employees.lastname
```

Since you're selecting columns from two tables, you need to identify which table a column comes from, which you do by prefixing the table name and a dot (.) to the column name. This is known as *disambiguation*, or removing ambiguity so the database manager knows which column to use. Though this has to be done only for columns that appear in both tables, the best practice is to qualify all columns with their table names.

The following FROM clause specifies both the tables you're joining and the kind of join you're using:

```
from
    orders inner join employees
    on
    orders.employeeid = employees.employeeid
```

It specifies an inner join of the Orders and Employees tables:

```
orders inner join employees
```

It also specifies the criteria for joining the primary key EmployeeId of the Employees table with the foreign key EmployeeId of the Orders table:

```
on
orders.employeeid = employees.employeeid
```

The inner join on EmployeeID produces a table composed of three columns: OrderID, CustomerID, and LastName. The data is retrieved from rows in Orders and Employees where their EmployeeID columns have the same value. Any rows in Orders that don't match rows in Employees are ignored, and vice versa. (This isn't the case here, but you'll see an example soon.) An inner join always produces only rows that satisfy the join specification.

■Tip Columns used for joining don't have to appear in the SELECT list. In fact, EmployeeID isn't in the SELECT list of the example query.

Try It Out: Writing an Inner Join Using Correlation Names

Joins can be quite complicated. Let's revise this one to simplify things a bit.

Open a New Query window in SSMSE (remember to make Northwind your query context). Enter the following query and click Execute. You should see the results shown in Figure 4-16.

```
select
    o.orderid,
    o.customerid,
    e.lastname
from
    orders o inner join employees e
    on
    o.employeeid = e.employeeid
```

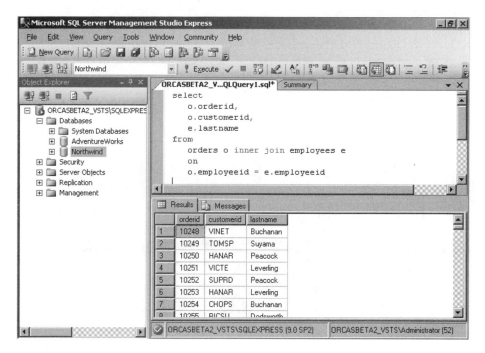

Figure 4-16. *Using correlation names*

How It Works

You simplify the table references by providing a *correlation name* for each table. (This is somewhat similar to providing column aliases, but correlation names are intended to be used as alternative names for tables. Column aliases are used more for labeling than for referencing columns.) You can now refer to Orders as o and to Employees as e. Correlation names can be as long as table names and can be in mixed case, but obviously the shorter they are, the easier they are to code.

You use the correlation names in both the SELECT list:

```
select
    o.orderid,
    o.customerid,
    e.lastname
```

and the ON clause:

```
on
o.employeeid = e.employeeid
```

Try It Out: Writing an Inner Join of Three Tables

Open a New Query window in SSMSE (remember to make Northwind your query context).
Enter the following query and click Execute. You should see the results shown in Figure 4-17.

```
select
    o.orderid      OrderID,
    c.companyname CustomerName,
    e.lastname     Employee
from
    orders o  inner join   employees e
    on  o.employeeid = e.employeeid
  inner join  customers c
    on    o.customerid = c.customerid
```

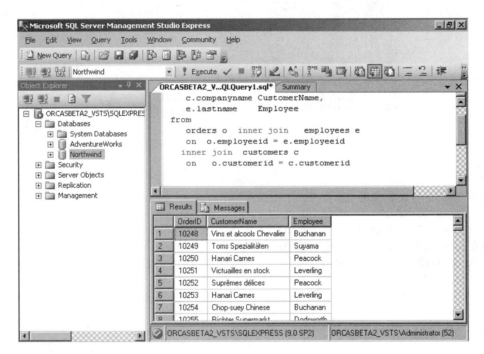

Figure 4-17. *Coding an* INNER JOIN *of three tables*

How It Works

First, you modify the SELECT list, replacing CustomerID from the Orders table with Company-
Name from the Customers table:

```
select
    o.orderid      OrderID,
    c.companyname CustomerName,
    e.lastname     Employee
```

Second, you add a second inner join, as always with two operands: the table produced by the first join and the base table Customers. You reformat the first JOIN operator, splitting it across three lines simply to make it easier to distinguish the tables and joins. You can also use parentheses to enclose joins, and you can make them clearer when you use multiple joins. (Furthermore, since joins produce tables, their results can also be associated with correlation names for reference in later joins and even in the SELECT list, but such complexity is beyond the scope of this discussion.)

```
from
    orders o  inner join   employees e
    on  o.employeeid = e.employeeid
    inner join  customers c
    on   o.customerid = c.customerid
```

The result of the first join, which matched orders to employees, is matched against the Customers table from which the appropriate customer name is retrieved for each matching row from the first join. Since referential integrity exists between Orders and both Employees and Customers, all Orders rows have matching rows in the other two tables.

How the database actually satisfies such a query depends on a number of things, but joins are such an integral part of relational database operations that query optimizers are themselves optimized to find efficient access paths among multiple tables to perform multiple joins. However, the fewer joins needed, the more efficient the query, so plan your queries carefully. Usually you have several ways to code a query to get the same data, but almost always only one of them is the most efficient.

Now you know how to retrieve data from two or more tables—when the rows match. What about rows that don't match? That's where outer joins come in.

Outer Joins

Outer joins return *all* rows from (at least) one of the joined tables even if rows in one table don't match rows in the other. Three types of outer joins exist: left outer join, right outer join, and full outer join. The terms *left* and *right* refer to the operands on the left and right of the JOIN operator. (Refer to the basic syntax for the inner join, and you'll see why we called the operands left-table and right-table.) In a left outer join, all rows from the left table will be retrieved whether they have matching rows in the right table. Conversely, in a right outer join, all rows from the right table will be retrieved whether they have matching rows in the left table. In a full outer join, all rows from both tables are returned.

■**Tip** Left and right outer joins are logically equivalent. It's always possible to convert a left join into a right join by changing the operator and flipping the operands or a right join into a left with a similar change. So, only one of these operators is actually needed. Which one you choose is basically a matter of personal preference, but a useful rule of thumb is to use either left or right, but not both in the same query. The query optimizer won't care, but humans find it much easier to follow a complex query if the joins always go in the same direction.

When is this useful? Quite frequently. In fact, whenever a parent-child relationship exists between tables, despite the fact that referential integrity is maintained, some parent rows may not have related rows in the child table, since child rows may be allowed to have null foreign key values and therefore not match any row in the parent table. This situation doesn't exist in the original `Orders` and `Employees` data, so you'll have to add some data before you can see the effect of outer joins.

You need to add an employee so you have a row in the Employees table that doesn't have related rows in Orders. To keep things simple, you'll provide data only for the columns that aren't nullable.

Try It Out: Adding an Employee with No Orders

To add an employee with no orders, open a New Query window in SSMSE (remember to make Northwind your query context). Enter the following query and click Execute. You should see the results shown in Figure 4-18.

```
insert into employees
(
  firstname,
  lastname
)
values ('Amy', 'Abrams')
```

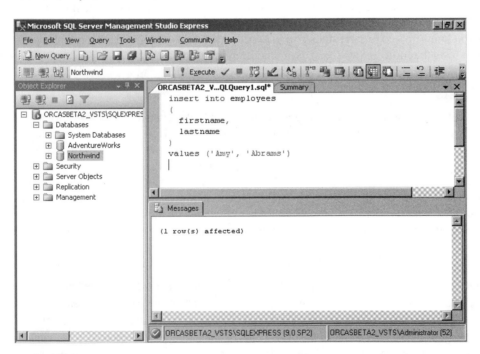

Figure 4-18. *Adding an employee with no orders*

How It Works

You submit a single INSERT statement, providing the two required columns. The first column, EmployeeID, is an IDENTITY column, so you can't provide a value for it, and the rest are nullable, so you don't need to provide values for them.

```
insert into employees
(
    firstname,
    lastname
)
values ('Amy', 'Abrams')
```

You now have a new employee, Amy Abrams, who has never taken an order.

Now, let's say you want a list of all orders taken by all employees—but this list must include *all* employees, even those who haven't taken any orders.

Try It Out: Using LEFT OUTER JOIN

To list all employees, even those who haven't taken any orders, open a New Query window in SSMSE (remember to make Northwind your query context). Enter the following query and click Execute. You should see the results shown in Figure 4-19.

```
select
  e.firstname,
  e.lastname,
  o.orderid
from
  employees e  left outer join  orders o
  on  e.employeeid = o.employeeid
  order by  2, 1
```

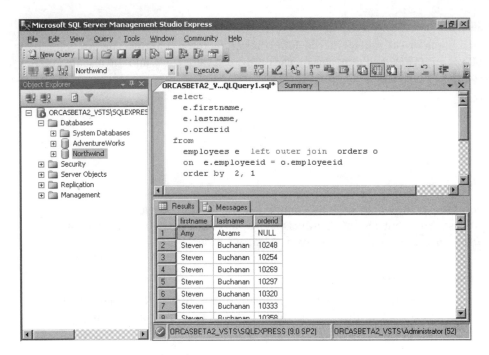

Figure 4-19. *Using* LEFT OUTER JOIN*s*

How It Works

Had you used an inner join you would have missed the row for the new employee. (Try it for yourself.) The only new SQL in the FROM clause is the JOIN operator itself:

```
left outer join
```

You also add an ORDER BY clause to sort the result set by first name within last name, to see that the kind of join has no effect on the rest of the query, and to see an alternative way to specify columns, by position number within the SELECT list rather than by name. This technique is convenient (and may be the only way to do it for columns that are produced by expressions, for example, by the SUM function):

```
order by
    2, 1
```

Note that the OrderID column for the new employee is null, since no value exists for it. The same holds true for any columns from the table that don't have matching rows (in this case, the right table).

You can obtain the same result by placing the Employees table on the right and the Orders table on the left of the JOIN operator and changing the operator to RIGHT OUTER JOIN. (Try it!) Remember to flip the correlation names, too.

The keyword OUTER is optional and is typically omitted. Left and right joins are *always* outer joins.

Other Joins

The SQL standard also provides for FULL OUTER JOIN, UNION JOIN, and CROSS JOIN (and even NATURAL JOIN, basically an inner join using equality predicates), but these are much less used and beyond the scope of this book. We won't provide examples, but this section contains a brief summary of them.

A FULL OUTER JOIN is like a combination of both the LEFT and RIGHT OUTER joins. All rows from both tables will be retrieved, even if they have no related rows in the other table.

A UNION JOIN is unlike outer joins in that it doesn't match rows. Instead, it creates a table that has all the rows from both tables. For two tables, it's equivalent to the following query:

```
select
    *
from
    table1
union all
select
    *
from
    table2
```

The tables must have the same number of columns, and the data types of corresponding columns must be compatible (able to hold the same types of data).

A CROSS JOIN combines all rows from both tables. It doesn't provide for a join specification, since this would be irrelevant. It produces a table with all columns from both tables and as many rows as the product of the number of rows in each table. The result is also known as a *Cartesian product*, since that's the mathematical term for associating each element (row) of one set (table) with all elements of another set. For example, if there are five rows and five columns in table A and ten rows and three columns in table B, the cross join of A and B would produce a table with fifty rows and eight columns. This join operation is not only virtually inapplicable to any real-world query, but it's also a potentially very expensive process for even small real-world databases. (Imagine using it for production tables with thousands or even millions of rows.)

Summary

In this chapter, we covered how to construct more sophisticated queries using SQL features such as aggregates, DATETIME functions, GROUP BY clauses, joins, and pattern matching. We also covered the features that are new in SQL Server 2005, such as common table expressions, the PIVOT operator, the ROW_NUMBER() function, and the PARTITION BY clause.

In the next chapter, you will learn about manipulating the database.

CHAPTER 5

■ ■ ■

Manipulating Database Data

Now that you know something about writing database queries, it's time to turn your attention to the different aspects of data modification, such as retrieving, inserting, updating, and deleting data.

In this chapter, we'll cover the following:

- Retrieving data

- Using SELECT INTO statements

- Inserting data

- Updating data

- Deleting data

Retrieving Data

A SQL query retrieves data from a database. Data is stored as *rows* in *tables*. Rows are composed of *columns*. In its simplest form, a query consists of two parts:

- A SELECT list, where the columns to be retrieved are specified

- A FROM clause, where the table or tables to be accessed are specified

---

Tip We've written SELECT and FROM in capital letters simply to indicate they're SQL keywords. SQL isn't case sensitive, and keywords are typically written in lowercase in code. In T-SQL, queries are called SELECT statements, but the ISO/ANSI standard clearly distinguishes "queries" from "statements." The distinction is conceptually important. A *query* is an operation on a table that produces a table as a result; *statements* may (or may not) operate on tables and don't produce tables as results. Furthermore, *subqueries* can be used in both queries and statements. So, we'll typically call queries "queries" instead of SELECT statements. Call queries whatever you prefer, but keep in mind that queries are a special feature of SQL.

Using two keywords, SELECT and FROM, here's the simplest possible query that will get all the data from the specified table:

```
Select *  from <table name>
```

The asterisk (*) means you want to select all the columns in the table.

You will be using a SQLEXPRESS instance of SQL Server 2005 in this chapter. Open SQL Server Management Studio Express and in the Connect to Server dialog box select *<ServerName>*\SQLEXPRESS as the server name and then click Connect. SQL Server Management Studio Express (SSMSE) will open. Expand the Databases node and select the Northwind database. Your screen should resemble that shown in Figure 5-1.

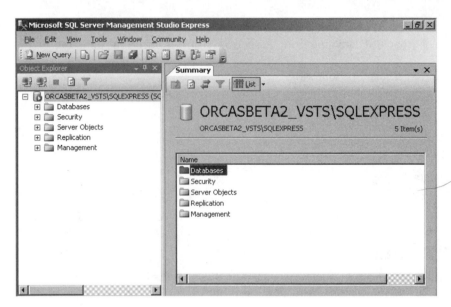

Figure 5-1. *Selecting a database to query*

Try It Out: Running a Simple Query

To submit a query to retrieve all employee data, open a New Query window in SSMSE (remember to make Northwind your query context). Enter the following query and click Execute. You should see the results shown in Figure 5-2.

```
Select * from employees
```

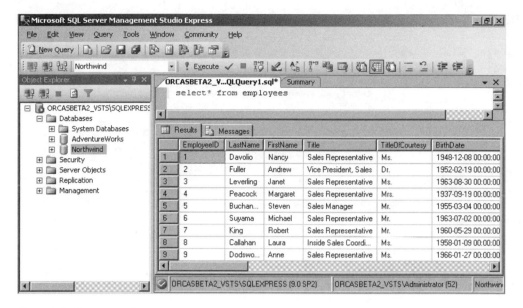

Figure 5-2. *Query results pane*

How It Works

You ask the database to return the data for all columns, and you get exactly that. If you scroll to the right, you'll find all the columns in the Employees table.

Most of the time, you should limit queries to only relevant columns. When you select columns you don't need, you waste resources. To explicitly select columns, enter the column names after the SELECT keyword, as shown in the following query, and click Execute. Figure 5-3 shows the results.

```
Select employeeid, firstname, lastname
from employees
```

This query selects all the rows from the Employees table but only the EmployeeID, First-Name, and LastName columns.

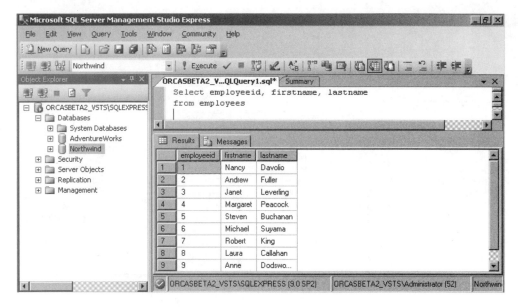

Figure 5-3. *Selecting specific columns*

Using the WHERE Clause

Queries can have WHERE clauses. The WHERE clause allows you to specify criteria for selecting rows. This clause can be complex, but we'll stick to a simple example for now. The syntax is as follows:

```
WHERE <column1> <operator> <column2 / Value>
```

Here, <operator> is a comparison operator (for example, =, <>, >, or <). (Table 5-1, later in the chapter, lists the T-SQL comparison operators.)

Try It Out: Refining Your Query

In this exercise, you'll see how to refine your query.

1. Add the following WHERE clause to the query in Figure 5-3.

   ```
   Where country = 'USA'
   ```

2. Run the query by pressing F5, and you should see the results shown in Figure 5-4.

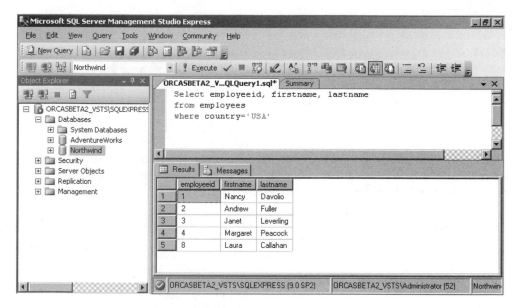

Figure 5-4. *Using a* WHERE *clause*

Caution SQL keywords and table and column names aren't case sensitive, but string literals (enclosed in single quotes) are. This is why we use 'USA', not 'usa', for this example.

How It Works

The new query returns the data for columns EmployeeID, FirstName, and LastName from the Employees table, but only for rows where the Country column value equals "USA".

Using Comparison Operators in a WHERE Clause

You can use a number of different comparison operators in a WHERE clause (see Table 5-1).

Table 5-1. *Comparison Operators*

Operator	Description	Example
=	Equals	EmployeeID = 1
<	Less than	EmployeeID < 1
>	Greater than	EmployeeID > 1
<=	Less than or equal to	EmployeeID <= 1
>=	Greater than or equal to	EmployeeID >= 1
<>	Not equal to	EmployeeID <> 1
!=	Not equal to	EmployeeID != 1
!<	Not less than	EmployeeID !< 1
!>	Not greater than	EmployeeID !> 1

■Tip As mentioned earlier, every database vendor has its own implementation of SQL. This discussion is specific to T-SQL; for example, standard SQL doesn't have the != operator and calls <> the *not equals operator*. In fact, standard SQL calls the expressions in a WHERE clause *predicates*; we'll use that term because predicates are either true or false, but other expressions don't have to be. If you work with another version of SQL, please refer to its documentation for specifics.

In addition to these operators, the LIKE operator (see Table 5-2) allows you to match patterns in character data. As with all SQL character data, strings must be enclosed in single quotes ('). (Chapter 4 covers the LIKE operator in more detail.)

Table 5-2. *The* LIKE *Operator*

Operator	Description	Example
LIKE	Allows you to specify a pattern	WHERE Title LIKE 'Sales%' selects all rows where the Title column contains a value that starts with the word "Sales" followed by zero or more characters.

You can use four different wildcards in the pattern. Chapter 4 covers these wildcards in detail, but to briefly review, we list them here in Table 5-3.

Table 5-3. *Wildcard Characters*

Wildcard	Description
%	Any combination of characters. Where FirstName LIKE 'Mc%' selects all rows where the FirstName column equals McDonald, McBadden, McMercy, and so on.
_	Any one character. WHERE Title LIKE '_ales' selects all rows where the Title column equals Aales, aales, Bales, bales, and so on.
[ ]	A single character within a range [a-d] or set [abcd]. WHERE Title LIKE '[bs]ales' selects all rows where the Title column equals either the bales or sales.
[^]	A single character not within a range [^a-d] or set [^abcd].

Sometimes it's useful to select rows where a value is unknown. When no value has been assigned to a column, the column is NULL. (This isn't the same as a column that contains the value 0 or a blank.) To select a row with a column that's NULL, use the IS [NOT] NULL operator (see Table 5-4).

Table 5-4. *The* IS [NOT] NULL *Operator*

Operator	Description	Example
IS NULL	Allows you to select rows where a column has no value	WHERE Region IS NULL returns all rows where Region has no value.
IS NOT NULL	Allows you to select rows where a column has a value	WHERE Region IS NOT NULL returns all rows where Region has a value.

> **Note** You must use the IS NULL and IS NOT NULL operators (collectively called the *null predicate* in standard SQL) to select or exclude NULL column values, respectively. The following is a valid query but always produces zero rows: SELECT * FROM employees WHERE Region = NULL. If you change = to IS, the query will read as SELECT * FROM employees WHERE Region IS NULL, and it will return rows where regions have no value.

To select values in a range or in a set, you can use the BETWEEN and IN operators (see Table 5-5). The negation of these two is NOT BETWEEN and NOT IN.

Table 5-5. *The* BETWEEN *and* IN *Operators*

Operator	Description	Example
BETWEEN	True if a value is within a range.	WHERE extension BETWEEN 400 AND 500 returns the rows where Extension is between 400 and 500, inclusive.
IN	True if a value is in a list. The list can be the result of a subquery.	WHERE city IN ('Seattle', 'London') returns the rows where City is either Seattle or London.

Combining Predicates

Quite often you'll need to use more than one predicate to filter your data. You can use the logical operators shown in Table 5-6.

Table 5-6. *SQL Logical Operators*

Operator	Description	Example
AND	Combines two expressions, evaluating the complete expression as true only if both are true	HERE (title LIKE 'Sales%' AND lastname ='Peacock')
NOT	Negates a Boolean value	WHERE NOT (title LIKE 'Sales%' AND lastname ='Peacock')
OR	Combines two expressions, evaluating the complete expression as true if either is true	WHERE (title = 'Peacock' OR title = 'King')

When you use these operators, it's often a good idea to use parentheses to clarify the conditions. In complex queries, this may be absolutely necessary.

Sorting Data

After you've filtered the data you want, you can sort the data by one or more columns and in a certain direction. Since tables are by definition unsorted, the order in which rows are retrieved by a query is unpredictable. To impose an ordering, you use the ORDER BY clause:

```
ORDER BY <column> [ASC | DESC] {, n}
```

The <column> is the column that should be used to sort the result. The {, n} syntax means you can specify any number of columns separated by commas. The result will be sorted in the order in which you specify the columns.

The following are the two sort directions:

- ASC: Ascending (1, 2, 3, 4, and so on)

- DESC: Descending (10, 9, 8, 7, and so on)

If you omit the ASC or DESC keywords, the sort order defaults to ASC.

The following is the basic syntax for queries:

```
SELECT <column>
FROM <table>
WHERE <predicate>
ORDER BY <column> ASC | DESC
```

Now that you've seen it, you'll put this syntax to use in an example.

Try It Out: Writing an Enhanced Query

In this example, you'll code a query that uses the basic syntax just shown. You want to do the following:

- Select all the orders that have been handled by employee 5.

- Select the orders shipped to either France or Brazil.

- Display only OrderID, EmployeeID, CustomerID, OrderDate, and ShipCountry.

- Sort the orders by the destination country and the date the order was placed.

Does this sound complicated? Give it a try. Open a New Query window in SSMSE. Enter the following query and click Execute. You should see the results shown in Figure 5-5.

```
select orderid,employeeid,customerid,orderdate,shipcountry
from orders
where employeeid = 5 and shipcountry in ('Brazil', 'France')
order by shipcountry asc,orderdate asc
```

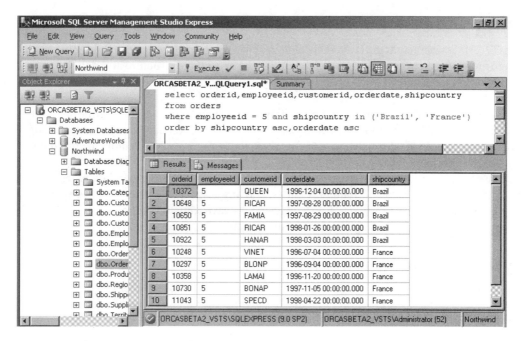

Figure 5-5. *Filtering and sorting data*

How It Works

Let's look at the clauses individually. The SELECT list specifies which columns you want to use:

```
select orderid,employeeid,customerid,orderdate,shipcountry
```

The FROM clause specifies that you want to use the Orders table:

```
from orders
```

The WHERE clause is a bit more complicated. It consists of two predicates that individually state the following:

- EmployeeID must be 5.

- ShipCountry must be in the list Brazil or France.

As these predicates are combined with AND, they both must evaluate to true for a row to be included in the result:

```
where employeeid = 5 and shipcountry in ('Brazil', 'France')
```

The ORDER BY clause specifies the order in which the rows are sorted. The rows will be sorted by ShipCountry first and then by OrderDate:

```
order by shipcountry asc,orderdate asc
```

Using SELECT INTO Statements

A SELECT INTO statement is used to create a new table containing (or not containing) the result set returned by a SELECT query. SELECT INTO copies the exact table structure and data into another table specified in the INTO clause. Usually, a SELECT query returns result sets to the client application.

Including the # (hash) symbol before the table name results in creating a temporary table, which ends up in the tempdb system database, regardless of which database you are working in. Specifying the table name without the # symbol gives you a permanent table in your database (not in tempdb).

The columns of the newly created table inherit the column names, their data types, whether or not columns can contain null values, and any associated IDENTITY property from the source table. However, the SELECT INTO clause does have some restrictions: it will not copy any constraints, indexes, or triggers from the source table.

Try It Out: Creating a New Table

In this exercise, you'll see how to create a table using a SELECT INTO statement. Open a New Query window in SSMSE (remember to make Northwind your query context). Enter the following query and click Execute. You should see the results shown in Figure 5-6.

```
select orderid,employeeid,customerid,orderdate,shipcountry
into #myorder
from orders
```

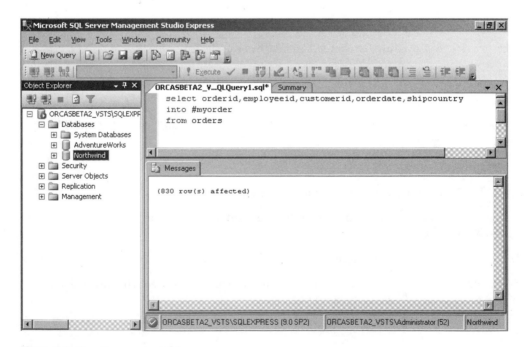

Figure 5-6. *Creating a new table*

How It Works

In the following statement:

```
select orderid,employeeid,customerid,orderdate,shipcountry
into #myorder
from orders
```

you define the SELECT list, the INTO clause with a table name prefixed by #, and then the FROM clause. This means that you want to retrieve all the specified columns from the Orders table and insert them into the #myorder table.

Even though you write the query in Northwind, the #myorder table gets created inside tempdb because of the prefixed # symbol (see Figure 5-7).

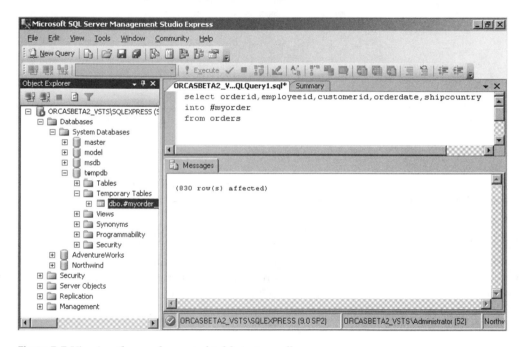

Figure 5-7. *Viewing the newly created table in tempdb*

A temporary table can reside in the tempdb database as long as you have the query window open. If you close the query window from which you created your temporary table, and regardless of whether you saved the query, the temporary table will be automatically deleted from tempdb.

Once the table is created, you can use it like any other table (see Figure 5-8).

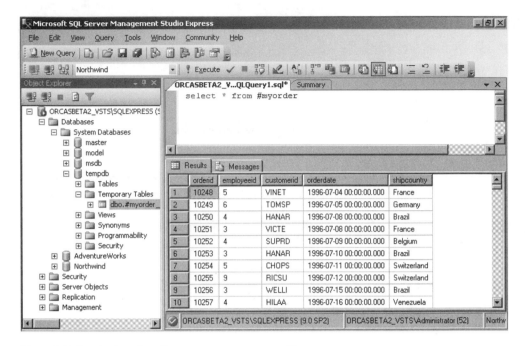

Figure 5-8. *Retrieving data from your temporary table*

Temporary tables will also be deleted if you close SSMSE, because the tempdb database gets rebuilt every time you close and open SSMSE again.

Try It Out: Using SELECT INTO to Copy Table Structure

Sometimes you will want to copy only the table structure, not the data inside the table (e.g., you only need an empty copy of the table). To do so, you need to include a condition that must not return true. In this case, you are free to insert your own data.

To try this out, enter the following query, and you should get the results shown in Figure 5-9.

```
select orderid,employeeid,customerid,orderdate,shipcountry
into #myemptyorder
from orders
where 0=1
```

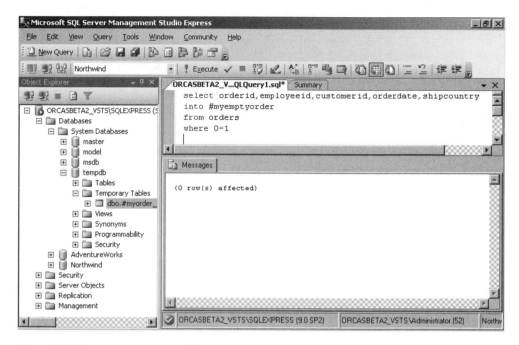

Figure 5-9. *Creating an empty table*

How It Works

The magic condition where 0=1, which is a false condition, has done all the work for you, and only table structure has been copied into the tempdb database.

To view this table, you can navigate to the tempdb database in Object Explorer, expand the Temporary Tables node if it isn't already expanded, select the node, right-click it, and select Refresh to refresh the tables list. You should see the newly created #myemptyorder table as shown in Figure 5-10.

As you can see, the table has structure but not data, the false condition you include.

If you were to run a SELECT query on the #myemptyorder table as shown in Figure 5-11, the query would return nothing, clearly demonstrating that only the table structure has been copied because only field names are displayed.

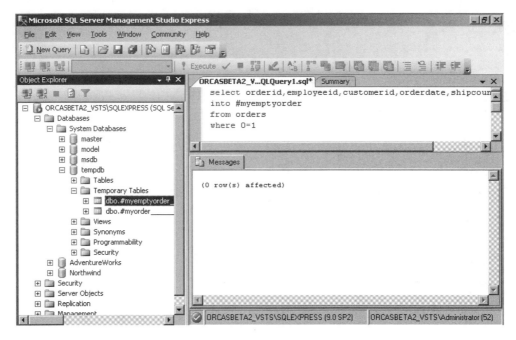

Figure 5-10. *Viewing a newly created empty table in tempdb*

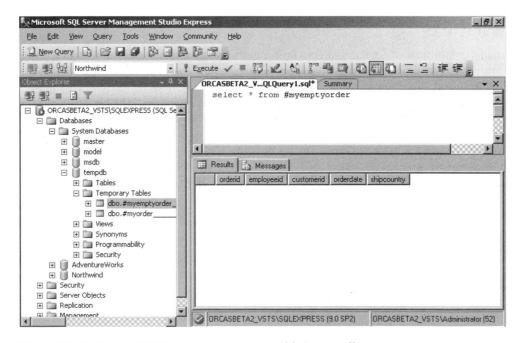

Figure 5-11. *Writing a* SELECT *query on an empty table in tempdb*

Inserting Data

The next important task you need to be able to do is add data (e.g., add rows) to a table. You do this with the INSERT statement. The INSERT statement is much simpler than a query, particularly because the WHERE and ORDER BY clauses have no meaning when inserting data and therefore aren't used.

A basic INSERT statement has these parts:

```
INSERT INTO <table>
(<column1>, <column2>, ..., <columnN>)
VALUES (<value1>, <value2>, ..., <valueN>)
```

Using this syntax, let's add a new row to the Shippers table of the Northwind database. Before you insert it, let's look at the table. In the SSMSE Object Explorer, select the Northwind database, right-click the Shippers table, and click Open Table. The table has three rows, which are displayed in a tabbed window (see Figure 5-12).

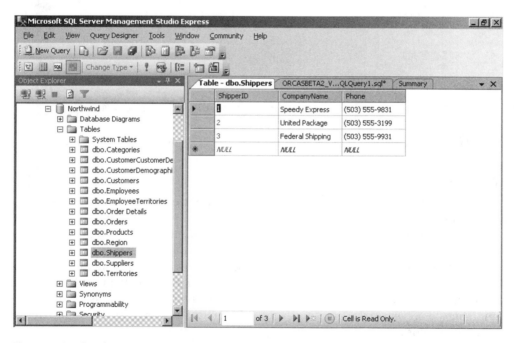

Figure 5-12. *The Shippers table before adding a row*

Try It Out: Inserting a New Row

To insert a new row into a table, open a New Query window in SSMSE. Enter the following query and click Execute.

```
insert into shippers ( companyname, phone )
values ('GUIPundits', '+91 9820801756')
```

Executing this statement in the query pane should produce a Messages window reporting "(1 row(s) affected)". You should see the results shown in Figure 5-13.

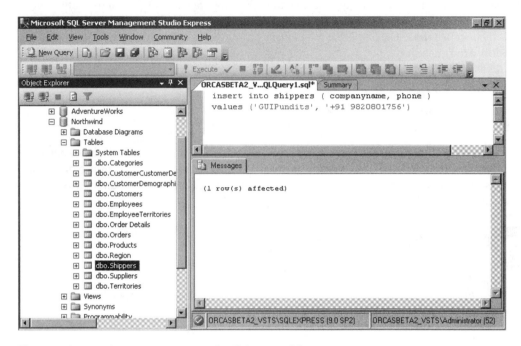

Figure 5-13. *Inserting a new row into the Shippers table*

How It Works

The first column, ShipperID, is an identity column, and you can't insert values into it explicitly—the SQL Server database engine will make sure that a unique and SQL Server–generated value is inserted for the ShipperID field. So, the INSERT statement needs to be written in such a way that you specify the column list you want to insert values for explicitly; though the Shippers table contains three fields, ShipperID is an identity column, and it does not expect any value to be inserted from the user. But by default, an INSERT statement cannot judge whether the column you are not passing a value for is an identity column. Thus, to prevent errors you specify the column list and then pass the respective values to these fields as shown in the following query:

```
insert into shippers( companyname, phone )
values ('GUIPundits', '+91 9820801756')
```

■**Note** INSERT statements have a limitation. When you try to insert data directly into a foreign key table, and the primary key table has no related parent record, you will receive an error because that value needs to be available in the primary key table before you insert it into the foreign key table. For example, the Shippers table is the PK table for the Orders table, which has an FK column named ShipVia that references the PK column ShipperID of Shippers table. In this scenario, you can't insert a row until you have inserted it into the Shippers table.

After inserting the row, return to the dbo.Shippers table in Object Explorer, right-click, and open the table again. You'll see that the new row has been added, as shown in Figure 5-14.

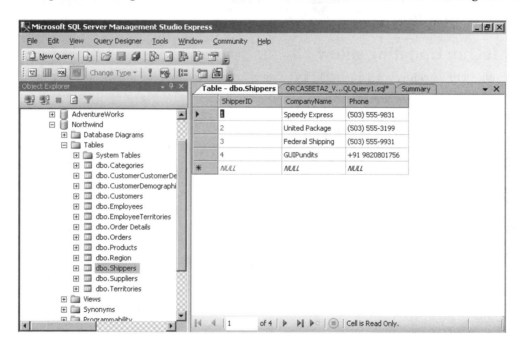

Figure 5-14. *The Shippers table after adding a row*

Be careful to insert data of the correct data type. In this example, both the columns are of the character type, so you inserted strings. If one of the columns had been of the integer type, you would have inserted an integer value instead.

Updating Data

Another important task you need to be able to do is change data. You do this with the UPDATE statement. When coding UPDATE statements, you must be careful to include a WHERE clause, or you'll update *all* the rows in a table. So, always code an appropriate WHERE clause, or you won't change the data you intend to change.

Now that you're aware of the implications of the UPDATE statement, let's take a good look at it. In essence, it's a simple statement that allows you to update values in one or more rows and columns:

```
UPDATE <table>
SET <column1> = <value1>, <column2> = <value2>, ..., <columnN> = <valueN>
WHERE <predicate>
```

As an example, imagine that the company you added earlier, GUIPundits, has realized that, though (unfortunately) accurate, its name isn't good for business, so it's changing its name to Pearl HR Solution. To make this change in the database, you first need to locate the row to change. More than one company could have the same name, so you shouldn't use the CompanyName column as the key. Instead, look back at Figure 5-10 and note the ShipperID value for GUIPundits.

Try It Out: Updating a Row

To change a row's value, open a New Query window in SSMSE. Enter the following query and click Execute:

```
update shippers
set companyname = 'PearlHRSolution'
where shipperid = 4
```

How It Works

The ShipperID is the primary key (unique identifier for rows) of the Shippers table, so you can use it to locate the one row we want to update. Running the query should produce a Messages pane reporting "(1 row(s) affected)". Switch back to Object Explorer and open the Shippers table, and you'll see that CompanyName has changed, as shown in Figure 5-15.

When you update more than one column, you still use the SET keyword only once, and separate column names and their respective values you want to set by comma. For example, the following statement would change both the name and the phone of the company:

```
update shippers
set companyname = 'PearlHRSolution',
phone = '+91 9819133949'
where  shipperid = 4
```

If you were to switch back to Object Explorer and open the Shippers table, you would see that the time value for Phone has also changed, as shown in Figure 5-16.

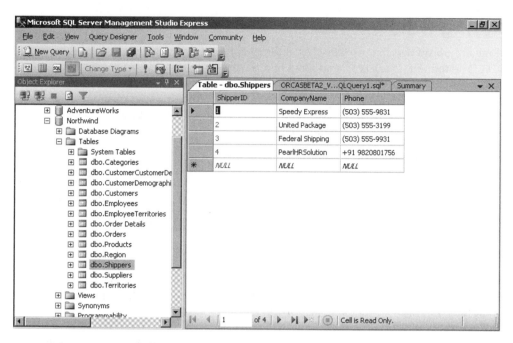

Figure 5-15. *The Shippers table after updating a row*

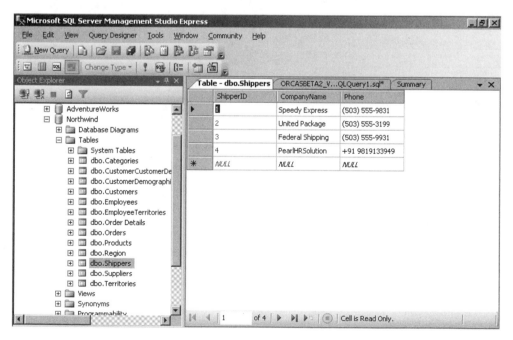

Figure 5-16. *The Shippers table after updating multiple columns of a row*

Deleting Data

The final important task that we'll discuss in this chapter is removing data. You do this with the DELETE statement. The DELETE statement has the same implications as the UPDATE statement. It's all too easy to delete every row (not just the wrong rows) in a table by forgetting the WHERE clause, so be careful. The DELETE statement removes entire rows, so it's not necessary (or possible) to specify columns. Its basic syntax is as follows (remember, the WHERE clause is optional, but without it *all* rows will be deleted):

```
DELETE FROM <table>
WHERE <predicate>
```

If you need to remove some records from the Shippers table, you need to determine the primary key of the row you want to remove and use that in the DELETE statement:

```
delete from shippers
where shipperid = 4
```

This should produce a Messages pane reporting "(1 row(s) affected)". Navigate to the Table – dbo.Shippers pane, right-click, and select Execute SQL, and you'll see that the company has been removed, as shown in Figure 5-17.

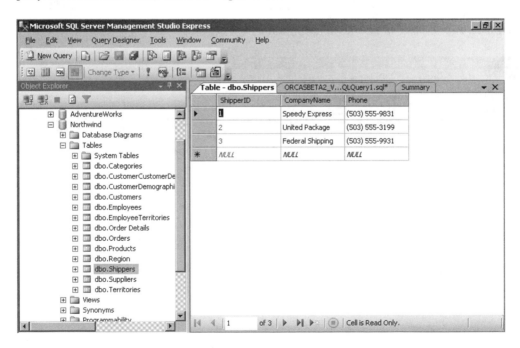

Figure 5-17. *The Shippers table after deleting a row*

If you try to delete one of the remaining three shippers, you'll get a database error. A foreign-key relationship exists from Orders (FK) to Shippers (PK), and SSMSE enforces it, preventing deletion of Shippers' rows that are referred to by Orders rows. If the database were to allow you to drop records from the PK table, the records in the FK table would be left as orphan records, leaving the database in an inconsistent state. (Chapter 3 discusses keys.)

Sometimes you do need to remove every row from a table. In such cases, the TRUNCATE TABLE statement may be preferable to the DELETE statement, since it performs better. The TRUNCATE TABLE statement is faster because it doesn't do any *logging* (saving each row in a log file before deleting it) to support recovery, while DELETE logs every row removed.

Summary

In this chapter, you saw how to use the following T-SQL keywords to perform data manipulation tasks against a database: SELECT INTO, SELECT, INSERT, UPDATE, and DELETE. You also saw how to use comparison and other operators to specify predicates that limit what rows are retrieved or manipulated.

In the next chapter, you will see how stored procedures work.

■ ■ ■

Using Stored Procedures

Stored procedures are SQL statements that allow you to perform a task repeatedly. You can create a procedure once and reuse it any number of times in your program. This can improve the maintainability of your application and allow applications to access the database in a uniform and optimized manner. The goal of this chapter is to get you acquainted with stored procedures and understand how Visual Basic .NET (VB .NET) programs can interact with them.

In this chapter, we'll cover the following:

- Creating stored procedures

- Modifying stored procedures

- Displaying definitions of stored procedures

- Renaming stored procedures

- Working with stored procedures in VB .NET

- Deleting stored procedures

Creating Stored Procedures

Stored procedures can have *parameters* that can be used for input or output and single-integer *return values* (that default to zero), and they can return zero or more result sets. They can be called from client programs or other stored procedures. Because stored procedures are so powerful, they are becoming the preferred mode for much database programming, particularly for multitier applications and web services, since (among their many benefits) they can dramatically reduce network traffic between clients and database servers.

Try It Out: Working with a Stored Procedure in SQL Server

Using SQL Server Management Studio Express (SSMSE), you'll create a stored procedure that produces a list of the names of employees in the Northwind database. It requires no input and doesn't need to set a return value.

1. Open SSMSE, and in the Connect to Server dialog box, select *<ServerName>*\SQLEX-PRESS as the server name and then click Connect.

2. In Object Explorer, expand the Databases node, select the Northwind database, and click the New Query button. Enter the following query and click Execute. You should see the results shown in Figure 6-1.

```
create procedure sp_Select_All_Employees
as
  select
     employeeid,
    firstname,
    lastname
  from
    employees
```

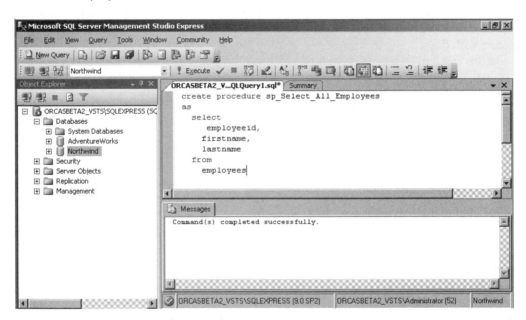

Figure 6-1. *Creating a stored procedure using SSMSE*

3. To execute the stored procedure, enter the following query and click Execute. You should see the results shown in Figure 6-2.

```
execute sp_Select_All_Employees
```

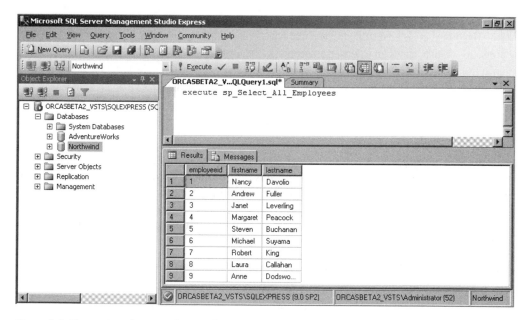

Figure 6-2. *Executing the stored procedure*

How It Works

The CREATE PROCEDURE statement creates stored procedures. The AS keyword separates the signature (the procedure's name and parameter list, but here you define no parameters) of the stored procedure from its body (the SQL that makes up the procedure):

```
create procedure sp_Select_All_Employees
as
```

After AS, the procedure body has just one component, a simple query:

```
Select
    employeeid,
    firstname,
    lastname
from
    employees
```

SSMSE submitted the CREATE PROCEDURE statement, and once the stored procedure is created, you run it from the query window by writing the statement

```
execute sp_Select_All_Employees
```

That's it. There's nothing complicated about creating stored procedures. The challenge is coding them when they're nontrivial, and stored procedures can be quite complicated and can do very powerful things, but that's well beyond the scope of this book.

Note The prefix `sp_` is a T-SQL convention that typically indicates the stored procedure is coded in SQL. The prefix `xp_` (which stands for extended procedure) is also used to indicate that the stored procedure isn't written in SQL. (However, not all `sp_` stored procedures provided by SQL Server are written in SQL.) By the way, hundreds of `sp_` (and other) stored procedures are provided by SQL Server 2005 to perform a wide variety of common tasks.

Although we use `sp_` for the purposes of these examples, it is a best practice not to create a stored procedure prefixed with `sp_`; doing so has a dramatic effect on the search mechanism and the way the SQL Server database engine starts searching for that particular procedure in order to execute.

The SQL Server follows this search order if you are executing a stored procedure that begins with `sp_`:

1. SQL Server will search the master database for the existence of the procedure, if it is available, and then it will call the procedure.

2. If the stored procedure is not available in the master database, SQL Server searches inside either the database from which you are calling it or the database whose name you provide as qualifier (`database_name.stored_procedure_name`).

Therefore, although a user-created stored procedure prefixed with `sp_` may exist in the current database, the *master* database (which is where the `sp_` prefixed stored procedures that come with SQL Server 2005 are stored) is always checked first, even if the stored procedure is qualified with the database name.

It is also important to note that if any user-defined stored procedure has the same name as a system stored procedure, and you try calling the user-defined stored procedure, it will never be executed, even you call it from inside the database where you have just created it. Only the master database's version will be called.

Try It Out: Creating a Stored Procedure with an Input Parameter

Here you'll create a stored procedure that produces a list of orders for a given employee. You'll pass the employee ID to the stored procedure for use in a query.

1. Enter the following query and click Execute. You should see the message "Command(s) completed successfully" in the results window.

```
create procedure sp_Orders_By_EmployeeId
        @employeeid int
as
        select  orderid, customerid
         from orders
         where  employeeid = @employeeid;
```

2. To execute the stored procedure, enter the following command along with the value for the parameter, select it, and then click Execute. You should see the results shown in Figure 6-3.

```
execute sp_Orders_By_EmployeeId 2
```

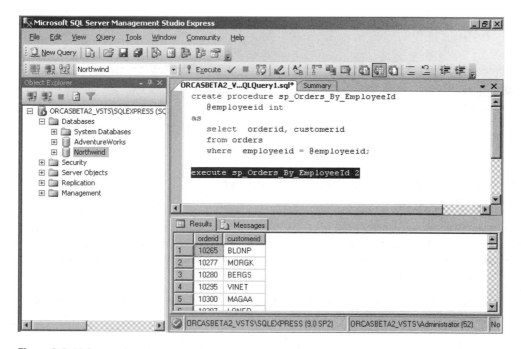

Figure 6-3. *Using an input parameter*

■**Tip** SQL Server has a very interesting behavior of executing a portion of a query or executing a particular query out of multiple SQL statements written in the query window, unlike other RDBMSs. This behavior is shown in the Figure 6-3, in which we have selected a particular statement. Click the Execute button, and SQL Server will process only the selected statement.

How It Works

The CREATE PROCEDURE statement creates a stored procedure that has one input parameter. Parameters are specified between the procedure name and the AS keyword. Here you specify only the parameter name and data type, so by default it is an input parameter. Parameter names start with @.

```
create procedure sp_Orders_By_EmployeeId
   @employeeid int
as
```

This parameter is used in the WHERE clause of the query.

```
where
   employeeid = @employeeid;
```

Note In this example, a semicolon terminates the query. It's optional here, but you'll see when it needs to be used in the next example.

Try It Out: Creating a Stored Procedure with an Output Parameter

Output parameters are usually used to pass values between stored procedures, but sometimes they need to be accessed from VB .NET, so here you'll see how to write a stored procedure with an output parameter so you can use it in a VB .NET program later. You'll also learn how to return a value other than zero.

1. Enter the following query and click Execute. You should see the message "Command(s) completed successfully" in the results window.

```
create procedure sp_Orders_By_EmployeeId2
    @employeeid int,
    @ordercount int = 0 output
as
    select orderid,customerid
    from orders
    where employeeid = @employeeid;
    select  @ordercount = count(*)
    from orders
    where  employeeid = @employeeid
    return @ordercount
```

2. Now you need to test your stored procedure. To do so, enter the following statements in the query window, making sure that you either replace the earlier statements or select only these statements while executing:

```
Declare @return_value int,
 @ordercount int

Execute @return_value=sp_Orders_By_EmployeeId2
@employeeId=2,
@ordercount=@ordercount output
```

```
Select @ordercount as '@ordercount'

Select 'Return value' =@return_value
```

You should get the results shown in Figure 6-4. Note that both the @ordercount and Return value rows show 96.

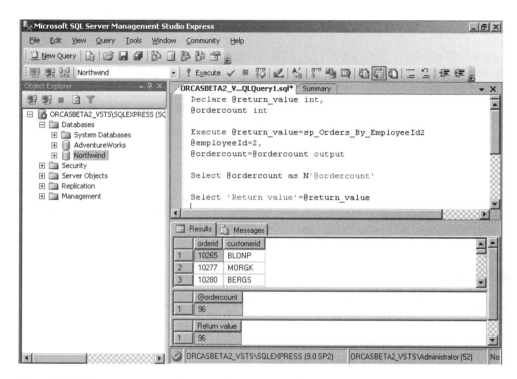

Figure 6-4. *Using an output parameter*

How It Works

You add an output parameter, @ordercount, assigning a default value of zero:

```
create procedure sp_Orders_By_EmployeeId2
    @employeeid int,
    @ordercount int = 0 output
as
    select orderid,customerid
    from orders
    where employeeid = @employeeid;
```

The keyword output marks it as an output parameter.
You also add an additional query:

```
select  @ordercount = count(*)
from  orders
    where  employeeid = @employeeid
```

In this example, you need the semicolon in sp_Orders_By_EmployeeId2 to separate the first query from the second. You assign the scalar returned by the new query to the output parameter in the SELECT list:

```
@ordercount = count(*)
```

and then you return the same value:

```
return @ordercount
```

The COUNT function returns an integer, which makes this a convenient way to demonstrate how to use the RETURN statement.

■Tip Input parameters can also be assigned default values.

There are other ways to do these (and many other) things with stored procedures. We've done all we need for this chapter, since our main objective is not teaching you how to write stored procedures, but how to use them in VB .NET. However, we'll show you how to modify and delete stored procedures in the remainder of this chapter.

Modifying Stored Procedures

Now we'll show you how to modify the sp_Select_All_Employees stored procedure you have created.

Try It Out: Modifying the Stored Procedure

To modify the sp_Select_All_Employees stored procedure you created earlier in the chapter, follow these steps:

1. Modify sp_Select_All_Employees as shown in the following code, and add an ORDER BY clause (see Figure 6-5):

```
Alter procedure sp_Select_All_Employees
as
    select employeeid,firstname,lastname
    from employees
    order by lastname,firstname
```

2. Execute the stored procedure using the statement shown in Figure 6-6. Notice that the employee names are now sorted by last name and then by first name; compare this to the results shown earlier in Figure 6-2, in which records are not sorted.

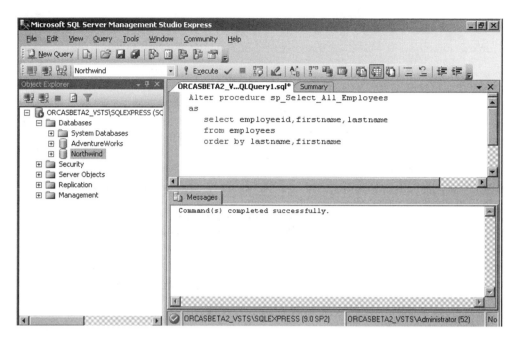

Figure 6-5. *Modifying the stored procedure*

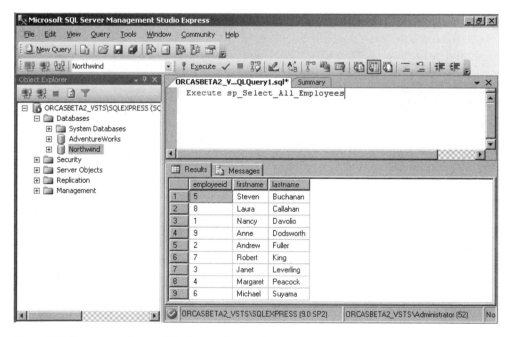

Figure 6-6. *Executing the modified stored procedure*

How It Works

After you execute the ALTER PROCEDURE statement, the stored procedure is updated in the database:

```
Alter procedure sp_Select_All_Employees
```

Including the ORDER BY clause while modifying the procedure results in the output being sorted in ascending order by last name and then by first name:

```
order by lastname,firstname
```

Displaying Definitions of Stored Procedures

SQL Server offers a mechanism of viewing the definition of the objects created in the database. This is known as *metadata retrieval*. The information about objects is stored in predefined system stored procedures that can be retrieved whenever required.

Try It Out: Viewing the Definition of Your Stored Procedure

To view the definition of your stored procedure, follow these steps:

1. Enter the following statement in the query window:

   ```
   Execute sp_helptext 'sp_Select_All_Employees'
   ```

2. Go to the Query menu, select Results To ➤ Results to Text, and then click Execute. You will see the same definition you specified for sp_Select_All_Employees. The output should be as shown in Figure 6-7.

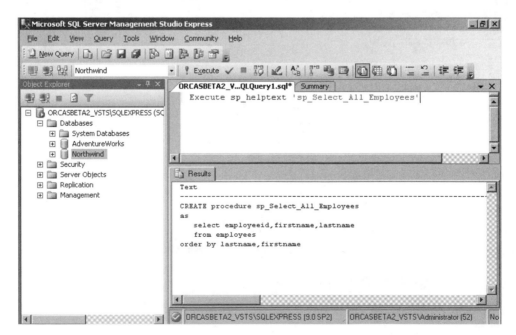

Figure 6-7. *Displaying the definition of a stored procedure*

How It Works

The statement sp_helptext is a predefined SQL Server stored procedure that accepts an object name as a parameter and shows the definition of that passed object:

```
Execute sp_helptext 'sp_Select_All_Employees'
```

■**Note** The sp_helptext statement doesn't work with table objects (e.g., you can't see the definition of the CREATE TABLE statement used while creating a table object).

Renaming Stored Procedures

SQL Server allows you to rename objects using the predefined stored procedure sp_rename. In the following example, you'll see how to use it to change a stored procedure's name.

Try It Out: Renaming a Stored Procedure

To rename a stored procedure, follow these steps:

1. Enter the following statement in the query window:

   ```
   Execute sp_rename 'sp_Select_All_Employees', 'sp_Select_Employees_Details'
   ```

2. Click Execute, and you will see the following message in the results window, even though sp_rename has been executed successfully: "Caution: Changing any part of an object name could break scripts and stored procedures."

3. Now go to Object Explorer, expand the Northwind database node, and then expand the Programmability node. Select the Stored Procedures node, right-click, and select Refresh.

4. Expand the Stored Procedures node and notice that sp_Select_All_Employees has been renamed to sp_Select_Employees_Details. Your screen should resemble Figure 6-8.

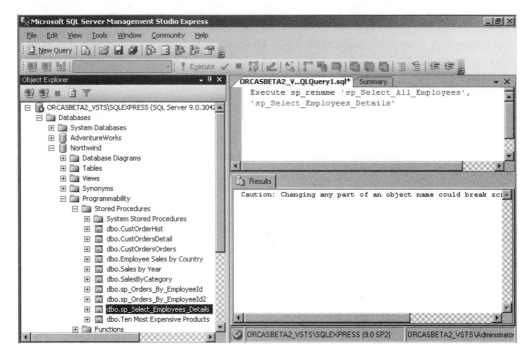

Figure 6-8. *Renaming a stored procedure*

How It Works

The sp_rename statement accepts an object's old name and then the object's new name as parameters:

```
Execute sp_rename 'sp_Select_All_Employees', 'sp_Select_Employees_Details'
```

■**Note** sp_rename works very well with most the objects, such as tables, columns, and others to rename them.

Working with Stored Procedures in VB .NET

Now that you've created some stored procedures, you can use them with VB .NET.

Try It Out: Executing a Stored Procedure with No Input Parameters

Here, you'll execute sp_Select_Employees_Details, which takes no input and returns only a result set: a list of all employees sorted by name.

1. Create a new Console Application project named CallSp1. Rename the CallSp1 Solution to Chapter6.

2. Rename the Module1.vb file to CallSp1.vb, and replace the generated code with the code in Listing 6-1.

▪**Note** You can easily rename the solution and project by selecting them, right-clicking, and selecting the Rename option.

Listing 6-1. CallSp1.vb

```vb
Imports System
Imports System.Data
Imports System.Data.SqlClient

Namespace Chapter6
    Class CallSp1
        Shared Sub Main()
            ' create connection
            Dim conn As New SqlConnection
            conn.ConnectionString = "Data Source=.\sqlexpress;➥
            Initial Catalog=Northwind;Integrated Security=True"

            ' open connection
            conn.Open()

            ' create command
            Dim cmd As SqlCommand = conn.CreateCommand()

            ' specify stored procedure to execute
            cmd.CommandType = CommandType.StoredProcedure
            cmd.CommandText = "sp_select_employees_details"

            ' execute command
            Dim rdr As SqlDataReader = cmd.ExecuteReader()

            ' Process the result set
            While rdr.Read()
```

```
                        Console.WriteLine("{0} {1} {2}",
            rdr(0).ToString().PadRight(5),➥
                        rdr(1).ToString(), rdr(2).ToString())
                End While
                'Console.ReadLine()
                rdr.Close()
                conn.Close()
            End Sub
        End Class
End Namespace
```

3. Build and run the solution by pressing Ctrl+F5. You should see the results in Figure 6-9.

Figure 6-9. *Running a stored procedure with VB .NET*

How It Works

You use the connection's CreateCommand method and then specify the command type is for a stored procedure call rather than a query. Finally, you set the command text to the stored procedure name.

```
' create command
Dim cmd As SqlCommand = conn.CreateCommand()

' specify stored procedure to execute
cmd.CommandType = CommandType.StoredProcedure
cmd.CommandText = "sp_select_employees_details"
```

The rest of the code changes only trivially to handle displaying the extra column. You used ExecuteReader just as you would for a query, which makes sense, since the stored procedure simply executes a query and returns a result set.

```
' execute command
Dim rdr As SqlDataReader = cmd.ExecuteReader()
```

Try It Out: Executing a Stored Procedure with Parameters

In this example, you'll call the sp_Orders_By_EmployeeId2 stored procedure, supplying the employee ID as an input parameter and displaying the result set, the output parameter, and the return value.

1. Add a new VB .NET Console Application project named CallSp2 to your Chapter6 solution. Rename Module1.vb to CallSp2.vb.

2. Replace the code in CallSp2.vb with the code in Listing 6-2.

Listing 6-2. CallSp2.vb

```vb
Imports System
Imports System.Data
Imports System.Data.SqlClient

Namespace Chapter6
    Class CallSp2
        Shared Sub Main()

            ' create connection
            Dim conn As New SqlConnection
            conn.ConnectionString = "Data Source=.\sqlexpress;Initial
            Catalog=Northwind;Integrated Security=True"

            Try
                ' open connection
                conn.Open()

                ' create command
                Dim cmd As SqlCommand = conn.CreateCommand()

                ' specify stored procedure to execute
                cmd.CommandType = CommandType.StoredProcedure
                cmd.CommandText = "sp_orders_by_employeeid2"

                ' create input parameter
                Dim inparm As SqlParameter = cmd.Parameters.Add( _
                "@employeeid", SqlDbType.Int)
                inparm.Direction = ParameterDirection.Input
                inparm.Value = 2

                ' create output parameter
                Dim ouparm As SqlParameter = cmd.Parameters.Add( _
                "@ordercount", SqlDbType.Int)
                ouparm.Direction = ParameterDirection.Output
```

```vb
            ' create return value parameter
            Dim retval As SqlParameter = cmd.Parameters.Add( _
            "return_value", SqlDbType.Int)
            retval.Direction = ParameterDirection.ReturnValue

            ' execute command
            Dim rdr As SqlDataReader = cmd.ExecuteReader()

            ' Process the result set
            While rdr.Read()
                Console.WriteLine("{0} {1}",
                    rdr(0).ToString().PadRight(5), rdr(1).ToString())
            End While
            rdr.Close()

            ' display output parameter value
            Console.WriteLine("The output parameter value is {0}" _
        , cmd.Parameters("@ordercount").Value)

            ' display return value
            Console.WriteLine( _
            "The return value is {0}" _
            , cmd.Parameters("return_value").Value)
        Catch ex As SqlException
            Console.WriteLine(ex.ToString())
        Finally
            conn.Close()
        End Try
    End Sub
    End Class
End Namespace
```

3. Make this the startup project and run it by pressing Ctrl+F5. You should see the results shown in Figure 6-10.

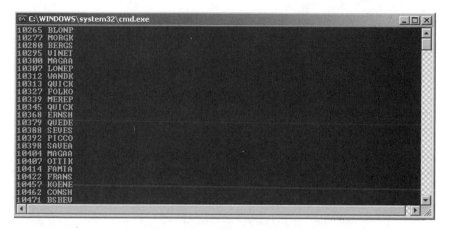

Figure 6-10. *Using parameters and the return value with VB .NET*

How It Works

This is very much like the previous example. The main difference is that you add three command parameters, specifying the kind of parameter with the `Direction` property:

```
' create input parameter
Dim inparm As SqlParameter = cmd.Parameters.Add( _
"@employeeid", SqlDbType.Int)
inparm.Direction = ParameterDirection.Input
inparm.Value = 2

' create output parameter
Dim ouparm As SqlParameter = cmd.Parameters.Add( _
"@ordercount", SqlDbType.Int)
ouparm.Direction = ParameterDirection.Output

' create return value parameter
Dim retval As SqlParameter = cmd.Parameters.Add( _
"return_value", SqlDbType.Int)
retval.Direction = ParameterDirection.ReturnValue
```

You set the input parameter value to 2 before the call:

```
inparm.Value = 2
```

and retrieve the values for the output parameter and return value by indexing into the command's parameters collection after the stored procedure is returned:

```
' display output parameter value
Console.WriteLine("The output parameter value is {0}" _
, cmd.Parameters("@ordercount").Value)
```

```
' display return value
Console.WriteLine( _
"The return value is {0}" _
, cmd.Parameters("return_value").Value)
```

You can create as many input and output parameters as you need. You *must* provide command parameters for all input parameters that don't have default values. You don't have to provide command parameters for any output parameters you don't need to use. Input and output parameter names must agree with the parameter names in the stored procedure, except for case (remember that T-SQL is not case sensitive).

Though it's handled in ADO.NET as a command parameter, there is always only one return value. Like output parameters, you don't need to create a command parameter for the return value unless you intend to use it. But unlike input and output parameters, you can give it whatever parameter name you choose.

Deleting Stored Procedures

Once a stored procedure is created, it can also be deleted if its functionality is not required.

Try It Out: Deleting a Stored Procedure

You'll delete your first stored procedure (sp_Select_All_Employees), which you renamed to sp_Select_Employees_Details.

1. Replace the query with the following statement in the query window and click Execute.

   ```
   Drop procedure sp_Select_Employees_Details
   ```

   You will see the following message: "Command(s) completed successfully."

2. Navigate to Object Explorer, expand the Northwind database node, and then expand the Programmability node. Select the Stored Procedures node, right-click, and select Refresh. Notice that the procedure sp_Select_Employees_Details has been deleted, as it is no longer listed in Object Explorer (see Figure 6-11).

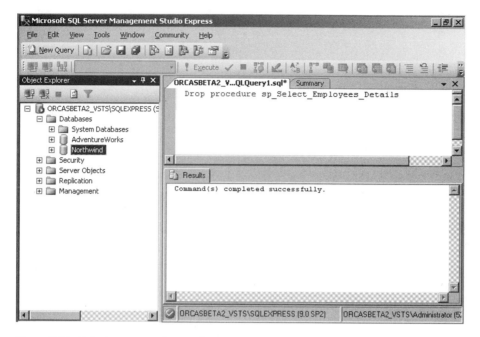

Figure 6-11. *Deleting a stored procedure*

How It Works

SQL Server offers the DROP statement to remove objects. To remove the stored procedure, you use

```
drop procedure sp_Select_Employees_Details
```

In this statement, DROP takes the procedure sp_Select_Employees_Details as its value and will thus remove it.

Summary

In this chapter, you created stored procedures; you developed an understanding of what's involved in calling stored procedures from VB .NET. You saw that calling stored procedures isn't inherently different from executing queries and statements; you simply create appropriate command parameters for the stored procedure parameters you need to use. You also learned about modifying a stored procedure, retrieving metadata information, and renaming and deleting a stored procedure, as well as calling a stored procedure from VB .NET applications using ADO .NET.

In the next chapter, you will see how to work with XML.

CHAPTER 7

■■■

Using XML

XML has been around for many years; with the release of Microsoft .NET technology, XML has become even more popular. Microsoft's development tools and technologies have built-in features to support XML. The advantages of using XML and its related technologies are major foundations of both the Internet and .NET.

Our goal in this chapter is to introduce you to the most essential XML concepts and terminology and the most basic techniques for using XML with SQL Server 2005. This will enable you to handle some common programming tasks while writing a software application.

In this chapter, we'll cover the following:

- Defining XML

- Why XML?

- Benefits of storing data as XML

- Understanding XML documents

- Understanding the XML declaration

- Converting relational data to XML

- How to store and retrieve XML documents using the xml data type

Defining XML

XML stands for eXtensible Markup Language. XML, which is derived from SGML (Standard Generalized Markup Language), is a metalanguage. A *metalanguage* isn't used for programming but rather for defining other languages, and the languages XML defines are known as *markup languages*. Markup is exactly what it implies: a means of "marking up" something. The XML document is in the form of a text document, and it can be read by both humans and computers.

■Note In essence, each XML document is an instance of a language defined by the XML elements used in the document. The specific language may or may not have been explicitly defined, but professional use of XML demands carefully planning one's XML *vocabulary* and specifying its definition in a *schema* that can be used to validate that documents adhere to both the syntax and semantics of a vocabulary. The XML Schema Definition language (usually referred to as XSD) is the language for defining XML vocabularies.

The World Wide Web Consortium (W3C) developed XML in 1996. Intended to support a wide variety of applications, XML was used by the W3C to create eXtensible HTML (XHTML), an XML vocabulary. Since 1996, the W3C has developed a variety of other XML-oriented technologies, including eXtensible Stylesheet Language (XSL), which provides the same kind of facility for XHTML that Cascading Style Sheets (CSS) does for HTML, and XSL Transformations (XSLT), which is a language for transforming XML documents into other XML documents.

Why XML?

XML is multipurpose, extensible data representation technology. XML increases the possibilities for applications to consume and manipulate data. XML data is different from relational data in that it can be structured, semistructured, or unstructured. XML support in SQL Server 2005 is fully integrated with the relational engine and query optimizer, allowing the retrieval and modification of XML data and even the conversion between XML and relational data representations.

Benefits of Storing Data As XML

XML is a platform-independent, data-representation format that offers certain benefits over a relational format for specific data representation requirements.

Storing data as XML offers many benefits, such as the following:

- Since XML is self-describing, applications can consume XML data without knowing the schema or structure. XML data is always arranged hierarchically in a tree structure form. XML tree structure must always have a root, or parent node, which is known as an *XML document*.

- XML maintains document ordering. Because XML is arranged in tree structure, maintaining node order becomes easy.

- XML Schema is used to define valid XML document structure.

- Because of XML's hierarchical structure, you can search inside the tree structures. XQuery and XPath are the query languages designed to search XML data.

- Data stored as XML is extensible. It is easy to manipulate XML data by inserting, modifying, and deleting nodes.

■**Note** Well-formed XML is an XML document that meets a set of constraints specified by the W3C recommendation for XML 1.0. For example, well-formed XML must contain a root-level element, and any other nested elements must open and close properly without intermixing.

SQL Server 2005 validates some of the constraints of well-formed XML. Some rules such as the requirement for a root-level element are not enforced. For a complete list of requirements for well-formed XML, refer to the W3C recommendations for XML 1.0 at `http://www.w3.org/TR/REC-xml`.

Understanding XML Documents

An XML document could be a physical file on a computer, a data stream over a network (in theory, formatted so a human could read it, but in practice, often in compressed binary form), or just a string in memory. It has to be complete in itself, however, and even without a schema, it must obey certain rules.

The most fundamental rule is that XML documents must be *well formed*. At its simplest, this means that overlapping elements aren't allowed, so you must close all *child* elements before the end tag of their *parent* element. For example, this XML document is well formed:

```
<states>
    <state>
        <name>Delaware</name>
        <city>Dover</city>
        <city>Wilmington</city>
    </state>
</states>
```

It has a *root* (or *document*) element, states, delimited by a start tag, `<states>`, and an end tag, `</states>`. The root element is the parent of the state element, which is in turn the parent of a name element and two city elements. An XML document can have only one root element.

Elements may have *attributes*. In the following example, name is used as an attribute with the state element:

```
<states>
    <state name="Delaware">
        <city>Dover</city>
        <city>Wilmington</city>
    </state>
</states>
```

This retains the same information as the earlier example, replacing the name element, which occurs only once, with a name attribute and changing the *content* of the original element (Delaware) into the *value* of the attribute ("Delaware"). An element may have any number of attributes, but it may not have duplicate attributes, so the city elements weren't candidates for replacement.

Elements may have content (text data or other elements), or they may be *empty*. For example, just for the sake of argument, if you want to keep track of how many states are in the document, you could use an empty element to do it:

```
<states>
   <controlinfo count="1"/>
   <state name="Delaware">
      <city>Dover</city>
      <city>Wilmington</city>
   </state>
</states>
```

The empty element, `controlinfo`, has one attribute, `count`, but no content. Note that it isn't delimited by start and end tags, but exists within an *empty element tag* (that starts with < and ends with />).

An alternative syntax for empty elements, using start and end tags, is also valid:

```
<controlinfo count="1"></controlinfo>
```

Many programs that generate XML use this form.

■**Note** Though it's easy to design XML documents, designing them well is as much a challenge as designing a database. Many experienced XML designers disagree over the best use of attributes and even whether attributes should be used at all (and without attributes, empty elements have virtually no use). While elements may in some ways map more ideally to relational data, this doesn't mean that attributes have no place in XML design. After all, XML isn't intended to (and in principle can't) conform to the relational model of data. In fact, you'll see that a "pure" element-only design can be more difficult to work with in T-SQL.

Understanding the XML Declaration

In addition to elements and attributes, XML documents can have other parts, but most of them are important only if you need to delve deeply into XML. Though it is optional, the *XML declaration* is one part that should be included in an XML document to precisely conform to the W3C recommendation. If used, it must occur before the root element in an XML document.

The XML declaration is similar in format to an element, but it has question marks immediately next to the angle brackets. It always has an attribute named `version`; currently, this has two possible values: "1.0" and "1.1". (A couple other attributes are defined but aren't required.) So, the simplest form of an XML declaration is

```
<?xml version="1.0" ?>
```

XML has other aspects, but this is all you need to get started. In fact, this may be all you'll ever need to be quite effective. As you'll see, we don't use any XML declarations (or even more important things such as XML schemas and namespaces) for our XML documents, yet our small examples work well, are representative of fundamental XML processing, and could be scaled up to much larger XML documents.

Converting Relational Data to XML

A SELECT query returns results as a row set. You can optionally retrieve results of a SQL query as XML by specifying the FOR XML clause in the query. SQL Server 2005 enables you to extract relational data into XML form, by using the FOR XML clause in the SELECT statement. SQL Server 2005 extends the FOR XML capabilities, making it easier to represent complex hierarchical structures and add new keywords to modify the resulting XML structure.

■**Note** In Chapter 13, we'll show how to extract data from a dataset, convert it into XML, and write it to a file with the dataset's WriteXml method.

The FOR XML clause converts result sets from a query into an XML structure, and it provides four modes of formatting:

- FOR XML RAW

- FOR XML AUTO

- FOR XML PATH

- FOR XML EXPLICIT

We'll use the first two in examples to show how to generate XML with a query.

Using FOR XML RAW

The FOR XML RAW mode transforms each row in the query result set into an XML element identified as row for each row displayed in the result set. Each column name in the SELECT statement is added as an attribute to the row element while displaying the result set.

By default, each column value in the row set that is not null is mapped to an attribute of the row element.

Try It Out: Using FOR XML RAW (Attribute Centric)

To use FOR XML RAW to transform returned rows into XML elements, follow these steps:

1. Open SQL Server Management Studio Express (SSMSE), and in the Connect to Server dialog box select *<ServerName>*\SQLEXPRESS as the server name and click Connect.

2. In Object Explorer, expand the Databases node, select the AdventureWorks database, and click the New Query button. Enter the following query and click Execute:

```
SELECT ProductModelID, Name
FROM Production.ProductModel
WHERE ProductModelID  between 98 and 101
FOR XML RAW
```

3. You will see a link in the results pane of the query window. Click the link, and you should see the results shown in Figure 7-1.

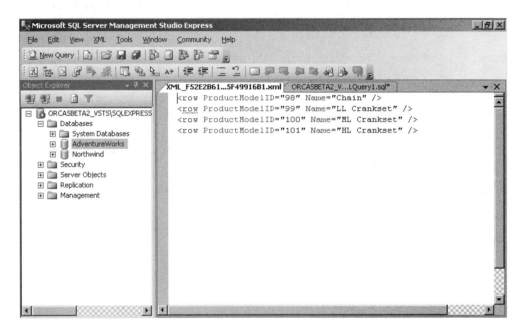

Figure 7-1. *Using* FOR XML RAW

How It Works

FOR XML RAW mode produces very "raw" XML. It turns each row in the result set into an XML row empty element and uses an attribute for each of the column values, using the alias names you specify in the query as the attribute names. It produces a string composed of all the elements.

FOR XML RAW mode doesn't produce an XML document, since it has as many root elements (raw) as there are rows in the result set, and an XML document can have only one root element.

Try It Out: Using FOR XML RAW (Element Centric)

To change the formatting from attribute centric (as shown in the previous example) to element centric, which means that a new element will be created for each column, you need to add the ELEMENTS keyword after the FOR XML RAW clause as shown in the following example:

1. Replace the existing query in the query window with the following query and click Execute:

```
SELECT ProductModelID, Name
FROM Production.ProductModel
WHERE ProductModelID  between 98 and 101
FOR XML RAW,ELEMENTS
```

2. You will see a link in the results pane of the query window. Click the link, and you should see the results shown in Figure 7-2.

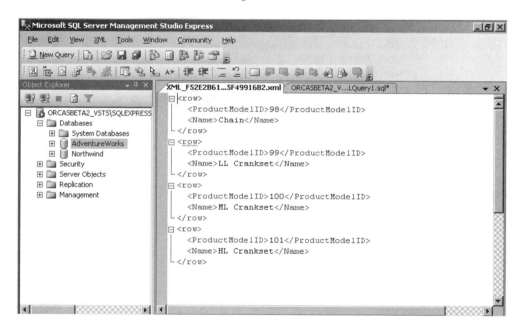

Figure 7-2. *Using* FOR XML RAW ELEMENTS

How It Works

FOR XML RAW ELEMENTS mode produces very "element-centric" XML. It turns each row in the result set where each column is converted into an attribute.

FOR XML RAW ELEMENTS mode also doesn't produce an XML document, since it has as many root elements (raw) as there are rows in the result set, and an XML document can have only one root element.

Try It Out: Renaming the row Element

For each row in the result set, the FOR XML RAW mode generates a row element. You can optionally specify another name for this element by including an optional argument in the FOR XML
RAW mode, as shown in the following example. To achieve this, you need to add an alias after
the FOR XML RAW clause, which you'll do now.

1. Replace the existing query in the query window with the following query, and click
   Execute:

   ```
   SELECT ProductModelID, Name
   FROM Production.ProductModel
   WHERE ProductModelID  between 98 and 101
   FOR XML RAW ('ProductModelDetail'),ELEMENTS
   ```

2. You will see a link in the results pane of the query window. Click the link, and you
   should see the results shown in Figure 7-3.

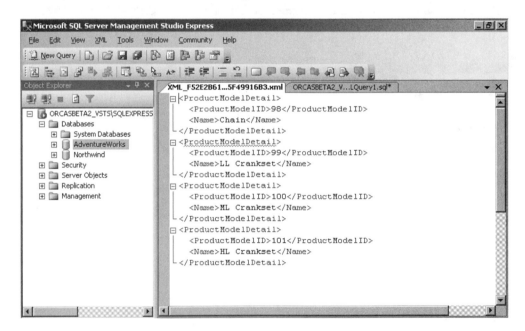

Figure 7-3. *Renaming the* row *element*

How It Works

FOR XML RAW ('alias') mode produces output where the row element is renamed to the alias
specified in the query.

Because the ELEMENTS directive is added in the query, the result is element centric, and
this is why the row element is renamed with the alias specified. If you don't add the ELEMENTS
keyword in the query, the output will be attribute centric, and the row element will be
renamed to the alias specified in the query.

Observations About FOR XML RAW Formatting

FOR XML RAW does not provide a root node, and this is why the XML structure is not a well-formed XML document.

FOR XML RAW supports attribute- and element-centric formatting, which means that all the columns must be formatted in the same way. Hence it is not possible to have the XML structure returned with both the XML attributes and XML elements.

FOR XML RAW generates a hierarchy in which all the elements in the XML structure are at the same level.

Using FOR XML AUTO

FOR XML AUTO mode returns query results as nested XML elements. This does not provide much control over the shape of the XML generated from a query result. FOR XML AUTO mode queries are useful if you want to generate simple hierarchies.

Each table in the FROM clause, from which at least one column is listed in the SELECT clause, is represented as an XML element. The columns listed in the SELECT clause are mapped to attributes or subelements.

Try It Out: Using FOR XML AUTO

To see how to use FOR XML AUTO to format query results as nested XML elements, follow these steps:

1. Replace the existing query in the query window with the following query and click Execute:

```
SELECT Cust.CustomerID,
OrderHeader.CustomerID,
OrderHeader.SalesOrderID,
OrderHeader.Status,
Cust.CustomerType
FROM Sales.Customer Cust, Sales.SalesOrderHeader
OrderHeader
WHERE Cust.CustomerID = OrderHeader.CustomerID
ORDER BY Cust.CustomerID
FOR XML AUTO
```

2. You will see a link in the results pane of the query window. Click the link, and you should see the results shown in Figure 7-4.

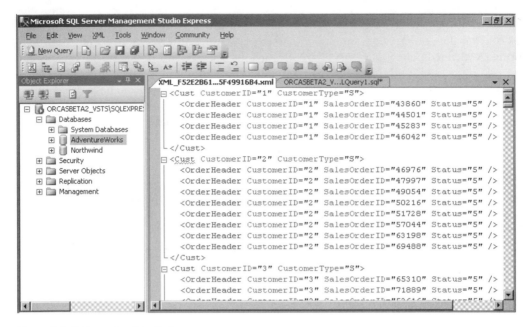

Figure 7-4. *Using* FOR XML AUTO

How It Works

The CustomerID references the Cust table. Therefore, a Cust element is created and CustomerID is added as its attribute.

Next, three columns, OrderHeader.CustomerID, OrderHeader.SaleOrderID, and Order-Header.Status, reference the OrderHeader table. Therefore, an OrderHeader element is added as a subelement of the Cust element, and the three columns are added as attributes of OrderHeader.

Next, the Cust.CustomerType column again references the Cust table that was already identified by the Cust.CustomerID column. Therefore, no new element is created. Instead, the CustomerType attribute is added to the Cust element that was previously created.

The query specifies aliases for the table names. These aliases appear as corresponding element names. ORDER BY is required to group all children under one parent.

Observations About FOR XML AUTO Formatting

FOR XML AUTO does not provide a root node, and this is why the XML structure is not a well-formed XML document.

FOR XML AUTO supports attribute- and element-centric formatting, which means that all the columns must be formatted in the same way. Hence it is not possible to have the XML structure returned with both the XML attributes and XML elements.

FOR XML AUTO does not provide a renaming mechanism the way FOR XML RAW does. However, FOR XML AUTO uses table and column names and aliases if present.

Using the xml Data Type

SQL Server 2005 has a new data type, xml, that is designed not only for holding XML documents (which are essentially character strings and can be stored in any character column big enough to hold them), but also for processing XML documents. When we discussed parsing an XML document into a DOM tree, we didn't mention that once it's parsed, the XML document can be updated. You can change element contents and attribute values, and you can add and remove element occurrences to and from the hierarchy.

We won't update XML documents here, but the xml data type provides methods to do it. It is a very different kind of SQL Server data type, and describing how to exploit it would take a book of its own—maybe more than one. Our focus here will be on what every database programmer needs to know: how to use the xml type to store and retrieve XML documents.

■Note There are so many ways to process XML documents (even in ADO.NET and with SQLXML, a support package for SQL Server 2000) that only time will tell if incorporating such features into a SQL Server data type was worth the effort. Because XML is such an important technology, being able to process XML documents purely in T-SQL does offer many possibilities, but right now it's unclear how much more about the xml data type you'll ever need to know. At any rate, this chapter will give you what you need to know to start experimenting with it.

Try It Out: Creating a Table to Store XML

To create a table to hold XML documents, replace the existing query in the query window with the following query and click Execute:

```
create table xmltest
(
   xid  int not null primary key,
   xdoc xml not null
)
```

How It Works

This works in the same way as a CREATE TABLE statement is expected to work. Though we've said the xml data type is different from other SQL Server data types, columns of xml type are defined just like any other columns.

■Note The xml data type cannot be used in primary keys.

Now, you'll insert your XML documents into xmltest and query it to see that they were stored.

Try It Out: Storing and Retrieving XML Documents

To insert your XML documents, follow these steps:

1. Replace the code in the SQL query window with the following two INSERT statements:

```
insert into xmltest
values(
1,
'
<states>
    <state>
        <abbr>CA</abbr>
        <name>California</name>
        <city>Berkeley</city>
        <city>Los Angeles</city>
        <city>Wilmington</city>
    </state>
    <state>
        <abbr>DE</abbr>
        <name>Delaware</name>
        <city>Newark</city>
        <city>Wilmington</city>
    </state>
</states>
'
)

insert into xmltest
values(
2,
'
<states>
    <state abbr="CA" name="California">
        <city name="Berkeley"/>
        <city name="Los Angeles"/>
        <city name="Wilmington"/>
    </state>
    <state abbr="DE" name="Delaware">
        <city name="Newark"/>
        <city name="Wilmington"/>
    </state>
</states>
'
)
```

2. Run the two INSERT statements by clicking Execute, and then display the table with select * from xmltest. You see the two rows displayed. Click the xdoc column in the first row, and you should see the XML shown in Figure 7-5.

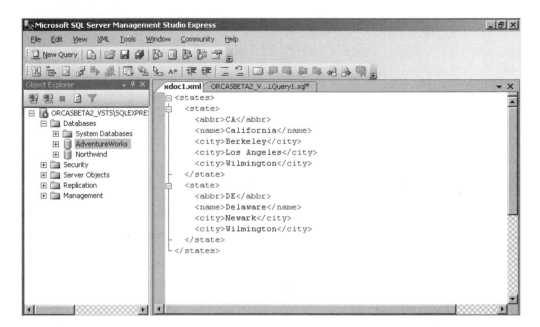

Figure 7-5. *Viewing an XML document*

How It Works

This works the same way all INSERTs work. You simply provide the primary keys as integers and the XML documents as strings. The query works just as expected, too.

Summary

This chapter covered the fundamentals of XML that every Visual Basic .NET programmer needs to know. It also showed you how to use the most frequently used T-SQL features for extracting XML from tables and querying XML documents like tables. Finally, we discussed the xml data type and gave you some practice using it.

How much more you need to know about XML or T-SQL and ADO.NET facilities for using XML documents depends on what you need to do. As for many developers, this chapter may be all you ever need to know and understand. If you do more sophisticated XML processing, you now have a strong foundation for experimenting on your own.

In the next chapter, you will learn about database transactions.

Understanding Transactions

For any business, transactions, which may comprise many individual operations and even other transactions, play a key role. Transactions are essential for maintaining data integrity, both for multiple related operations and when multiple users update the database concurrently.

This chapter will discuss the concepts related to transactions and how transactions can be used in SQL Server 2005 and VB.NET.

In this chapter, we'll cover the following:

- What is a transaction?

- When to use transactions

- Understanding ACID properties

- Transaction design

- Transaction state

- Specifying transaction boundaries

- T-SQL statements allowed in a transaction

- Local transactions in SQL Server 2005

- Distributed transactions in SQL Server 2005

- Guidelines to code efficient transactions

- How to code transactions

What Is a Transaction?

A *transaction* is a set of operations performed so all operations are guaranteed to succeed or fail as one unit.

A common example of a transaction is the process of transferring money from a checking account to a savings account. This involves two operations: deducting money from the checking account and adding it to the savings account. Both must succeed together and be *committed* to the accounts, or both must fail together and be *rolled back* so that the accounts are maintained in a consistent state. Under no circumstances should money be deducted from the checking account but not added to the savings account (or vice versa)—at least you would not want this to happen with the transactions occurring with your bank accounts. By using a transaction, both the operations, namely debit and credit, can be guaranteed to succeed or fail together. So both accounts remain in a consistent state all the times.

When to Use Transactions

You should use transactions when several operations must succeed or fail as a unit. The following are some frequent scenarios where use of transactions is recommended:

- In batch processing, where multiple rows must be inserted, updated, or deleted as a single unit

- Whenever a change to one table requires that other tables be kept consistent

- When modifying data in two or more databases concurrently

- In distributed transactions, where data is manipulated in databases on different servers

When you use transactions, you place locks on data pending permanent change to the database. No other operations can take place on locked data until the lock is released. You could lock anything from a single row up to the whole database. This is called *concurrency*, which means how the database handles multiple updates at one time.

In the bank example, locks ensure that two separate transactions don't access the same accounts at the same time. If they did, either deposits or withdrawals could be lost.

■**Note** It's important to keep transactions pending for the shortest period of time. A lock stops others from accessing the locked database resource. Too many locks, or locks on frequently accessed resources, can seriously degrade performance.

Understanding ACID Properties

A transaction is characterized by four properties, often referred to as the *ACID properties*: atomicity, consistency, isolation, and durability.

■**Note** The term ACID was coined by Andreas Reuter in 1983.

Atomicity: A transaction is atomic if it's regarded as a single action rather than a collection of separate operations. So, only when all the separate operations succeed does a transaction succeed and is committed to the database. On the other hand, if a single operation fails during the transaction, everything is considered to have failed and must be undone (rolled back) if it has already taken place. In the case of the order-entry system of the Northwind database, when you enter an order into the Orders and Order Details tables, data will be saved together in both tables, or it won't be saved at all.

Consistency: The transaction should leave the database in a consistent state—whether or not it completed successfully. The data modified by the transaction must comply with all the constraints placed on the columns in order to maintain data integrity. In the case of Northwind, you can't have rows in the Order Details table without a corresponding row in the Orders table, as this would leave the data in an inconsistent state.

Isolation: Every transaction has a well-defined boundary—that is, it is isolated from another transaction. One transaction shouldn't affect other transactions running at the same time. Data modifications made by one transaction must be isolated from the data modifications made by all other transactions. A transaction sees data in the state it was in before another concurrent transaction modified it, or it sees the data after the second transaction has completed, but it doesn't see an intermediate state.

Durability: Data modifications that occur within a successful transaction are kept permanently within the system regardless of what else occurs. Transaction logs are maintained so that should a failure occur the database can be restored to its original state before the failure. As each transaction is completed, a row is entered in the database transaction log. If you have a major system failure that requires the database to be restored from a backup, you could then use this transaction log to insert (roll forward) any successful transactions that have taken place.

Every database server that offers support for transactions enforces these four ACID properties automatically.

Transaction Design

Transactions represent real-world events such as bank transactions, airline reservations, remittance of funds, and so forth.

The purpose of transaction design is to define and document the high-level characteristics of transactions required on the database system, including the following:

- Data to be used by the transaction

- Functional characteristics of the transaction

- Output of the transaction

- Importance to users

- Expected rate of usage

There are three main types of transactions:

- *Retrieval transactions*: Retrieves data from display on the screen

- *Update transactions*: Inserts new records, deletes old records, or modifies existing records in the database

- *Mixed transactions*: Involves both retrieval and updating of data

Transaction State

In the absence of failures, all transactions complete successfully. However, a transaction may not always complete its execution successfully. Such a transaction is termed *aborted*.

A transaction that completes its execution successfully is said to be *committed*. Figure 8-1 shows that if a transaction has been partially committed, it will be committed but only if it has not failed; and if the transaction has failed, it will be aborted.

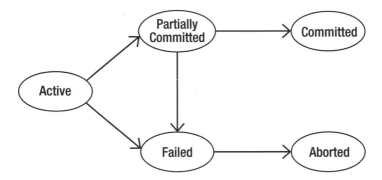

Figure 8-1. *States of a transaction*

Specifying Transaction Boundaries

SQL Server transaction boundaries help you to identify when SQL Server transactions start and end by using API functions and methods:

- *Transact-SQL statements*: Use the BEGIN TRANSACTION, COMMIT TRANSACTION, COMMIT WORK, ROLLBACK TRANSACTION, ROLLBACK WORK, and SET IMPLICIT_TRANSACTIONS statements to delineate transactions. These are primarily used in DB-Library applications and in T-SQL scripts, such as the scripts that are run using the osql command-prompt utility.

- *API functions and methods*: Database APIs such as ODBC, OLE DB, ADO, and the .NET Framework SQLClient namespace contain functions or methods used to delineate transactions. These are the primary mechanisms used to control transactions in a database engine application.

Each transaction must be managed by only one of these methods. Using both methods on the same transaction can lead to undefined results. For example, you should not start a transaction using the ODBC API functions, and then use the T-SQL COMMIT statement to complete the transaction. This would not notify the SQL Server ODBC driver that the transaction was committed. In this case, use the ODBC SQLEndTran function to end the transaction.

T-SQL Statements Allowed in a Transaction

You can use all T-SQL statements in a transaction, except for the following statements: ALTER DATABASE, RECONFIGURE, BACKUP, RESTORE, CREATE DATABASE, UPDATE STATISTICS, and DROP DATABASE.

Also, you cannot use sp_dboption to set database options or use any system procedures that modify the master database inside explicit or implicit transactions.

Local Transactions in SQL Server 2005

All database engines are supposed to provide built-in support for transactions. Transactions that are restricted to only a single resource or database are known as *local transactions*. Local transactions can be in one of the following four transaction modes:

Autocommit Transactions   Autocommit mode is the default transaction management mode of SQL Server. Every T-SQL statement is committed or rolled back when it is completed. If a statement completes successfully, it is committed; if it encounters any errors, it is bound to roll back. A SQL Server connection operates in autocommit mode whenever this default mode has not been overridden by any type transactions.

Explicit Transactions   Explicit transactions are those in which you explicitly control when the transaction begins and when it ends. Prior to SQL Server 2000, explicit transactions were also called *user-defined* or *user-specified* transactions.

T-SQL scripts for this mode use the BEGIN TRANSACTION, COMMIT TRANSACTION, and ROLLBACK TRANSACTION statements. Explicit transaction mode lasts only for the duration of the transaction. When the transaction ends, the connection returns to the transaction mode it was in before the explicit transaction was started.

Implicit Transactions   When you connect to a database using SQL Server Management Studio Express and execute a DML query, the changes are automatically saved. This occurs because, by default, the connection is in autocommit transaction mode. If you want no changes to be committed unless you explicitly indicate so, you need to set the connection to implicit transaction mode.

You can set the database connection to implicit transaction mode by using SET IMPLICIT _TRANSACTIONS ON|OFF.

After implicit transaction mode has been set to ON for a connection, SQL Server automatically starts a transaction when it first executes any of the following statements: ALTER TABLE, CREATE, DELETE, DROP, FETCH, GRANT, INSERT, OPEN, REVOKE, SELECT, TRUNCATE TABLE, and UPDATE.

The transaction remains in effect until a COMMIT or ROLLBACK statement has been explicitly issued. This means that when, say, an UPDATE statement is issued on a particular record in a database, SQL Server will maintain a lock on the data scoped for data modification until either a COMMIT or ROLLBACK is issued. In case neither of these commands is issued, the transaction will be automatically rolled back when the user disconnects. This is why it is not a best practice to use implicit transaction mode on a highly concurrent database.

Batch-Scoped Transactions   A connection can be in batch-scoped transaction mode, if the transaction running in it is Multiple Active Result Sets (MARS) enabled. Basically MARS has an associated batch execution environment, as it allows ADO.NET to take advantage of SQL Server 2005's capability of having multiple active commands on a single connection object.

When MARS is enabled, you can have multiple interleaved batches executing at the same time, so all the changes made to the execution environment are scoped to the specific batch until the execution of the batch is complete. Once the execution of the batch completes, the execution settings are copied to the default environment. Thus a connection is said to be using batch-scoped transaction mode if it is running a transaction, has MARS enabled on it, and has multiple batches running at the same time.

MARS allows executing multiple interleaved batches of commands. However, MARS does not let you have multiple transactions on the same connection; it only allows you to have Multiple Active Result Sets.

Distributed Transactions in SQL Server 2005

In contrast to local transactions, which are restricted to a single resource or database, *distributed transactions* span two or more servers, which are known as *resource managers*. Transaction management needs to be coordinated among the resource managers via a server component known as a *transaction manager* or *transaction coordinator*. SQL Server can operate as a resource manager for distributed transactions coordinated by transaction managers such as the Microsoft Distributed Transaction Coordinator (MS DTC).

A transaction with a single SQL Server that spans two or more databases is actually a distributed transaction. SQL Server, however, manages the distributed transaction internally.

At the application level, a distributed transaction is managed in much the same way as a local transaction. At the end of the transaction, the application requests the transaction to be either committed or rolled back. A distributed commit must be managed differently by the transaction manager to minimize the risk that a network failure might lead you to a situation when one of the resource managers is committing instead of rolling back the transactions due to failure caused by various reasons. This critical situation can be handled by managing the commit process in two phases, also known as *two-phase commit*:

Prepare phase: When the transaction manager receives a commit request, it sends a prepare command to all of the resource managers involved in the transaction. Each resource manager then does everything required to make the transaction durable, and all buffers holding any of the log images for other transactions are flushed to disk. As each resource manager completes the prepare phase, it returns success or failure of the prepare phase to the transaction manager.

Commit phase: If the transaction manager receives successful prepares from all of the resource managers, it sends a COMMIT command to each resource manager. If all of the resource managers report a successful commit, the transaction manager sends notification of success to the application. If any resource manager reports a failure to prepare, the transaction manager sends a ROLLBACK statement to each resource manager and indicates the failure of the commit to the application.

Guidelines to Code Efficient Transactions

We recommend you use the following guidelines while coding transactions to make them as efficient as possible:

- *Do not require input from users during a transaction.*

  Get all required input from users before a transaction is started. If additional user input is required during a transaction, roll back the current transaction and restart the transaction after the user input is supplied. Even if users respond immediately, human reaction times are vastly slower than computer speeds. All resources held by the transaction are held for an extremely long time, which has the potential to cause blocking problems. If users do not respond, the transaction remains active, locking critical resources until they respond, which may not happen for several minutes or even hours.

- *Do not open a transaction while browsing through data, if at all possible.*

  Transactions should not be started until all preliminary data analysis has been completed.

- *Keep the transaction as short as possible.*

  After you know the modifications that have to be made, start a transaction, execute the modification statements, and then immediately commit or roll back. Do not open the transaction before it is required.

- *Make intelligent use of lower cursor concurrency options, such as optimistic concurrency options.*

  In a system with a low probability of concurrent updates, the overhead of dealing with an occasional "somebody else changed your data after you read it" error can be much lower than the overhead of always locking rows as they are read.

- *Access the least amount of data possible while in a transaction.*

  The smaller the amount of data that you access in the transaction, the fewer the number of rows that will be locked, reducing contention between transactions.

How to Code Transactions

The following three T-SQL statements control transactions in SQL Server:

- BEGIN TRANSACTION: This marks the beginning of a transaction.

- COMMIT TRANSACTION: This marks the successful end of a transaction. It signals the database to save the work.

- ROLLBACK TRANSACTION: This denotes that a transaction hasn't been successful and signals the database to roll back to the state it was in prior to the transaction.

Note that there is no END TRANSACTION statement. Transactions end on (explicit or implicit) commits and rollbacks.

Coding Transactions in T-SQL

You'll use a stored procedure to practice coding transactions in SQL. It's an intentionally artificial example but representative of transaction processing fundamentals. It keeps things simple so you can focus on the important issue of what can happen in a transaction. That's what you really need to understand, especially when you later code the same transaction in VB.NET.

■**Warning** Using ROLLBACK and COMMIT inside stored procedures typically requires careful consideration of what transactions may already be in progress and have led to the stored procedure call. The example runs by itself, so you don't need to be concerned with this here, but you should always consider whether it's a potential issue.

Try It Out: Coding a Transaction in T-SQL

Here, you'll code a transaction to both add a customer to and delete one from the Northwind Customers table. The Customers table has eleven columns; two columns, CustomerID and

CompanyName, don't allow null values, whereas the rest do, so you'll use just the CustomerID and CompanyName columns for inserting values. You'll also use arbitrary customer IDs to make it easy to find the rows you manipulate when viewing customers sorted by ID.

1. Open SQL Server Management Studio Express (SSMSE), and in the Connect to Server dialog box, select *<ServerName>*\SQLEXPRESS as the server name and then click Connect.

2. In Object Explorer, expand the Databases node, select the Northwind database, and click the New Query button.

3. Create a stored procedure named sp_Trans_Test using the code in Listing 8-1.

Listing 8-1. sp_Trans_Test

```
create procedure sp_Trans_Test
    @newcustid nchar(5),
    @newcompname nvarchar(40),
    @oldcustid nchar(5)
as
    declare @inserr int
    declare @delerr int
    declare @maxerr int

    set @maxerr = 0

    begin transaction

    -- Add a customer
    insert into customers (customerid, companyname)
    values(@newcustid, @newcompname)

    -- Save error number returned from Insert statement
    set @inserr = @@error
    if @inserr > @maxerr
        set @maxerr = @inserr

    -- Delete a customer
    delete from customers
    where customerid = @oldcustid

    -- Save error number returned from Delete statement
    set @delerr = @@error
    if @delerr > @maxerr
        set @maxerr = @delerr
```

```
-- If an error occurred, roll back
if @maxerr <> 0
  begin
     rollback
     print 'Transaction rolled back'
  end
else
  begin
     commit
     print 'Transaction committed'
  end

print 'INSERT error number:' + cast(@inserr as nvarchar(8))
print 'DELETE error number:' + cast(@delerr as nvarchar(8))

return @maxerr
```

4. Enter the following query in the same query window as the Listing 8-1 code. Select the
statement as shown in Figure 8-2, and then click Execute to run the query.

```
exec sp_Trans_Test 'a ', 'a ', 'z '
```

The results window should show a return value of zero, and you should see the same
messages as shown in Figure 8-2.

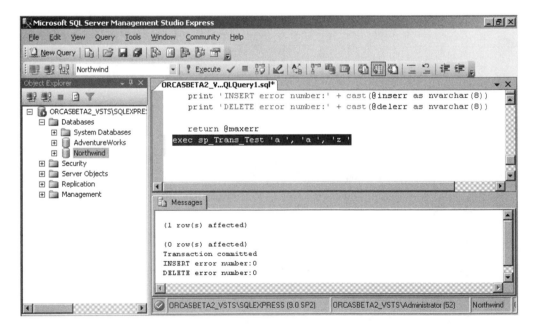

Figure 8-2. *Executing the stored procedure*

5. In the same query window, enter the following SELECT statement:

```
Select * from Customers
```

Select the statement as shown in Figure 8-3 and then click the Execute button. You will see that the customer named "a" has been added to the table, as shown in the Results tab in Figure 8-3.

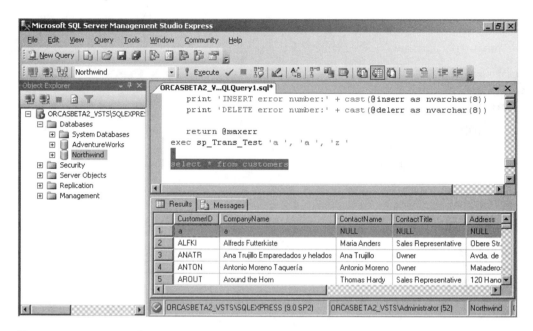

Figure 8-3. *Row inserted in a transaction*

6. Add another customer with parameter value "aa" for both @newcustid and @newcompname and "z" for @oldcustid. Enter the following statement and execute it as you've done previously with other similar statements:

```
exec sp_Trans_Test 'aa ', 'aa ', 'z '
```

You should get the same results shown earlier in Figure 8-2 in the Messages tab.

7. Try the SELECT statement shown in Figure 8-3 one more time. You should see that customer "aa" has been added to the Customers table. Both customer "a" and "aa" have no child records in the Orders table.

How It Works

In the stored procedure, you define three input parameters:

```
create procedure sp_Trans_Test
   @newcustid nchar(5),
   @newcompname nvarchar(40),
   @oldcustid nchar(5)
as
```

You also declare three local variables:

```
declare @inserr int
declare @delerr int
declare @maxerr int
```

These local variables will be used with the stored procedure, so you can capture and display the error numbers returned, if any, from the INSERT and DELETE statements.

You mark the beginning of the transaction with a BEGIN TRANSACTION statement and follow it with the INSERT and DELETE statements that are part of the transaction. After each statement, you save the return number for it.

```
begin transaction

-- Add a customer
insert into customers (customerid, companyname)
values(@newcustid, @newconame)

-- Save error number returned from Insert statement
set @inserr = @@error
if @inserr > @maxerr
   set @maxerr = @inserr

-- Delete a customer
delete from customers
where customerid = @oldcustid

-- Save error number returned from Delete statement
set @delerr = @@error
if @delerr > @maxerr
   set @maxerr = @delerr
```

Error handling is important at all times in SQL Server, and it's never more so than inside transactional code. When you execute any T-SQL statement, there's always the possibility that it may not succeed. The T-SQL @@ERROR function returns the error number for the last T-SQL statement executed. If no error occurred, @@ERROR returns zero.

@@ERROR is reset after every T-SQL statement (even SET and IF) is executed, so if you want to save an error number for a particular statement, you must store it before the next statement executes. That's why you declare the local variables @inserr, @delerr, and @maxerr.

If `@@ERROR` returns any value other than 0, an error has occurred, and you want to roll back the transaction. You also include `PRINT` statements to report whether a rollback or commit has occurred.

```
-- If an error occurred, roll back
if @maxerr <> 0
   begin
      rollback
      print 'Transaction rolled back'
   end
else
   begin
      commit
      print 'Transaction committed'
   end
```

▆Tip T-SQL (and standard SQL) supports various alternative forms for keywords and phrases. You've used just ROLLBACK and COMMIT here.

Then you add some more instrumentation, so you could see what error numbers are encountered during the transaction:

```
print 'INSERT error number:' + cast(@inserr as nvarchar(8))
print 'DELETE error number:' + cast(@delerr as nvarchar(8))

return @maxerr
```

Now let's look at what happens when you execute the stored procedure. You run it twice, first by adding customer "a" and next by adding customer "aa", but you also enter the same nonexistent customer to delete each time. If all statements in a transaction are supposed to succeed or fail as one unit, why does the `INSERT` succeed when the `DELETE` doesn't delete anything?

Figure 8-2 should make everything clear. Both the `INSERT` and `DELETE` return error number zero. The reason `DELETE` returns error number zero even though it has not deleted any rows is that when a `DELETE` doesn't find any rows to delete, T-SQL doesn't treat that as an error. In fact, that's why you use a nonexistent customer. The rest of the customers (well, all but the two you have just added) have child orders, and you can't delete these existing customers unless you delete their orders first.

Try It Out: What Happens When the First Operation Fails

In this example, you'll try to insert a duplicate customer and delete an existing customer.

Add customer "a" and delete customer "aa" by entering the following statement, and then click the Execute button:

```
exec sp_Trans_Test 'a', 'a ', 'aa '
```

The result should appear as in Figure 8-4.

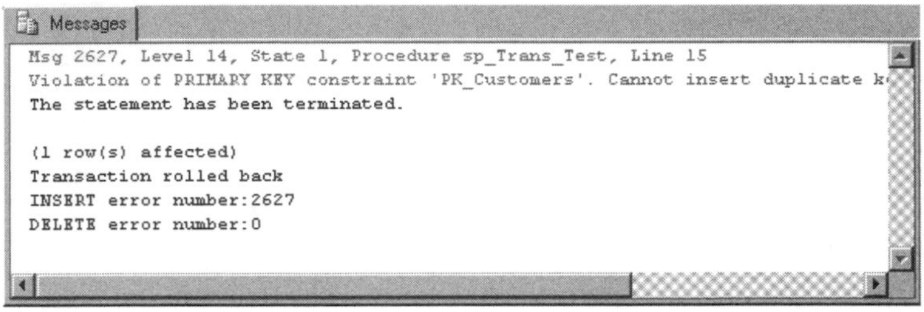

Figure 8-4. *Second operation rolled back*

In the Messages pane shown in Figure 8-4, note that the transaction was rolled back because the INSERT failed and was terminated with error number 2627 (whose error message appears at the top of the window). The DELETE error number was 0, meaning it executed successfully but was rolled back. (If you check the table, you'll find that customer "aa" still exists in the Customers table.)

How It Works

Since customer "a" already exists, SQL Server prevents the insertion of a duplicate, so the first operation fails. The second DELETE statement in the transaction is executed, and customer "aa" is deleted since it doesn't have any child records in the Orders table; but because @maxerr isn't zero (it's 2627, as you see in the Results pane), you roll back the transaction by undoing the deletion of customer "aa".

Try It Out: What Happens When the Second Operation Fails

In this example, you'll insert a valid new customer and try to delete a customer who has child records in Orders table.

Add customer "aaa" and delete customer ALFKI by entering the following statement, and then click the Execute button:

```
exec sp_Trans_Test 'aaa', 'aaa ', 'ALFKI'
```

The result should appear as in Figure 8-5.

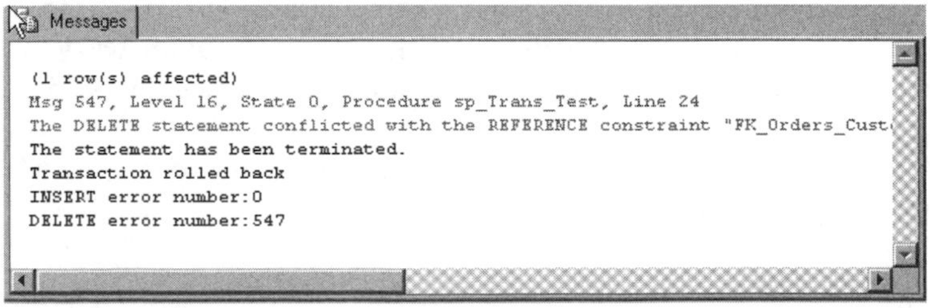

Figure 8-5. *First operation rolled back*

In the Messages pane shown in Figure 8-5, note that the transaction was rolled back because the DELETE failed and was terminated with error number 547 (the message for which appears at the top of the window). The INSERT error number was 0, so it apparently executed successfully but was rolled back. (If you check the table, you'll find "aaa" is not a customer.)

How It Works

Since customer "aaa" doesn't exist, SQL Server inserts the row, so the first operation succeeds. When the second statement in the transaction is executed, SQL Server prevents the deletion of customer ALFKI because it has child records in the Orders table, but since @maxerr isn't zero (it's 547, as you see in the Results pane), the entire transaction is rolled back.

Try It Out: What Happens When Both Operations Fail

In this example, you'll try to insert an invalid new customer and try to delete an undeletable one.

Add customer "a" and delete customer ALFKI by entering the following statement, and then click the Execute button:

```
exec sp_Trans_Test 'a ', 'a ', 'ALFKI'
```

The result should appear as in Figure 8-6.

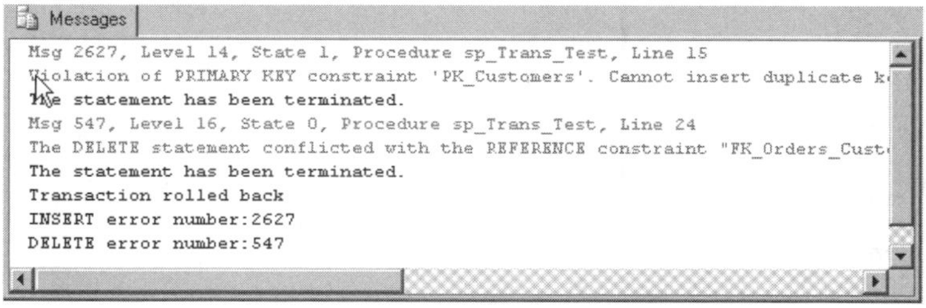

Figure 8-6. *Both operations rolled back*

In the Messages pane shown in Figure 8-6, note that the transaction was rolled back (even though neither statement succeeded, so there was nothing to roll back) because @maxerr returns 2627 for the INSERT and 547 for the DELETE. Error messages for both failing statements are displayed at the top of the window.

How It Works

By now, you should understand why both statements failed. This example proves that even when the first statement fails, the second is executed (and in this case fails with error number 547). Our original example, where the error code is zero when there are no rows to delete, didn't necessarily prove this since the error number there may have come from the line

```
set @maxerr = @inserr
```

immediately before the DELETE statement.

Coding Transactions in ADO.NET

In ADO.NET, a transaction is an instance of a class that implements the interface System. Data.IDbTransaction. Like a data reader, a transaction has no constructor of its own but is created by calling another object's method—in this case, a connection's BeginTransaction method. Commands are associated with a specific transaction for a specific connection, and any SQL submitted by these commands is executed as part of the same transaction.

Try It Out: Working with ADO.NET Transactions

In this ADO.NET example, you'll code a VB .NET equivalent of sp_Trans_Test.

1. Create a new Windows Forms Application project named Chapter8. When Solution Explorer opens, save the solution.

2. Rename Form1.vb to Transaction.vb.

3. Change the Text property of Transaction form to ADO.NET Transaction in VB .NET.

4. Add three labels, three text boxes, and a button to the form as shown in Figure 8-7.

Figure 8-7. *ADO.NET transaction form*

5. Add an Imports directive to Transaction.vb:

   Imports System.Data.SqlClient

6. Next you want to add a click event for the button. Double-click button1, and it will open the code editor with the button1_click event. Insert the code in Listing 8-2 into the code editor.

   Listing 8-2. button1_Click()

   ```
   Dim conn As New SqlConnection
   conn.ConnectionString = "Data Source=.\sqlexpress;" & _
   "Initial Catalog=Northwind;Integrated Security=True"
           ' INSERT
   ```

```vbnet
    Dim sqlins As String = "insert into customers" & _
    "(customerid, CompanyName)values(@newcustid, @newconame)"
        ' DELETE
        Dim sqldel As String = "delete from customers "& _
        " where customerid = @oldcustid "

        ' Open connection
        conn.Open() '

        ' Begin transaction
        Dim sqltrans As SqlTransaction = conn.BeginTransaction()

        Try
            ' create insert command
            Dim cmdins As SqlCommand = conn.CreateCommand()
            cmdins.CommandText = sqlins
            cmdins.Transaction = sqltrans
            cmdins.Parameters.Add("@newcustid",
System.Data.SqlDbType.NVarChar, 5)
            cmdins.Parameters.Add("@newconame", System.Data.SqlDbType.NVar ➡
Char, 30)

            ' create delete command
            Dim cmddel As SqlCommand = conn.CreateCommand()
            cmddel.CommandText = sqldel
            cmddel.Transaction = sqltrans
            cmddel.Parameters.Add("@oldcustid", System.Data.SqlDbType.NVar ➡
Char, 5)

            ' add customer
            cmdins.Parameters("@newcustid").Value = TextBox1.Text
            cmdins.Parameters("@newconame").Value = TextBox2.Text
            cmdins.ExecuteNonQuery()

            ' delete customer
            cmddel.Parameters("@oldcustid").Value = TextBox3.Text
            cmddel.ExecuteNonQuery()

            'Commit transaction
            sqltrans.Commit()

            ' No exception, transaction committed, give message
            MessageBox.Show("Transaction committed")
        Catch ex As System.Data.SqlClient.SqlException
            'Roll back transaction
            sqltrans.Rollback()
```

```
                    MessageBox.Show("Transaction rolled back" + ControlChars.Lf + _
                        ex.Message, "Rollback Transaction")
                Catch ex As System.Exception
                    MessageBox.Show("System Error" + ControlChars.Lf + ex.Message, ➥
        "Error")
                Finally
                    ' Close connection
                    conn.Close()
                End Try
```

7. Run the program by pressing Ctrl+F5. Try the same kinds of insertions and deletions as you did with sp_Trans_Test, but use "b", "bb", and "bbb", instead of "a", "aa", and "aaa", for the new customers.

How It Works

After you open the connection, you create a transaction. Note that transactions are connection specific. You can't create a second transaction for the same connection before committing or rolling back the first one. Though the BeginTransaction method begins a transaction, the transaction itself performs no work until the first SQL statement is executed by a command.

```
' open connection
 conn.Open();

' begin transaction
Dim sqltrans As SqlTransaction = conn.BeginTransaction()
```

You create separate commands for the INSERT and DELETE statements and associate them with the same transaction by setting their Transaction property to the same transaction, sqltrans:

```
                ' create insert command
                Dim cmdins As SqlCommand = conn.CreateCommand()
                cmdins.CommandText = sqlins
                cmdins.Transaction = sqltrans
                cmdins.Parameters.Add("@newcustid", System.Data.SqlDbType.NVarChar, 5)
                cmdins.Parameters.Add("@newconame", System.Data.SqlDbType.NVarChar, 30)

                ' create delete command
                Dim cmddel As SqlCommand = conn.CreateCommand()
                cmddel.CommandText = sqldel
                cmddel.Transaction = sqltrans
                cmddel.Parameters.Add("@oldcustid", System.Data.SqlDbType.NVarChar, 5)
```

■**Tip** You could use the same command object for both commands, but this doesn't save you anything, and it would prevent you from preparing the commands if the program were designed to do this.

You then assign values to the parameters and execute the commands:

```
' add customer
cmdins.Parameters("@newcustid").Value = TextBox1.Text
cmdins.Parameters("@newconame").Value = TextBox2.Text
cmdins.ExecuteNonQuery()

' delete customer
cmddel.Parameters("@oldcustid").Value = TextBox3.Text
cmddel.ExecuteNonQuery()
```

You then commit the transaction after the second command:

```
'Commit transaction
sqltrans.Commit()
```

or roll it back in the database exception handler:

```
Catch ex As System.Data.SqlClient.SqlException
'Roll back transaction
sqltrans.Rollback()
```

Summary

This chapter covered the fundamentals of transactions, from concepts such as understanding what transactions are, to ACID properties, local and distributed transactions, guidelines for writing efficient transactions, and coding transactions in T-SQL and ADO.NET using VB .NET 2008. Although this chapter provides just the fundamentals of transactions, you now know enough about coding transactions to handle basic transactional processing.

In the next chapter, we'll look at the fundamentals of ADO.NET.

CHAPTER 9

■ ■ ■

Getting to Know ADO.NET

In industry, most applications can't be built without having interaction with a database. Databases solve the purpose of retrieval and storage of data. Almost every software application running interacts with either one or multiple databases. The front end needs a mechanism to connect with databases, and ADO.NET serves the purpose. Each .NET application that requires database functionality is dependent on ADO.NET.

In this chapter, we'll cover the following:

- Understanding ADO.NET
- The motivation behind ADO.NET
- Moving from ADO to ADO.NET
- Understanding ADO.NET architecture
- Working with the SQL Server Data Provider
- Working with the OLE DB Data Provider
- Working with the ODBC Data Provider
- Data providers as APIs

Understanding ADO.NET

Before .NET, developers used data access technologies such as ODBC, OLE DB, and ActiveX Data Objects (ADO). With the introduction of .NET, Microsoft created a new way to work with data, called *ADO.NET*.

ADO.NET is a set of classes that exposes data access services to the .NET programmer, providing a rich set of components for creating distributed, data-sharing applications. ADO.NET is an integral part of the .NET Framework that provides access to relational, XML, and application data. ADO.NET classes are found in `System.Data.dll`. This technology supports a variety of development needs, including the creation of front-end database clients and middle-tier business objects used by applications, tools, languages, and Internet browsers.

The Motivation Behind ADO.NET

With the evolution of application development, applications have become *loosely coupled*, an architecture where components are easier to maintain and reuse (for more information, please refer to `http://www.serviceoriented.org/loosely_coupled.html`). More and more of today's applications use XML to encode data to be passed over network connections, and that is how different applications running on different platforms can interoperate.

ADO.NET was designed to support the disconnected data architecture, tight integration with XML, common data representation with the ability to combine data from multiple and varied data sources, and optimized facilities for interacting with a database, all native to the .NET Framework.

During the development of ADO.NET, Microsoft wanted to include the following features:

Leverage for the Current ADO Knowledge   ADO.NET's design addresses many of the requirements of today's application development model. At the same time, the programming model stays as similar as possible to ADO, so current ADO developers do not have to start from scratch. ADO.NET is an intrinsic part of the .NET Framework, yet is familiar to the ADO programmer.

ADO.NET also coexists with ADO. Although most new .NET-based applications will be written using ADO.NET, ADO remains available to the .NET programmer through .NET COM interoperability services.

Support for the N-Tier Programming Model   The concept of working with a disconnected record set has become a focal point in the programming model. ADO.NET provides premium class support for the disconnected, n-tier programming environment. ADO.NET's solution for building n-tier database applications is the dataset.

Integration of XML Support   XML and data access are closely tied. XML is about encoding data, and data access is increasingly becoming about XML. The .NET Framework not only supports web standards, but also is built entirely on top of them.

XML support is built into ADO.NET at a very fundamental level. The XML classes in the .NET Framework and ADO.NET are part of the same architecture; they integrate at many different levels. You therefore no longer have to choose between the data access set of services and their XML counterparts; the ability to cross over from one to the other is inherent in the design of both.

Moving from ADO to ADO.NET

ADO is a collection of ActiveX objects that are designed to work in a constantly *connected* environment. It was built on top of OLE DB (which we'll look at in the "Working with the OLE DB Data Provider" section). OLE DB provides access to non-SQL data as well as SQL databases, and ADO provides an interface designed to make it easier to work with OLE DB providers.

However, accessing data with ADO (and OLE DB under the hood) means you have to go through several layers of connectivity before you reach the data source. Just as OLE DB is there to connect to a large number of data sources, an older data access technology, Open Database Connectivity (ODBC), is still there to connect to even older data sources such as dBASE and

Paradox. To access ODBC data sources using ADO, you use an OLE DB provider for ODBC (since ADO only works directly with OLE DB), thus adding more layers to an already multi-layered model.

With the multilayered data access model and the connected nature of ADO, you could easily end up sapping server resources and creating a performance bottleneck. ADO served well in its time, but ADO.NET has some great features that make it a far superior data access technology.

ADO.NET Isn't a New Version of ADO

ADO.NET is a completely new data access technology, with a new design that was built entirely from scratch. Let's first get this cleared up: ADO.NET *doesn't* stand for ActiveX Data Objects .NET. Why? For many reasons, but the following are the two most important ones:

- ADO.NET is an integral part of .NET, not an external entity.

- ADO.NET isn't a collection of ActiveX components.

The name ADO.NET is analogous to ADO because Microsoft wanted developers to feel at home using ADO.NET and didn't want them to think they'd need to "learn it all over again," as mentioned earlier, so it purposely named and designed ADO.NET to offer similar features implemented in a different way.

During the design of .NET, Microsoft realized that ADO wasn't going to fit in. ADO was available as an external package based on Component Object Model (COM) objects, requiring .NET applications to explicitly include a reference to it. In contrast, .NET applications are designed to share a single model, where all libraries are integrated into a single framework, organized into logical namespaces, and declared public to any application that wants to use them. It was wisely decided that the .NET data access technology should comply with the .NET architectural model. So, ADO.NET was born.

ADO.NET is designed to accommodate both connected and disconnected access. Also, ADO.NET embraces the fundamentally important XML standard, much more than ADO did, since the explosion in XML use came about after ADO was developed. With ADO.NET, not only can you use XML to transfer data between applications, but you can also export data from your application into an XML file, store it locally on your system, and retrieve it later when you need it.

Performance usually comes at a price, but in the case of ADO.NET, the price is definitely reasonable. Unlike ADO, ADO.NET doesn't transparently wrap OLE DB providers; instead, it uses *managed data providers* that are designed specifically for each type of data source, thus leveraging their true power and adding to overall application speed and performance.

ADO.NET also works in both connected and disconnected environments. You can connect to a database, remain connected while simply reading data, and then close your connection, which is a process similar to ADO. Where ADO.NET really begins to shine is in the disconnected world. If you need to edit database data, maintaining a continuous connection would be costly on the server. ADO.NET gets around this by providing a sophisticated disconnected model. Data is sent from the server and cached locally on the client. When you're ready to update the database, you can send the changed data back to the server, where updates and conflicts are managed for you.

In ADO.NET, when you retrieve data, you use an object known as a *data reader*. When you work with disconnected data, the data is cached locally in a relational data structure, either a *data table* or a *dataset*.

ADO.NET and the .NET Base Class Library

A dataset (a `DataSet` object) can hold large amounts of data in the form of tables (`DataTable` objects), their relationships (`DataRelation` objects), and constraints (`Constraint` objects) in an in-memory cache, which can then be exported to an external file or to another dataset. Since XML support is integrated into ADO.NET, you can produce XML schemas and transmit and share data using XML documents.

Table 9-1 describes the namespaces in which ADO.NET components are grouped.

Table 9-1. *ADO.NET Namespaces*

Namespace	Description
System.Data	Classes, interfaces, delegates, and enumerations that define and partially implement the ADO.NET architecture
System.Data.Common	Classes shared by .NET Framework data providers
System.Data.Design	Classes that can be used to generate a custom-typed dataset
System.Data.Odbc	The .NET Framework data provider for ODBC
System.Data.OleDb	The .NET Framework data provider for OLE DB
System.Data.Sql	Classes that support SQL Server–specific functionality
System.Data.OracleClient	The .NET Framework data provider for Oracle
System.Data.SqlClient	The .NET Framework data provider for SQL Server
System.Data.SqlServerCe	The .NET Compact Framework data provider for SQL Server Mobile
System.Data.SqlTypes	Classes for native SQL Server data types
Microsoft.SqlServer.Server	Components for integrating SQL Server and the CLR

Since XML support has been closely integrated into ADO.NET, some ADO.NET components in the System.Data namespace rely on components in the System.Xml namespace. So, you sometimes need to include both namespaces as references in Solution Explorer.

These namespaces are physically implemented as assemblies, and if you create a new application project in Visual Studio 2008, references to the assemblies should automatically be created, along with the reference to the System assembly. However, if they're not present, simply perform the following steps to add the namespaces to your project:

1. Right-click the References item in Solution Explorer, and then click Add Reference.

2. A dialog box with a list of available references displays. Select System.Data, System.Xml, and System (if not already present) one by one (hold down the Ctrl key for multiple selections), and then click the Select button.

3. Click OK, and the references will be added to the project.

Tip Though we don't use it in this book, if you use the command-line VB .NET compiler, you can use the following compiler options to include the reference of the required assemblies: `/r:System.dll` `/r:System.Data.dll /r:System.Xml.dll`.

As you can see from the namespaces, ADO.NET can work with older technologies such as OLE DB and ODBC. However, the SQL Server data provider communicates directly with SQL Server without adding an OLE DB or ODBC layer, so it's the most efficient form of connection. Likewise, the Oracle data provider accesses Oracle directly.

Note All major DBMS vendors support their own ADO.NET data providers. We'll stick to SQL Server in this book, but the same kind of VB .NET code is written regardless of the provider.

Understanding ADO.NET Architecture

Figure 9-1 presents the most important architectural features of ADO.NET. We'll discuss them in far greater detail in later chapters.

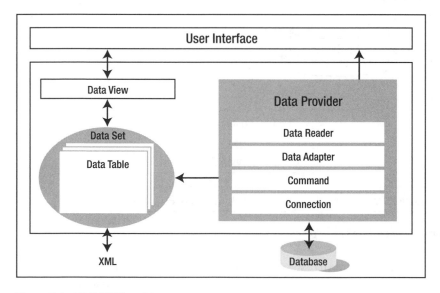

Figure 9-1. *ADO.NET architecture*

ADO.NET has two central components: data providers and datasets.

A *data provider* connects to a data source and supports data access and manipulation. You'll play with three different ones later in this chapter.

A *dataset* supports disconnected, independent caching of data in a relational fashion, updating the data source as required. A dataset contains one or more data tables. A *data table* is a row-and-column representation that provides much the same logical view as a physical table in a database. For example, you can store the data from the Northwind database's Employees table in an ADO.NET data table and manipulate the data as needed. You'll learn about datasets and data tables starting in Chapter 13.

In Figure 9-1, notice the DataView class (in the System.Data namespace). This isn't a data provider component. Data views are used primarily to bind data to Windows and web forms.

As you saw in Table 9-1, each data provider has its own namespace. In fact, each data provider is essentially an implementation of interfaces in the System.Data namespace, specialized for a specific type of data source.

For example, if you use SQL Server, you should use the SQL Server data provider (System. Data.SqlClient) because it's the most efficient way to access SQL Server.

The OLE DB data provider supports access to older versions of SQL Server as well as to other databases, such as Access, DB2, MySQL, and Oracle. However, native data providers (such as System.Data.OracleClient) are preferable for performance, since the OLE DB data provider works through two other layers, the OLE DB service component and the OLE DB provider, before reaching the data source.

Figure 9-2 illustrates the difference between using the SQL Server and OLE DB data providers to access a SQL Server database.

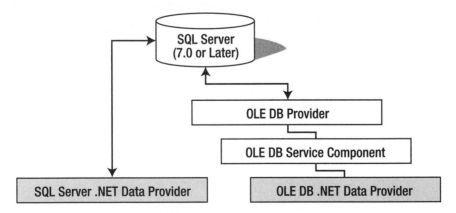

Figure 9-2. *SQL Server and OLE DB data provider differences*

If your application connects to an older version of SQL Server (6.5 or older) or to more than one kind of database server at the same time (for example, an Access and an Oracle database connected simultaneously), only then should you choose to use the OLE DB data provider.

No hard-and-fast rules exist; you can use both the OLE DB data provider for SQL Server and the Oracle data provider (System.Data.OracleClient) if you want, but it's important you choose the best provider for your purpose. Given the performance benefits of the server-specific data providers, if you use SQL Server, 99% of the time you should be using the System.Data.SqlClient classes.

Before we look at what each kind of data provider does and how it's used, you need to be clear on its core functionality. Each .NET data provider is designed to do the following two things very well:

- Provide access to data with an active connection to the data source

- Provide data transmission to and from disconnected datasets and data tables

Database connections are established by using the data provider's connection class (for example, System.Data.SqlClient.SqlConnection). Other components such as data readers, commands, and data adapters support retrieving data, executing SQL statements, and reading or writing to datasets or data tables, respectively.

As you've seen, each data provider is prefixed with the type of data source it connects to (for instance, the SQL Server data provider is prefixed with Sql), so its connection class is named SqlConnection. The OLE DB data provider's connection class is named OleDbConnection.

Let's see how to work with the three data providers that can be used with SQL Server.

Working with the SQL Server Data Provider

The .NET data provider for SQL Server is in the System.Data.SqlClient namespace. Although you can use System.Data.OleDb to connect with SQL Server, Microsoft has specifically designed the System.Data.SqlClient namespace to be used with SQL Server, and it works in a more efficient and optimized way than System.Data.OleDb. The reason for this efficiency and optimized approach is that this data provider communicates directly with the server using its native network protocol instead of through multiple layers.

Table 9-2 describes some important classes in the SqlClient namespace.

Table 9-2. *Commonly Used* SqlClient *Classes*

Classes	Description
SqlCommand	Executes SQL queries, statements, or stored procedures
SqlConnection	Represents a connection to a SQL Server database
SqlDataAdapter	Represents a bridge between a dataset and a data source
SqlDataReader	Provides a forward-only, read-only data stream of the results
SqlError	Holds information on SQL Server errors and warnings
SqlException	Defines the exception thrown on a SQL Server error or warning
SqlParameter	Represents a command parameter
SqlTransaction	Represents a SQL Server transaction

Another namespace, `System.Data.SqlTypes`, maps SQL Server data types to .NET types, both enhancing performance and making developers' lives a lot easier.

Let's look at an example that uses the SQL Server data provider. It won't cover connections and data retrieval in detail, but it will familiarize you with what you'll encounter in upcoming chapters.

Try It Out: Creating a Simple Console Application Using the SQL Server Data Provider

You'll build a simple Console Application project that opens a connection and runs a query, using the `SqlClient` namespace against the SQL Server Management Studio Express (SSMSE) Northwind database. You'll display the retrieved data in a console window.

1. Open Visual Studio 2008 and create a new Visual Basic Console Application project named Chapter09.

2. Right-click the Chapter09 project and rename it to SqlServerProvider.

3. Right-click the `Module1.vb` file and rename it to `SqlServerProvider.vb`. When prompted to rename all references to Program, you can click either Yes or No.

4. Since you'll be creating this example from scratch, open `SqlServerProvider.vb` in the code editor and replace it with the code in Listing 9-1.

Listing 9-1. `SqlServerProvider.vb`

```
Imports System
Imports System.Data
Imports System.Data.SqlClient

Module SqlServerProvider
    Sub Main()

        'Set up connection string
        Dim conn As New SqlConnection
        conn.ConnectionString = "Data Source=.\sqlexpress;" & _
        "Initial Catalog=Northwind;Integrated Security=True"

        'Set up query string
        Dim sql As String = "select * from employees"
    'Declare data reader variables
    Dim reader As SqlDataReader = Nothing
        Try
            ' Open connection
            conn.Open()
```

```
            ' Execute the query
            Dim cmd As New SqlCommand(sql, conn)
            reader = cmd.ExecuteReader()

            ' Display output header
            Console.WriteLine("This program demonstrates the use of " & _
            "the SQL Server Data Provider.")
            Console.WriteLine("Querying database {0} with query {1}" & _
            ControlChars.NewLine, conn.Database, cmd.CommandText)
            Console.WriteLine("First Name" + ControlChars.Tab & _
            "Last Name" + ControlChars.Lf)

            ' Process the result set
            While reader.Read()
                Console.WriteLine("{0} | {1}", _
                reader("FirstName").ToString().PadLeft(10), _
                reader(1).ToString().PadLeft(10))
            End While
        Catch e As Exception
            Console.WriteLine("Error: ", e)

        Finally
            ' Close reader and connection
            reader.Close()
            conn.Close()
        End Try
    End Sub
End Module
```

5. Save the project, and press Ctrl+F5 to run it. The results should appear as in Figure 9-3.

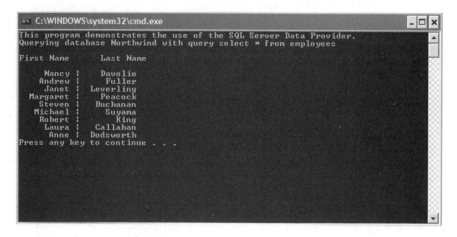

Figure 9-3. *Accessing Northwind via the SQL Server data provider*

How It Works

Let's take a look at how the code works, starting with the using directives:

```
Imports System
Imports System.Data
Imports System.Data.SqlClient
```

The reference to System.Data is not needed in this small program, since you don't explicitly use any of its members, but it's a good habit to always include it. The reference to System.Data.SqlClient is necessary since you want to use the simple names of its members.

You specify the connection string with *parameters* (key-value pairs) suitable for a SQL Server Express session:

```
'Set up connection string
 Dim conn As New SqlConnection
conn.ConnectionString = "Data Source=.\sqlexpress;" & _
"Initial Catalog=Northwind;Integrated Security=True"
```

The connection string contains this parameter:

```
Integrated Security=True
```

which specifies Windows Authentication, so any user logged on to Windows can access the SQLEXPRESS instance.

You then code the SQL query:

```
'Set up query string
Dim sql As String = "select * from employees"
```

You next declare variables for data reader, so that becomes available to the rest of your code:

```
'Declare data reader variables
Dim reader As SqlDataReader = Nothing
```

You then create the connection and open it:

```
Try
    ' Open connection
    conn.Open()
```

You do this (and the rest of your database work) in a try block to handle exceptions, in particular exceptions thrown by ADO.NET in response to database errors. Here, ADO.NET will throw an exception if the connection string parameters aren't syntactically correct, so you may as well be prepared. If you had waited until you entered the try block to declare the connection (and data reader) variable, you wouldn't have it available in the finally block to close the connection. Note that creating a connection doesn't actually connect to the database. You need to call the Open method on the connection.

To execute the query, you first create a command object, passing its constructor the SQL to run and the connection on which to run it. Next, you create a data reader by calling ExecuteReader() on the command object. This not only executes the query, but also sets up the data reader. Note that unlike with most objects, you have no way to create a data reader with a new expression.

```
' Execute the query
Dim cmd As New SqlCommand(sql, conn)
reader = cmd.ExecuteReader()
```

You then produce a header for your output, using connection and command properties (Database and CommandText, respectively) to get the database name and query text:

```
' Display output header
Console.WriteLine("This program demonstrates the use of " & _
"the SQL Server Data Provider.")
Console.WriteLine("Querying database {0} with query {1}" & _
ControlChars.NewLine, conn.Database, cmd.CommandText)
Console.WriteLine("First Name" + ControlChars.Tab & _
"Last Name" + ControlChars.Lf)
```

You retrieve all the rows in the result set by calling the data reader's Read method, which returns true if there are more rows and false otherwise. Note that the data reader is positioned immediately *before* the first row prior to the first call to Read:

```
' Process the result set
While reader.Read()
    Console.WriteLine("{0} | {1}", _
    reader("FirstName").ToString().PadLeft(10), _
    reader(1).ToString().PadLeft(10))
End While
```

You access each row's columns with the data reader's *indexer* (here, the SqlDataReader. Item property), which is overloaded to accept either a column name or a zero-based integer index. You use both so you can see the indexer's use, but using column numbers is more efficient than using column names.

Next you handle any exceptions, quite simplistically, but at least you're developing a good habit. We'll cover exception handling much more thoroughly in Chapter 16.

```
Catch e As Exception
        Console.WriteLine("Error: ", e)
```

At last, in a finally block, you close the data reader and the connection by calling their Close methods. As a general rule, you should close things in a finally block to be sure they get closed no matter what happens within the try block.

```
Finally
    ' Close reader and connection
    reader.Close()
    conn.Close()
End Try
```

Technically, closing the connection also closes the data reader, but closing both (in the previous order) is another good habit. A connection with an open data reader can't be used for any other purpose until the data reader has been closed.

Working with the OLE DB Data Provider

Outside .NET, OLE DB is still Microsoft's high-performance data access technology. The OLEDB data provider has been around for many years. If you've programmed Microsoft Access in the past, you may recall using Microsoft Jet OLE DB 3.5 or 4.0 to connect with an Access database. You can use this data provider to access data stored in any format, so even in ADO.NET it plays an important role in accessing data sources that don't have their own ADO.NET data providers.

The .NET Framework data provider for OLE DB is in the namespace System.Data.OleDb. Table 9-3 describes some important classes in the OleDb namespace.

Table 9-3. *Commonly Used* OleDb *Classes*

Classes	Description
OleDbCommand	Executes SQL queries, statements, or stored procedures
OleDbConnection	Represents a connection to an OLE DB data source
OleDbDataAdapter	Represents a bridge between a dataset and a data source
OleDbDataReader	Provides a forward-only, read-only data stream of rows from a data source
OleDbError	Holds information on errors and warnings returned by the data source
OleDbParameter	Represents a command parameter
OleDbTransaction	Represents a SQL transaction

Notice the similarity between the two data providers, SqlClient and OleDb. The differences in their implementations are transparent, and the user interface is fundamentally the same.

The ADO.NET OLE DB data provider requires that an OLE DB provider be specified in the connection string. Table 9-4 describes some OLE DB providers.

Table 9-4. *Some OLE DB Providers*

Provider	Description
DB2OLEDB	Microsoft OLE DB provider for DB2
SQLOLEDB	Microsoft OLE DB provider for SQL Server
Microsoft.Jet.OLEDB.4.0	Microsoft OLE DB provider for Access (which uses the Jet engine)
MSDAORA	Microsoft OLE DB provider for Oracle
MSDASQL	Microsoft OLE DB provider for ODBC

Let's use the OLE DB data provider (SQLOLEDB) to access the Northwind database, making a few straightforward changes to the code in Listing 9-1. (Of course, you'd use the SQL Server data provider for real work since it's more efficient.)

Try It Out: Creating a Simple Console Application Using the OLE DB Data Provider

In this example, you'll see how to access Northwind with OLE DB.

1. In Solution Explorer, add a new Visual Basic Console Application project named OleDbProvider to the Chapter09 solution. Rename the Module1.vb file to OleDbProvider.vb. In the code editor, replace the generated code with the code in Listing 9-2, which shows the changes to Listing 9-1 in bold.

Listing 9-2. OleDbProvider.vb

```vb
Imports System
Imports System.Data
Imports System.Data.OleDb

Module OleDbProvider
    Sub Main()

        'Set up connection string
        Dim conn As New OleDbConnection
        conn.ConnectionString = "Provider=sqloledb;Data Source=. ➥
\sqlexpress;" & _
        "Initial Catalog=Northwind;Integrated Security=sspi"

        'Set up query string
        Dim sql As String = "select * from employees"

        'Declare data reader variable
        Dim reader As OleDbDataReader = Nothing
        Try
            ' Open connection
            conn.Open()

            ' Execute the query
            Dim cmd As New OleDbCommand(sql, conn)
            reader = cmd.ExecuteReader()

            ' Display output header
            Console.WriteLine("This program demonstrates the use of " & _
            "the OLE DB Data Provider.")
            Console.WriteLine("Querying database {0} with query {1}" & _
            ControlChars.NewLine, conn.Database, cmd.CommandText)
            Console.WriteLine("First Name" + ControlChars.Tab & _
            "Last Name" + ControlChars.Lf)

            ' Process the result set
```

```
            While reader.Read()
                Console.WriteLine("{0} | {1}", _
                reader("FirstName").ToString().PadLeft(10), _
                reader(1).ToString().PadLeft(10))
            End While
        Catch e As Exception
            Console.WriteLine("Error: ", e)

        Finally
            ' Close reader and connection
            reader.Close()
            conn.Close()
        End Try
    End Sub
End Module
```

2. Since you now have two projects in your solution, you need to make this project the startup project so it runs when you press Ctrl+F5. Right-click the project name in Solution Explorer, and then click Set As StartUp Project (see Figure 9-4).

Figure 9-4. *Setting the startup project*

3. Run the application by pressing Ctrl+F5. The results should appear as in Figure 9-5.

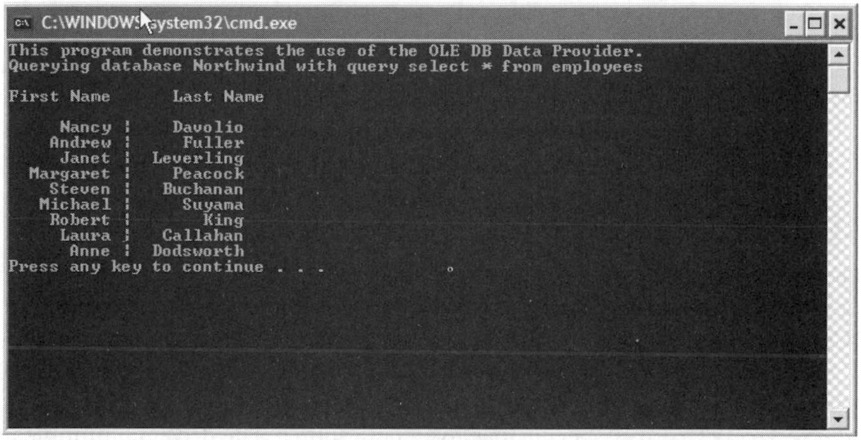

Figure 9-5. *Accessing Northwind via OLE DB*

How It Works

This program does the same thing as the first example, so we'll discuss only the things that changed. First, you replace SqlClient with OleDb in the third using directive:

```
Imports System
Imports System.Data
Imports System.Data.OleDb;
```

The connection string requires the most change, since the OLE DB data provider doesn't accept the same parameters as the SQL Server data provider. In addition, it requires a provider parameter:

```
'Set up connection string
Dim conn As New OleDbConnection
conn.ConnectionString = "Provider=sqloledb;Data Source=.\sqlexpress;" & _
"Initial Catalog=Northwind;Integrated Security=sspi"
```

Only four other lines had to change to use the OLE DB data provider classes for the connection, command, and data reader.

```
'Declare data reader variable
Dim reader As OleDbDataReader = Nothing

Try
    ' Open connection
    conn.Open()

    ' Execute the query
    Dim cmd As New OleDbCommand(sql, conn)
    reader = cmd.ExecuteReader()
```

The final change was a semantic one and wasn't required by ADO.NET:

```
' Display output header
            Console.WriteLine("This program demonstrates the use of " & _
            "the OLE DB Data Provider.")
```

Working with the ODBC Data Provider

ODBC was Microsoft's original general-purpose data access technology. It's still widely used for data sources that don't have OLE DB providers or .NET Framework data providers. ADO.NET includes an ODBC data provider in the namespace System.Data.Odbc.

The ODBC architecture is essentially a three-tier process. An application uses ODBC functions to submit database requests. ODBC converts the function calls to the protocol (*call-level interface*) of a *driver* specific to a given data source. The driver communicates with the data source, passing any results or errors back up to ODBC. Obviously this is less efficient than a database-specific data provider's direct communication with a database, so for performance it's preferable to avoid the ODBC data provider, since it merely offers a simpler interface to ODBC but still involves all the ODBC overhead. Table 9-5 describes some important classes in the Odbc namespace.

Table 9-5. *Commonly Used* Odbc *Classes*

Classes	Description
OdbcCommand	Executes SQL queries, statements, or stored procedures
OdbcConnection	Represents a connection to an ODBC data source
OdbcDataAdapter	Represents a bridge between a dataset and a data source
OdbcDataReader	Provides a forward-only, read-only data stream of rows from a data source
OdbcError	Holds information on errors and warnings returned by the data source
OdbcParameter	Represents a command parameter
OdbcTransaction	Represents a SQL transaction

Let's use the ODBC data provider to access the Northwind database, making the same kind of straightforward changes (highlighted later in this chapter in Listing 9-3) to the code in Listing 9-1 as you did in using the OLE DB data provider.

Before you do, though, you need to create an ODBC data source—actually, you configure a DSN (data source name) for use with a data source accessible by ODBC—for the Northwind database, since, unlike the SQL Server and OLE DB data providers, the ODBC data provider doesn't let you specify the server or database in the connection string. (The following works on Windows XP, and the process is similar for other versions of Windows.)

Creating an ODBC Data Source

To create an ODBC data source, follow these steps:

1. In the Control Panel, double-click Administrative Tools (see Figure 9-6).

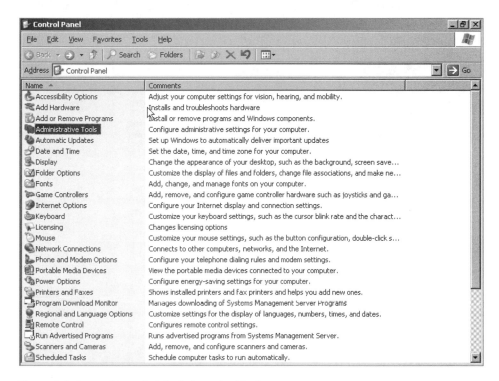

Figure 9-6. *Control Panel: Administrative Tools*

2. In Administrative Tools, double-click Data Sources (ODBC) (see Figure 9-7).

3. When the ODBC Data Source Administrator window opens, click the User DSN tab and then click Add (see Figure 9-8).

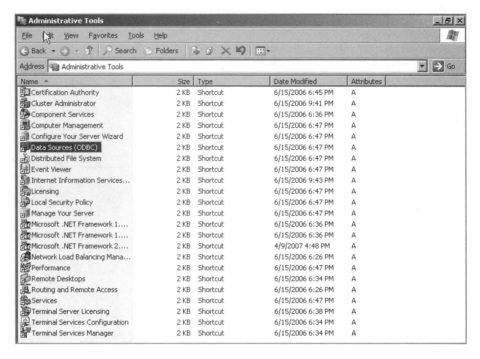

Figure 9-7. *Administrative Tools: Data Sources (ODBC)*

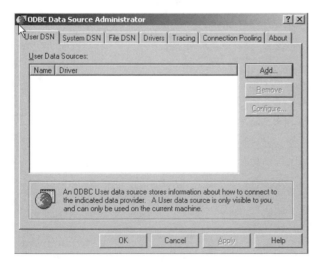

Figure 9-8. *ODBC Data Source Administrator dialog box*

4. The Create New Data Source wizard starts. Follow its instructions carefully! First, select the SQL Server driver; second, click Finish (see Figure 9-9).

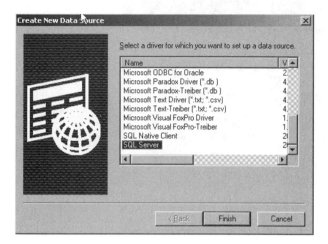

Figure 9-9. *Create New Data Source wizard*

5. The next window prompts for the data source name and server. Specify the values for Name and Server as **NorthwindOdbc** and **.\sqlexpress**, respectively, as shown in Figure 9-10, and then click Next.

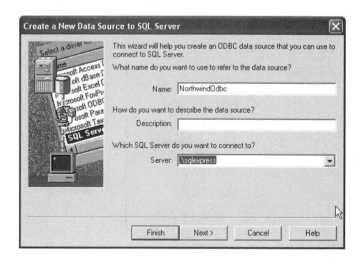

Figure 9-10. *Specifying the data source name and SQL Server to connect to*

6. Accept the defaults in the authentication window by clicking Next (see Figure 9-11).

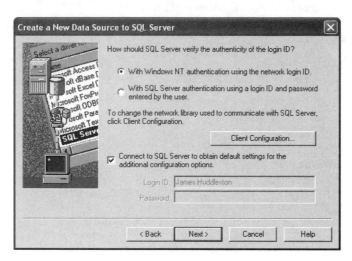

Figure 9-11. *Specifying SQL Server authentication*

7. In the next window, check the Change the Default Database To option, select the Northwind database from the provided drop-down list, and click Next (see Figure 9-12).

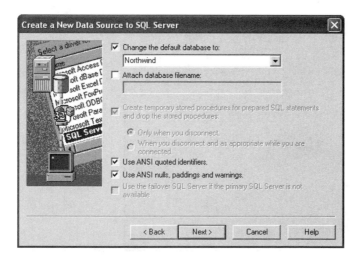

Figure 9-12. *Specifying the default database*

8. In the next window, simply click Finish (see Figure 9-13).

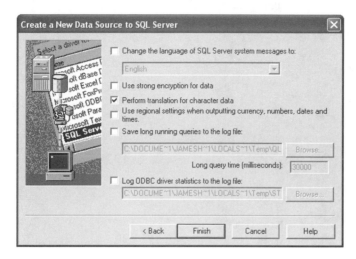

Figure 9-13. *Finishing DSN creation*

9. A confirmation window appears, describing the new data source. Click Test Data Source (see Figure 9-14).

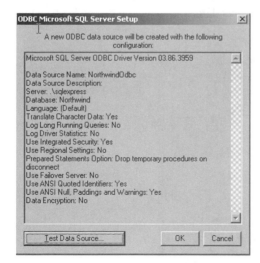

Figure 9-14. *Testing the Northwind data source connection*

10. A window reporting a successful test should appear (see Figure 9-15). (If it doesn't, cancel your work and *carefully* try again.) Click OK.

Figure 9-15. *Connection to Northwind was successful.*

11. When the confirmation window reappears, click OK. When the ODBC Data Source Administrator window reappears, the new data source will be on the list (see Figure 9-16). Click OK.

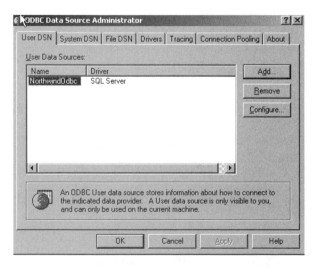

Figure 9-16. *New data source appearing in the data source list*

Now you have your NorthwindOdbc data source ready to work with. Next, you will use it in code for setting up the connection string.

Try It Out: Creating a Simple Console Application Using the ODBC Data Provider

Let's access Northwind with ODBC:

1. In Solution Explorer, add a new Visual Basic Console Application project named OdbcProvider to the Chapter09 solution. Rename the Module1.vb file to OdbcProvider.vb. In the code editor, replace the generated code with the code in Listing 9-3, which shows the changes to Listing 9-1 in bold.

Listing 9-3. OdbcProvider.vb

```vb
Imports System
Imports System.Data
Imports System.Data.Odbc

Module OdbcProvider
    Sub Main()

        'Set up connection string
        Dim connString As String = "dsn=northwindodbc"

        'Set up query string
        Dim sql As String = "select * from employees"

        'Declare data reader variable
        Dim reader As OdbcDataReader = Nothing
        Try
            ' Open connection
            Dim conn As New OdbcConnection(connString)
            conn.Open()

            ' Execute the query
            Dim cmd As New OdbcCommand(sql, conn)
            reader = cmd.ExecuteReader()

            ' Display output header
            Console.WriteLine("This program demonstrates the use of " & _
            "the ODBC Data Provider.")
            Console.WriteLine("Querying database {0} with query {1}" & _
            ControlChars.NewLine, conn.Database, cmd.CommandText)
            Console.WriteLine("First Name" + ControlChars.Tab & _
            "Last Name" + ControlChars.Lf)
```

```
                    ' Process the result set
                    While reader.Read()
                        Console.WriteLine("{0} | {1}", _
                        reader("FirstName").ToString().PadLeft(10), _
                        reader(1).ToString().PadLeft(10))
                    End While
                Catch e As Exception
                    Console.WriteLine("Error: ", e)

                Finally
                    ' Close reader
                    reader.Close()
                End Try
            End Sub
        End Module
```

2. Make this project the startup program by right-clicking the project name in Solution Explorer and then clicking Set As StartUp Project as shown earlier in Figure 9-4.

3. Run the application with Ctrl+F5. The results should appear as in Figure 9-17.

Figure 9-17. *Accessing Northwind via ODBC.*

How It Works

Once you create a DSN, the rest is easy. You simply change Sql to Odbc in the class names (and, of course, the output header), just as you did to modify the program to work with OLE DB. The biggest change, and the only one that really deserves attention, is to the connection string:

```
        'Set up connection string
        Dim connString As String = "dsn=northwindodbc"
```

The ODBC connection string isn't limited only to the DSN, but it doesn't allow blanks or newlines anywhere in the string.

Tip Each data provider has its own rules regarding both the parameters and syntax of its connection string. Consult the documentation for the provider you're using when coding connection strings. Connection strings can be very complicated. We don't cover the details here, but documentation for connection strings is included with the description of the `ConnectionString` property for the connection class for each data provider.

Now that you've played with all the data providers that access SQL Server (the SQL Server CE data provider is beyond the scope of this book), let's make sure you clearly understand what a data provider is and how different data providers can be used to access data.

Data Providers As APIs

The .NET Framework data providers, sophisticated as they are (and you'll learn plenty about exploiting their sophistication later), are simply APIs for accessing data sources, most often relational databases. (ADO.NET is essentially one big API of which data providers are a major part.)

Newcomers to ADO.NET are often understandably confused by the Microsoft documentation. They read about `Connection`, `Command`, `DataReader`, and other ADO.NET objects, but they see no classes named `Connection`, `Command`, or `DataReader` in any of the ADO.NET namespaces. The reason is that data provider classes implement *interfaces* in the `System.Data` namespace. These interfaces define the data provider methods of the ADO.NET API.

The key concept is simple. A data provider, such as `System.Data.SqlClient`, consists of classes whose methods provide a uniform way of accessing a specific kind of data source. In this chapter, you used three different data providers (SQL Server, OLE DB, and ODBC) to access the same SSE database. The only real difference in the code was the connection string. Except for choosing the appropriate data provider, the rest of the programming was effectively the same. This is true of all ADO.NET facilities, whatever kind of data source you need to access.

The SQL Server data provider is optimized to access SQL Server and can't be used for any other DBMS. The OLE DB data provider can access any OLE DB data source—and you used it without knowing anything about OLE DB (a major study in itself). The ODBC data provider lets you use an even older data access technology, again without knowing anything about it. Working at such an abstract level enabled you to do a lot more, a lot more quickly, than you could have otherwise.

ADO.NET is not only an efficient data access technology, but also an elegant one. Data providers are only one aspect of it. The art of ADO.NET programming is founded more on conceptualizing than on coding. First get a clear idea of what ADO.NET offers, and then look for the right method in the right class to make the idea a reality.

Since conceptual clarity is so important, you can view (and refer to) connections, commands, data readers, and other ADO.NET components primarily as abstractions rather than merely objects used in database programs. If you concentrate on concepts, learning when and how to use relevant objects and methods will be easy.

Summary

In this chapter, you saw why ADO.NET was developed and how it supersedes other data access technologies in .NET. We gave an overview of its architecture and then focused on one of its core components, the data provider. You built three simple examples to practice basic data provider use and experience the uniform way data access code is written, regardless of the data provider. Finally, we offered the opinion that conceptual clarity is the key to understanding and using both data providers and the rest of the ADO.NET API.

Next, we'll study the details of ADO.NET, starting with connections.

CHAPTER 10

■ ■ ■

Making Connections

Before you can do anything useful with a database, you need to establish a *session* with the database server. You do this with an object called a *connection*, which is an instance of a class that implements the System.Data.IDbConnection interface for a specific data provider. In this chapter, you'll use various data providers to establish connections and look at problems that may arise and how to solve them.

In this chapter, we'll cover the following:

- Introducing data provider connection classes

- Connecting to SQL Server Express with SqlConnection

- Improving your use of connection objects

- Connecting to SQL Server Express with OleDbConnection

Introducing the Data Provider Connection Classes

As you saw in Chapter 9, each data provider has its own namespace. Each has a connection class that implements the System.Data.IDbConnection interface. Table 10-1 summarizes the data providers supplied by Microsoft.

Table 10-1. *Data Provider Namespaces and Connection Classes*

Data Provider	Namespace	Connection Class
ODBC	System.Data.Odbc	OdbcConnection
OLE DB	System.Data.OleDb	OleDbConnection
Oracle	System.Data.OracleClient	OracleConnection
SQL Server	System.Data.SqlClient	SqlConnection
SQL Server CE	System.Data.SqlServerCe	SqlCeConnection

As you can see, the names follow a convention, using Connection prefixed by an identifier for the data provider. Since all connection classes implement System.Data.IDbConnection, the use of each one is similar. Each has additional members that provide methods specific to a particular database. You used connections in Chapter 9. Let's take a closer look at one of them, SqlConnection, in the namespace System.Data.SqlClient.

Connecting to SQL Server Express with SqlConnection

In this example, you'll again connect to the SQL Server Management Studio Express (SSMSE) Northwind database.

Try It Out: Using SqlConnection

You'll write a very simple program, just to open and check a connection:

1. In Visual Studio 2008, create a new Visual Basic Console Application project named Chapter10. When Solution Explorer opens, save the solution.

2. Rename the Chapter10 project to ConnectionSQL. Rename the Module1.vb file to ConnectionSql.vb, and replace the generated code with the code in Listing 10-1.

Listing 10-1. ConnectionSql.vb

```vb
Imports System
Imports System.Data
Imports System.Data.SqlClient

Module ConnectionSQL
    Sub Main()

        'Set up connection string
        Dim connstring As String
        connstring = "Data Source=.\sqlexpress;Integrated Security=True"

    'Create connection
        Dim conn As SqlConnection = New SqlConnection(connstring)

        Try
            ' Open connection
            conn.Open()
            Console.WriteLine("Connection opened")

        Catch e As SqlException
            Console.WriteLine("Error: " &  e.ToString)

        Finally
            ' Close connection
            conn.Close()
            Console.WriteLine("Connection closed.")
        End Try
    End Sub
End Module
```

3. Run the application by pressing Ctrl+F5. If the connection is successful, you'll see the output in Figure 10-1.

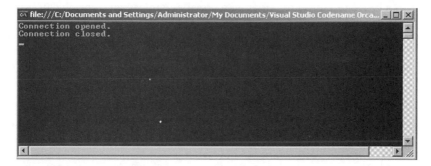

Figure 10-1. *Connecting and disconnecting*

If the connection failed, you'll see an error message, as shown in Figure 10-2. (You can get this by shutting down SSMSE first, entering net stop mssql$sqlexpress at a command prompt. If you try this, remember to restart it by typing net start mssql$sqlexpress.)

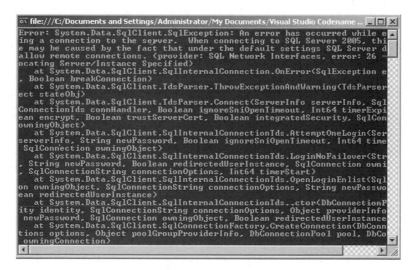

Figure 10-2. *Error if connection failed while connecting to SQL Server*

Don't worry about the specifics of this message right now. Connections often fail for reasons that have nothing to do with your code. It may be because a server isn't started, as in this case, or because a password is wrong, or some other configuration problem exists. You'll soon look at common problems in establishing database connections.

How It Works

Let's examine the code in Listing 10-1 to understand the steps in the connection process. First, you specify the ADO.NET and the SQL Server data provider namespaces, so you can use the simple names of their members:

```
Imports System
Imports System.Data
Imports System.Data.SqlClient
```

Then you create a connection string. A *connection string* consists of parameters—in other words, key=value pairs separated by semicolons—that specify connection information. Although some parameters are valid for all data providers, each data provider has specific parameters it will accept, so it's important to know what parameters are valid in a connection string for the data provider you're using.

```
Dim connstring As String
connstring = "Data Source=.\sqlexpress;Integrated Security=True"
```

Let's briefly examine each of the connection string parameters in this example. The data source parameter specifies the SQL Server instance to which you want to connect:

```
Data Source=.\sqlexpress
```

In this statement, . (dot) represents the local server, and the name followed by the \ (backslash) represents the instance name running on the database server. So here you have an instance of SQL Server Express named sqlexpress running on the local server.

■**Tip** (local) is an alternative to the . (dot) to specify the local machine, so .\sqlexpress can be replaced with (local)\sqlexpress.

The next clause indicates that you should use Windows Authentication (i.e., any valid logged-on Windows user can log on to SSE):

```
integrated security = true
```

You could alternatively have used sspi instead of true, as they both have the same effect. Other parameters are available. You'll use one later to specify the database to which you want to connect.

Next you create a connection (a SqlConnection object), passing it the connection string. This doesn't create a database session. It simply creates the object you'll use later to open a session:

```
'Create connection
Dim conn As SqlConnection = New SqlConnection(connstring)
```

Now you have a connection, but you still need to establish a session with the database by calling the Open method on the connection. If the attempt to open a session fails, an exception will be thrown, so you use a try statement to enable exception handling. You display a message after calling Open, but this line will be executed only if the connection was successfully opened.

```
Try
    ' Open connection
    conn.Open()
    Console.WriteLine("Connection opened")
```

At this stage in the code, you'd normally issue a query or perform some other database operation over the open connection. However, we'll save that for later chapters and concentrate here on just connecting.

Next comes an exception handler in case Open() fails:

```
Catch e As SqlException
        Console.WriteLine("Error: " &  e.ToString)
```

Each data provider has a specific exception class for its error handling; SqlException is the class for the SQL Server data provider. Specific information about database errors is available from the exception, but here you're just displaying its raw contents.

When you've finished with the database, you call Close() to terminate the session and then print a message to show that Close() was called:

```
Finally
    ' Close connection
    conn.Close()
    Console.WriteLine("Connection closed.")
End Try
```

You call Close() within the finally block to ensure it *always* gets called.

■**Note** Establishing connections (database sessions) is relatively expensive. They use resources on both the client and the server. Although connections may eventually get closed through garbage collection or by timing out, leaving one open when it's no longer needed is a bad practice. Too many open connections can slow a server down or prevent new connections from being made.

Note that you can call Close() on a closed connection, and no exception will be thrown. So, your message would have been displayed if the connection had been closed earlier or even if it had never been opened. See Figure 10-2, where the connection failed but the close message is still displayed.

In one typical case, multiple calls to both Open() and Close() make sense. ADO.NET supports disconnected processing of data, even when the connection to the data provider has been closed. The pattern looks like this:

```
Try
    ' Open connection
    conn.Open()

    'online processing (e.g., queries) here
    'close connection
    conn.Close()

    'offline processing here
    'reopen connection
    conn.Open()

    'online processing(e.g., INSERT/UPDATE/DELETE) here
    'reclose connection
    conn.Close()

Finally
    ' Close connection
    conn.Close()
End Try
```

The `finally` block still calls `Close()`, calling it unnecessarily if no exceptions are encountered, but this isn't a problem or expensive, and it ensures the connection will be closed. Although many programmers hold connections open until program termination, this is usually wasteful in terms of server resources. With *connection pooling*, opening and closing a connection as needed is actually more efficient than opening it once and for all.

That's it! You've finished with the first connection example. However, since you saw a possible error, let's look at typical causes of connection errors.

Debugging Connections to SQL Server

Writing the VB.NET code to use a connection is usually the easy part of getting a connection to work. Problems often lie not in the code, but rather in a mismatch in the connection parameters between the client (your VB.NET program) and the database server. All appropriate connection parameters must be used and must have correct values. Even experienced database professionals often have problems getting a connection to work the first time.

More parameters are available than the ones shown here, but you get the idea. A corollary of Murphy's Law applies to connections: if several things can go wrong, surely one of them will. Your goal is to check both sides of the connection to make sure all of your assumptions are correct and that everything the client program specifies is matched correctly on the server.

Often the solution is on the server side. If the SQL Server instance isn't running, the client will be trying to connect to a server that doesn't exist. If Windows Authentication isn't used and the user name and password on the client don't match the name and password of a user authorized to access the SQL Server instance, the connection will be rejected. If the database requested in the connection doesn't exist, an error will occur. If the client's network information doesn't match the server's, the server may not receive the client's connection request, or the server response may not reach the client.

For connection problems, using the debugger to locate the line of code where the error occurs usually doesn't help—the problem almost always occurs on the call to the `Open` method. The question is, why? You need to look at the error message.

A typical error is as follows:

```
Unhandled Exception: System.ArgumentException: Keyword not supported...
```

The cause for this is either using an invalid parameter or value or misspelling a parameter or value in your connection string. Make sure you've entered what you really meant to enter.

Figure 10-2 earlier showed probably the most common message when trying to connect to SQL Server. In this case, most likely SQL Server simply isn't running. Restart the SSE service with `net start mssql$sqlexpress`.

Other possible causes of this message are as follows:

- The SQL Server instance name is incorrect. For example, you used `.\sqlexpress`, but SSE was installed with a different name. It's also possible that SSE was installed as the default instance (with no instance name) or is on another machine (see the next section); correct the instance name if this is the case.

- SSE hasn't been installed—go back to Chapter 1 and follow the instructions there for installing SSE.

- A security problem exists—your Windows login and password aren't valid on the server. This is unlikely to be the problem when connecting to a local SSE instance, but it might happen in trying to connect to a SQL Server instance on another server.

- A hardware problem exists—again unlikely if you're trying to connect to a server on the same machine.

Security and Passwords in SqlConnection

There are two kinds of user authentication in SSE. The preferred way is to use Windows Authentication (integrated security), as you do when following the examples in this book. SQL Server uses your Windows login to access the instance. Your Windows login must exist on the machine where SQL Server is running, and your login must be authorized to access the SQL Server instance or be a member of a user group that has access.

If you don't include the `Integrated Security = true` (or `Integrated Security = sspi`) parameter in the connection string, the connection defaults to SQL Server security, which uses a separate login and password within SQL Server.

How to Use SQL Server Security

If you really did intend to use SQL Server security because that's how your company or department has set up access to your SQL Server (perhaps because some clients are non-Microsoft), you need to specify a user name and password in the connection string, as shown here:

```
thisConnection.ConnectionString = "server = .\sqlexpress"& _
"user id = sa;   password = x1y2z3"
```

The sa user name is the default system administrator account for SQL Server. If a specific user has been set up, such as george or payroll, specify that name. The password for sa is set when SQL Server is installed. If the user name you use has no password, you can omit the password clause entirely or specify an empty password, as follows:

password =

However, a blank password is bad practice and should be avoided, even in a test environment.

Connection String Parameters for SqlConnection

Table 10-2 summarizes the basic parameters for the SQL Server data provider connection string.

Table 10-2. *SQL Server Data Provider Connection String Parameters*

Name	Alias	Default Value	Allowed Values	Description
Application Name		.Net SqlClient Data Provider	Any string	Name of application
AttachDBFileName	extended properties, Initial File Name	None	Any path	Full path of an attachable database file
Connect Timeout	Connection Timeout	15	0–32767	Seconds to wait to connect
Data Source	Server, Address, Addr, Network Address	None	Server name or network address	Name of the target SQL Server instance
Encrypt		false	true, false, yes, no	Whether to use SSL encryption
Initial Catalog	Database	None	Any database that exists on server	Database name
Integrated Security	Trusted_ Connection	false	true, false, yes, no, sspi	Authentication mode
Network Library	Net	dbmssocn	dbnmpntw, dbmsrpcn, dbmsadsn, dbmsgnet, dbmslpcn, dbmsspxn, dbmssocn	Network .dll
Packet Size		8192	Multiple of 512	Network packet size in bytes
Password	PWD	None	Any string	Password if not using Windows Authentication
Persist Security Info		false	true, false, yes, no	Whether sensitive information should be passed back after connecting
User ID	UID		None	User name if not using Windows Authentication
Workstation ID		Local computer name	Any string	Workstation connecting to SQL Server

The Alias column in Table 10-2 gives alternate parameter names. For example, you can specify the server using any of the following:

```
data source = .\sqlexpress
server = .\sqlexpress
address = .\sqlexpress
addr = .\sqlexpress
network address = .\sqlexpress
```

Connection Pooling

One low-level detail that's worth noting—even though you shouldn't change it—is *connection pooling*. Recall that creating connections is expensive in terms of memory and time. With pooling, a closed connection isn't immediately destroyed but is kept in memory in a pool of unused connections. If a new connection request comes in that matches the properties of one of the unused connections in the pool, the unused connection is used for the new database session.

Creating a totally new connection over the network can take seconds, whereas reusing a pooled connection can happen in milliseconds; it's much faster to use pooled connections. The connection string has parameters that can change the size of the connection pool or even turn off connection pooling. The default values (for example, connection pooling is on by default) are appropriate for the vast majority of applications.

Improving Your Use of Connection Objects

The code in the first sample program was trivial, so you could concentrate on how connections work. Let's enhance it a bit.

Using the Connection String in the Connection Constructor

In the ConnectionSql project, you created the connection and specified the connection string in separate steps. Since you always have to specify a connection string, you can use an overloaded version of the constructor that takes the connection string as an argument:

```
'Set up connection string
Dim conn As SqlConnection= New SqlConnection _
("server=(local)\sqlexpress;Integrated Security=True")
```

This constructor sets the `ConnectionString` property when creating the `SqlConnection` object. You will try it in the next examples and use it in later chapters.

Displaying Connection Information

Connections have several properties that provide information about the connection. Most of these properties are read-only, since their purpose is to display rather than set information. (You set connection values in the connection string.) These properties are often useful when debugging, to verify that the connection properties are what you expect them to be.

Here, we'll describe the connection properties common to most data providers.

Try It Out: Displaying Connection Information

In this example, you'll see how to write a program to display connection information.

1. Add a VB.NET Console Application project named ConnectionDisplay to the Chapter10 solution.

2. Rename Module1.vb to ConnectionDisplay.vb. When prompted to rename all references to Program, you can click either Yes or No. Replace the code with that in Listing 10-2.

Listing 10-2. ConnectionDisplay.vb

```vb
Imports System
Imports System.Data
Imports System.Data.SqlClient

Module ConnectionDisplay
    Sub Main()

        'Set up connection string
        Dim connstring As String
        connstring = "data source = .\sqlexpress;" & _
        "Integrated Security=True"

        'Create connection
        Dim conn As SqlConnection = New SqlConnection(connstring)

        Try
        ' Open connection
          conn.Open()
         Console.WriteLine("Connection opened")

         'Display connection properties
         Console.WriteLine("Connection Properties:")
        Console.WriteLine("Connection String: {0}", conn.ConnectionString)
        Console.WriteLine("Database: {0}", conn.Database)
        Console.WriteLine("DataSource: {0}", conn.DataSource)
        Console.WriteLine("ServerVersion: {0}", conn.ServerVersion)
        Console.WriteLine("State: {0}", conn.State)
       Console.WriteLine("WorkstationId: {0}", conn.WorkstationId)

        Catch e As SqlException
            Console.WriteLine("Error:" & e.ToString)
```

```
        Finally
            ' Close connection
            conn.Close()
            Console.WriteLine("Connection closed.")
        End Try
    End Sub
End Module
```

3. Make ConnectionDisplay the startup project, and run it by pressing Ctrl+F5. If the connection is successful, you'll see output like that shown in Figure 10-3.

Figure 10-3. *Displaying connection information*

How It Works

The ConnectionString property can be both read and written. Here you just display it:

```
Console.WriteLine("Connection String: {0}", conn.ConnectionString)
```

You can see the value you assign to it, including the whitespace, in the verbatim string.

What's the point? Well, it's handy when debugging connections to verify that the connection string really contains the values you thought you assigned. For example, if you're trying out different connection options, you may have different connection string parameters in the program. You may have commented out one, intending to use it later, but forgot about it. Displaying the ConnectionString property helps you to see whether a parameter is missing.

The next statement displays the Database property. Since each SQL Server instance has several databases, this property shows which one you're initially using when you connect:

```
Console.WriteLine("Database: {0}", conn.Database)
```

In this program, it displays

```
Database: master
```

---

since you didn't specify a database in the connection string, so you were connected to the SQL Server's default database master. If you wanted to connect to the Northwind database, you'd need to specify the database property, for example:

```
'connection string
Dim connstring As String
connstring = "data source = .\sqlexpress;" & _
"Integrated Security=True;database=northwind"
```

You can also change the default database from the master database to some other database, say, AdventureWorks, by executing the following statement:

```
exec sp_defaultdb 'sa','adventureworks'
```

Again, this is a handy property to display for debugging purposes. If you get an error saying that a particular table doesn't exist, often the problem isn't that the table doesn't exist but that it isn't in the database to which you're connected. Displaying the database property helps you to find that kind of error quickly.

■**Tip** If you specify a database in the connection string that doesn't exist on the server, you may see the following error message: "System.Data.SqlClient.SqlException: Cannot open database 'database' requested by the login. The login failed."

You can change the database currently used on a connection with the ChangeDatabase method.

The next statement displays the DataSource property, which gives the server instance name for SQL Server database connections.

```
Console.WriteLine("DataSource: {0}", conn.DataSource)
```

This displays the same SQL Server instance name you've used in all the examples so far:

```
DataSource: .\sqlexpress
```

The utility of this, again, is mainly for debugging purposes.

The ServerVersion property displays the server version information:

```
Console.WriteLine("ServerVersion: {0}", conn.ServerVersion)
```

It shows the version of SSE you installed in Chapter 1. (Your version may differ.)

```
ServerVersion: 09.00.3042
```

The version number is useful for debugging. This information actually comes from the server, so it indicates the connection is working.

■**Note** SQL Server 2005 (and SSE) is Version 9. SQL Server 2000 is version 8.

The State property indicates whether the connection is open or closed:

```
Console.WriteLine("State: {0}", conn.State)
```

Since you display this property after the Open() call, it shows that the connection is open:

```
State: Open
```

You've been displaying your own message that the connection is open, but this property contains the current state. If the connection is closed, the State property would be Closed.

You then display the workstation ID, which is a string identifying the client computer. The WorkstationId property is specific to SQL Server and can be handy for debugging:

```
Console.WriteLine("WorkstationId: {0}", conn.WorkstationId)
```

It defaults to the computer name. Our computer is named VIDYAVRAT, but yours, of course, will be different:

```
WorkstationId: <YourComputerName>
```

What makes this useful for debugging is that the SQL Server tools on the server can display which workstation ID issued a particular command. If you don't know which machine is causing a problem, you can modify your programs to display the WorkstationId property and compare them to the workstation IDs displayed on the server.

You can also set this property with the workstation ID connection string parameter as follows, so if you want all the workstations in, say, Building B to show that information on the server, you can indicate that in the program:

```
// connection string
string connString = @"
    server = .\sqlexpress;
    workstation id = Building B;
    integrated security = true;
";
```

That completes the discussion of the fundamentals of connecting to SQL Server with SqlClient. Now let's look at connecting with another data provider.

Connecting to SQL Server Express with OleDbConnection

As you saw in Chapter 9, you can use the OLE DB data provider to work with any OLE DB–compatible data store. Microsoft provides OLE DB data providers for Microsoft SQL Server, Microsoft Access (Jet), Oracle, and a variety of other database and data file formats.

If a native data provider is available for a particular database or file format (such as the SqlClient data provider for SQL Server), it's generally better to use it rather than the generic OLE DB data provider. This is because OLE DB introduces an extra layer of indirection between the VB.NET program and the data source. One common database format for which no native data provider exists is the Microsoft Access database (.mdb file) format, also known as the Jet database engine format, so in this case you need to use the OLE DB (or the ODBC) data provider.

We don't assume you have an Access database to connect to, so you'll use OLE DB with SSMSE, as you did in Chapter 9.

Try It Out: Connecting to SQL Server Express with the OLE DB Data Provider

To connect to SSMSE with the OLE DB data provider, follow these steps:

1. Add a VB.NET Console Application project named ConnectionOleDb, and rename Module1.vb to ConnectionOleDb.vb.

2. Replace the code in ConnectionOleDb.vb with that in Listing 10-3. This is basically the same code as Connection.vb, with the changed code in bold.

Listing 10-3. ConnectionOleDb.vb

```vb
Imports System
Imports System.Data
Imports System.Data.OleDb

Module ConnectionOleDb
    Sub Main()

        'Set up connection string
        Dim connstring As String
        connstring = "data source = .\sqlexpress;" & _
        "provider = sqloledb;integrated security = sspi"

        'Create connection
        Dim conn As OleDbConnection = New OleDbConnection(connstring)

        Try
            ' Open connection
            conn.Open()
            Console.WriteLine("Connection opened")

            'Display connection properties
            Console.WriteLine("Connection Properties:")
            Console.WriteLine("Connection String: {0}", conn.ConnectionString)
            Console.WriteLine("Database: {0}", conn.Database)
            Console.WriteLine("DataSource: {0}", conn.DataSource)
            Console.WriteLine("ServerVersion: {0}", conn.ServerVersion)
            Console.WriteLine("State: {0}", conn.State)
```

```
        Catch e As OleDbException
            Console.WriteLine("Error:" & e.ToString)

        Finally
            ' Close connection
            conn.Close()
            Console.WriteLine("Connection closed.")
        End Try
    End Sub
End Module
```

3. Make ConnectionOleDb the startup project, and run it by pressing Ctrl+F5. If the connection is successful, you'll see output like that shown in Figure 10-4.

Figure 10-4. *Displaying OLE DB connection information*

How It Works

We'll discuss only the differences between this example and the previous one.

The first step is to reference the OLE DB data provider namespace, System.Data.OleDb:

```
Imports System.Data.OleDb
```

Next, you create an OleDbConnection object instead of a SqlConnection object. Note the changes to the connection string. Instead of the server parameter, you use Provider and Data Source. Notice the value of the Integrated Security parameter must be sspi, not true.

```
'connection string
Dim connstring As String
connstring = "data source = .\sqlexpress;" & _
"provider = sqloledb;integrated security = sspi"
```

Finally, note that you omit the WorkstationId property in your display. The OLE DB data provider doesn't support it.

This is the pattern for accessing any data source with any .NET data provider. Specify the connection string with parameters specific to the data provider. Use the appropriate objects from the data provider namespace. Use only the properties and methods provided by that data provider.

Summary

In this chapter, you created, opened, and closed connections using two data providers and their appropriate connection strings parameters and values. You displayed information about connections after creating them using connection properties. You also saw how to handle various exceptions associated with connections.

In the next chapter, you'll look at ADO.NET *commands* and see how to use them to access data.

■ ■ ■

Executing Commands

Once you've established a connection to the database, you want to start interacting with it and getting it doing something useful for you. You may need to add, update, or delete some data, or perhaps modify the database in some other way, usually by running a query. Whatever the task, it will inevitably involve a *command*.

In this chapter, we'll explain commands, which are objects that encapsulate the SQL for the action you want to perform and that provide methods for submitting it to the database. Each data provider has a command class that implements the System.Data. IDbCommand interface.

In this chapter, we'll cover the following:

- Creating commands

- Executing commands

- Executing commands with multiple results

- Executing statements

- Command parameters

We'll use the SQL Server data provider (System.Data.SqlClient) in our examples. Its command is named SqlCommand. The commands for the other data providers work the same way.

Creating a Command

You can create a command either using the SqlCommand constructor or using methods that create the object for you. Let's look at the first of these alternatives.

Try It Out: Creating a Command with a Constructor

In this example, you'll create a SqlCommand object but not yet do anything with it.

1. Create a new Visual Basic Console Application project named Chapter11. When Solution Explorer opens, save the solution.

2. Rename the Chapter11 project to CommandSql. Rename the Module1.vb file to CommandSql.vb, and replace the generated code with the code in Listing 11-1.

Listing 11-1. CommandSql.vb

```vb
Imports System
Imports System.Data
Imports System.Data.SqlClient

Module ConnectionSQL
    Sub Main()

        'create connection
        Dim conn As SqlConnection = New SqlConnection _
        ("Data Source=.\sqlexpress;" & _
         "Integrated Security=True;" & _
         "database=northwind")

        'create command
        Dim cmd As SqlCommand = New SqlCommand
        Console.WriteLine("Command created.")

        Try
            ' Open connection
            conn.Open()

        Catch ex As SqlException
            Console.WriteLine(ex)

        Finally
            ' Close connection
            conn.Close()
            Console.WriteLine("Connection closed.")
        End Try
    End Sub
End Module
```

3. Run the program by pressing Ctrl+F5. You should see the output in Figure 11-1.

Figure 11-1. *Connecting after creating a command*

How It Works

You create a SqlCommand object using the default constructor and print a message indicating you've created it:

```
'create command
Dim cmd As SqlCommand = New SqlCommand
Console.WriteLine("Command created.")
```

In this example, the command is empty. It isn't associated with a connection, and it doesn't have its text (in other words, the SQL) set. You can't do much with it here, so let's move on and see how you can associate a command with a connection.

Associating a Command with a Connection

For your commands to be executed against a database, each command must be associated with a connection to the database. You do this by setting the Connection property of the command, and in order to save resources, multiple commands can use the same connection. You have a couple of ways to set up this association, so next you'll modify the example to try them.

Try It Out: Setting the Connection Property

To set the Connection property, follow these steps:

1. Add the following bold code to the try block of Listing 11-1.

```
 'Open connection
conn.Open()
 'connect command to connection
 cmd.Connection = conn
 Console.WriteLine("Connnected command to this connection.")
```

2. Run the code by pressing Ctrl+F5. You should see the results in Figure 11-2.

Figure 11-2. *Connecting a command to a connection*

How It Works

As you saw in the previous example, you start the code by creating the connection and command:

```
'create connection
        Dim conn As SqlConnection = New SqlConnection _
        ("Data Source=.\sqlexpress;" & _
         "Integrated Security=True;" & _
         "database=northwind")

        Dim cmd As SqlCommand = New SqlCommand
        Console.WriteLine("Command created.")
```

At this point, both the connection and command exist, but they aren't associated with each other in any way. It's only when you assign the connection to the command's Connection property that they become associated:

```
'connect command to connection
   cmd.Connection = conn
  Console.WriteLine("Connnected command to this connection.")
```

The actual assignment occurs after the call to conn.Open in this particular example, but you could have done it before calling Open method; the connection doesn't have to be open for the Connection property of the command to be set.

As mentioned earlier, you have a second option for associating a connection with a command; calling the connection's CreateCommand method will return a new command with the Connection property set to that connection:

```
   Dim cmd As SqlCommand = New SqlCommand
cmd = conn.CreateCommand
```

This is equivalent to

```
   Dim cmd As SqlCommand = New SqlCommand
cmd.Connection = conn
```

In both cases, you end up with a command associated with a connection.

You still need one more thing in order to use the command, and that's the text of the command. Let's see how to set that next.

Assigning Text to a Command

Every command has a property, CommandText, that holds the SQL to execute. You can assign to this property directly or specify it when constructing the command. Let's look at these alternatives.

Try It Out: Setting the CommandText Property

To set the CommandText property, follow these steps:

1. Modify the try block with the following bold code:

```
Try
  'Open connection
conn.Open()
  'connect command to connection
  cmd.Connection = conn
  Console.WriteLine("Connnected command to this connection.")

         ' associate SQL with command
         cmd.CommandText = "select count(*)from employees"

         Console.WriteLine("Ready to execute SQL:" & _
            cmd.CommandText)
         End Try
```

2. Run the code by pressing Ctrl+F5. You should see the result in Figure 11-3.

Figure 11-3. *Setting command text*

How It Works

CommandText is just a string, so you can print it with Console.WriteLine() just like any other string. The SQL will return the number of employees in the Northwind Employees table when you eventually execute it.

■**Note** You must set both the Connection and the CommandText properties of a command before the command can be executed.

You can set both of these properties when you create the command with yet another variation of its constructor, as shown here:

```
'create command (with both text and connection)
Dim sql As String = "select count(*) from employees"
Dim cmd As SqlCommand = New SqlCommand(sql, conn)
```

This is equivalent to the previous code that assigns each property explicitly. This is the most commonly used variation of the SqlCommand constructor, and you'll use it for the rest of the chapter.

Executing Commands

Commands aren't much use unless you can execute them, so let's look at that now. Commands have several different methods for executing SQL. The differences between these methods depend on the results you expect from the SQL. Queries return rows of data (*result sets*), but the INSERT, UPDATE, and DELETE statements don't. You determine which method to use by considering what you expect to be returned (see Table 11-1).

Table 11-1. *Command Execution Methods*

If the Command Is Going to Return . . .	You Should Use . . .
Nothing (It isn't a query)	ExecuteNonQuery
Zero or more rows	ExecuteReader
XML	ExecuteXmlReader

The SQL you just used in the example should return one value, the number of employees. Looking at Table 11-1, you can see that you should use the ExecuteScalar method of SqlCommand to return this one result. Let's try it.

Try It Out: Using the ExecuteScalar Method

To use the ExecuteScalar method, follow these steps:

1. Add a new Visual Basic Console Application project named CommandScalar to your Chapter11 solution. Rename Module1.vb to CommandScalar.vb.

2. Replace the code in CommandScalar.vb with the code in Listing 11-2.

   Listing 11-2. CommandScalar.vb

   ```
   Imports System
   Imports System.Data
   Imports System.Data.SqlClient

   Module CommandScalar
       Sub Main()
   ```

```
        'create connection
        Dim conn As SqlConnection = New SqlConnection _
        ("Data Source=.\sqlexpress;" & _
         "Integrated Security=True;" & _
         "database=northwind")
        'create command (with both text and connection)
        Dim sql As String = "select count(*) from employees"

        Dim cmd As SqlCommand = New SqlCommand(sql, conn)
        Console.WriteLine("Command created and connected.")

        Try
            'Open connection
            conn.Open()

            'execute query
            Console.WriteLine("Number of Employees is {0}", _
            cmd.ExecuteScalar())

        Catch ex As SqlException
            Console.WriteLine(ex)

        Finally
            ' Close connection
            conn.Close()
            Console.WriteLine("Connection closed.")
        End Try
    End Sub
End Module
```

3. Make CommandScalar the startup project, and then run it by pressing Ctrl+F5. You should see the results in Figure 11-4.

Figure 11-4. *Executing a scalar command*

How It Works

All you do is add a call to ExecuteScalar() within a call to WriteLine():

```
'execute query
Console.WriteLine("Number of Employees is {0}", _
cmd.ExecuteScalar())
```

ExecuteScalar() takes the CommandText property and sends it to the database using the command's Connection property. It returns the result (9) as a single object, which you display with Console.WriteLine().

This is pretty simple to follow, but it's worth noting this is simpler than usual because Console.WriteLine() takes any kind of object as its input. In fact, ExecuteScalar()'s return type is object, the base class of all types in the .NET Framework, which makes perfect sense when you remember that a database can hold any type of data. So, if you want to assign the returned object to a variable of a specific type (Integer, for example), you must cast the object to the specific type. If the types aren't compatible, the system will generate a runtime error that indicates an invalid cast.

The following is an example that demonstrates this idea. In it, you store the result from ExecuteScalar() in the variable count, casting it to the specific type Integer:

```
Dim count As Integer = cmd.ExecuteScalar()
Console.WriteLine("Number of Employees is: {0}", count)
```

If you're sure the type of the result will always be an Integer (a safe bet with COUNT(*)), the previous code is safe. However, if you left the cast to Integer in place and changed the CommandText of the command to the following:

```
select
  firstname
from
  employees
where
  lastname = 'Davolio'
```

ExecuteScalar() would return the string Nancy instead of an integer, and you'd get this exception:

```
Unhandled Exception: System.InvalidCastException: Specified cast is not valid.
```

because you can't cast a string to an Integer.

Another problem may occur if a query actually returns multiple rows where you thought it would return only one; for example, what if there were multiple employees with the last name Davolio? In this case, ExecuteScalar() just returns the first row of the result and ignores the rest. If you use ExecuteScalar(), make sure you not only expect but actually get a single value returned.

Executing Commands with Multiple Results

For queries where you're expecting multiple rows and columns to be returned, use the command's ExecuteReader() method.

ExecuteReader() returns a data reader, an instance of the SqlDataReader class that you'll study in the next chapter. Data readers have methods that allow you to read successive rows in result sets and retrieve individual column values.

We'll leave the details of data readers for the next chapter, but for comparison's sake, we'll give a brief example here of using the ExecuteReader() method to create a SqlDataReader from a command to display query results.

Try It Out: Using the ExecuteReader Method

To use the ExecuteReader method, follow these steps:

1. Add a new Visual Basic Console Application project named CommandReader to your Chapter11 solution. Rename Module1.vb to CommandReader.vb.

2. Replace the code in CommandReader.vb with the code in Listing 11-3.

   Listing 11-3. CommandReader.vb

```
Imports System
Imports System.Data
Imports System.Data.SqlClient

Module CommandReader
    Sub Main()

        'create connection
        Dim conn As SqlConnection = New SqlConnection _
        ("Data Source=.\sqlexpress;" & _
         "Integrated Security=True;" & _
         "database=northwind")

        'create command (with both text and connection)
        Dim sql As String = "select firstname,lastname from employees"


        Dim cmd As SqlCommand = New SqlCommand(sql, conn)
        Console.WriteLine("Command created and connected.")

        Try
            'Open connection
            conn.Open()
```

```
        'execute query
        Dim rdr As SqlDataReader = cmd.ExecuteReader

        While (rdr.Read)
            Console.WriteLine("Employee name: {0} {1}", _
            rdr.GetValue(0), rdr.GetValue(1))
        End While

    Catch ex As SqlException
        Console.WriteLine(ex)

    Finally
        ' Close connection
        conn.Close()
        Console.WriteLine("Connection closed.")
    End Try
End Sub
End Module
```

3. Make CommandReader the startup project, and then run it by pressing Ctrl+F5. You should see the output in Figure 11-5, the first and last names of all nine employees.

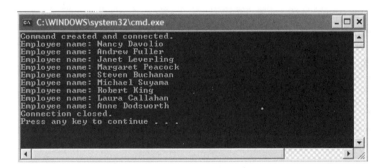

Figure 11-5. *Using a data reader*

How It Works

In this example, you use the ExecuteReader method to retrieve and then output the first and last names of all the employees in the Employees table. As with ExecuteScalar(), ExecuteReader() takes the CommandText property and sends it to the database using the connection from the Connection property.

When you use the ExecuteScalar method, you produce only a single scalar value. In contrast, using ExecuteReader() returns a SqlDataReader object.

```
'execute query
Dim rdr As SqlDataReader = cmd.ExecuteReader

While (rdr.Read)
    Console.WriteLine("Employee name: {0} {1}", _
    rdr.GetValue(0), rdr.GetValue(1))
End While
```

The SqlDataReader object has a Read method that gets each row in turn and a GetValue method that gets the value of a column in the row. The particular column whose value it retrieves is given by the integer parameter indicating the index of the column. Note that GetValue uses a zero-based index, so the first column is column 0, the second column is column 1, and so on. Since the query asked for two columns, FirstName and LastName, these are the columns numbered 0 and 1 in this query result.

Executing Statements

The ExecuteNonQuery method of the command executes SQL statements instead of queries. Let's try it.

Try It Out: Using the ExecuteNonQuery Method

To use the ExecuteNonQuery method, follow these steps:

1. Add a new Visual Basic Console Application project named CommandNonQuery to your Chapter11 solution. Rename Module1.vb to CommandNonQuery.vb.

2. Replace the code in CommandNonQuery.vb with the code in Listing 11-4.

Listing 11-4. CommandNonQuery.vb

```
Imports System
Imports System.Data
Imports System.Data.SqlClient

Module CommandNonQuery
    Sub Main()

        'create connection
        Dim conn As SqlConnection = New SqlConnection _
        ("Data Source=.\sqlexpress;" & _
         "Integrated Security=True;" & _
         "database=northwind")
```

```vbnet
'define scalar query
Dim sqlqry As String = "select count(*)from employees"

'define insert statement
Dim sqlins As String = "insert into employees " & _
"(firstname,lastname)values('Zachariah', 'Zinn')"

'define delete statement
Dim sqldel As String = "delete from employees " & _
"where firstname = 'Zachariah'" & _
"and lastname = 'Zinn'"

'create commands
Dim cmdqry As SqlCommand = New SqlCommand(sqlqry, conn)
Dim cmdnon As SqlCommand = New SqlCommand(sqlins, conn)
Console.WriteLine("Command created and connected.")

Try
    'Open connection
    conn.Open()

    'execute query to get number of employees
    Console.WriteLine("Before INSERT: Number of employees {0}" _
    , cmdqry.ExecuteScalar())

    'execute nonquery to insert an employee
    Console.WriteLine("Executing statement {0}" _
    , cmdnon.CommandText)

    cmdnon.ExecuteNonQuery()

    Console.WriteLine("After INSERT: Number of employees {0}" _
    , cmdqry.ExecuteScalar())

    'execute nonquery to delete an employee
    cmdnon.CommandText = sqldel
    Console.WriteLine("Executing statement {0}" _
     , cmdnon.CommandText)
    cmdnon.ExecuteNonQuery()
    Console.WriteLine("After DELETE: Number of employees {0}" _
    , cmdqry.ExecuteScalar())

Catch ex As SqlException
    Console.WriteLine(ex)
```

```
        Finally
            ' Close connection
            conn.Close()
            Console.WriteLine("Connection closed.")
        End Try
    End Sub
End Module
```

3. Make CommandNonQuery the startup project, and then run it by pressing Ctrl+F5. You should see the results in Figure 11-6.

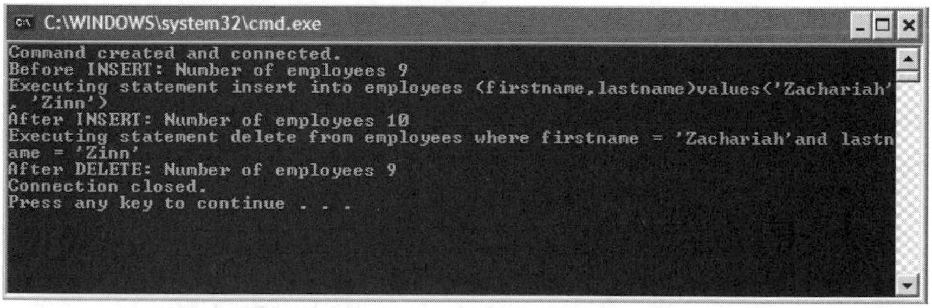

Figure 11-6. *Executing statements*

How It Works

In this program, you use a scalar query and two statements, storing the SQL in three string variables:

```
'define scalar query
Dim sqlqry As String = "select count(*)from employees"

'define insert statement
Dim sqlins As String = "insert into employees " & _
"(firstname,lastname)values('Zachariah', 'Zinn')"

'define delete statement
Dim sqldel As String = "delete from employees " & _
"where firstname = 'Zachariah'" & _
"and lastname = 'Zinn'"
```

Then you create two commands. The first is cmdqry, which encapsulates the scalar query to count the rows in the Employees table. You use this command several times to monitor the number of rows as you insert and delete employees. The second is cmdnon, which you use twice, first to insert a row and then to delete the same row. You initially set its CommandText to the INSERT statement SQL:

```
Dim cmdnon As SqlCommand = New SqlCommand(sqlins, conn)
```

and later reset it to the DELETE statement SQL:

```
cmdnon.CommandText = sqldel
```

executing the SQL statements with two calls to

```
cmdnon.ExecuteNonQuery()
```

ExecuteNonQuery() returns an int indicating how many rows are affected by the command. Since you want to display the number of affected rows, you put the call to ExecuteNonQuery() within a call to Console.WriteLine(). You used ExecuteScalar() to display the number of rows, before and after the INSERT and DELETE operations:

```
Console.WriteLine("After INSERT: Number of employees {0}\n" _
cmdqry.ExecuteScalar())
```

Note that both cmdqry and cmdnon are SqlCommand objects. The difference between submitting queries and statements is the method you use to submit them.

■**Note** With ExecuteNonQuery() you can submit virtually any SQL statement, including Data Definition Language (DDL) statements, to create and drop database objects like tables and indexes.

Command Parameters

When you inserted the new row into Employees, you hard-coded the values. Although this was perfectly valid SQL, it's something you almost never want (or need) to do. You must be able to store whatever values are appropriate at any given time. There are two approaches to doing this. Both are reasonable, but one is far more efficient than the other.

The less efficient alternative is to dynamically build an SQL statement, producing a string that contains all the necessary information in the CommandText property. For example, you could do something like this:

```
Dim fname As String = "Zachariah"
Dim lname As String = "Zinn"
  Dim vals As String = "('" & fname & "'," & "'" & lname & "')"
  Dim sqlins As String = "insert into employees" & _
  "(firstname,lastname)values" & vals
```

and then assign sqlins to some command's CommandText before executing the statement.

■**Note** Of course, we're using `fname` and `lname` simply as rudimentary sources of data. Data most likely comes from some dynamic input source and involves many rows over time, but the technique is nonetheless the same: building an SQL string from a combination of hard-coded SQL keywords and values contained in variables.

You should take care when inserting values that consist of single quotes, for example, a possessive form of the surname Agarwal's. To insert this string, you must include two single quotes—Agarwal"s—to prevent a syntax error. However, this is not recommended as best practice due to the risk of SQL injection attacks.

A much better way to handle this is with *command parameters*. A command parameter is a placeholder in the command text where a value will be substituted. In SQL Server, *named parameters* are used. They begin with @ followed by the parameter name with no intervening space. So, in the following INSERT statement, @MyName and @MyNumber are both parameters:

```
INSERT INTO MyTable VALUES (@MyName, @MyNumber)
```

■**Note** Some data providers use the standard SQL *parameter marker*, a question mark (?), instead of named parameters.

Command parameters have several advantages:

- The mapping between the variables and where they're used in SQL is clearer.

- Parameters let you use the type definitions that are specific to a particular ADO.NET data provider to ensure that your variables are mapped to the correct SQL data types.

- Parameters let you use the Prepare method, which can make your code run faster because the SQL in a "prepared" command is parsed by SQL Server only the first time it's executed. Subsequent executions run the same SQL, changing only parameter values.

- Parameters are used extensively in other programming techniques, such as using stored procedures and working with irregular data.

Try It Out: Using Command Parameters

To try out using command parameters, follow these steps:

1. Add a new Visual Basic Console Application project named CommandParameters to your Chapter11 solution. Rename Module1.vb to CommandParameters.vb.

2. Replace the code in CommandParameters.vb with the code in Listing 11-5. This is a variation of Listing 11-4, with salient changes highlighted in bold.

Listing 11-5. CommandParameters.vb

```
Imports System
Imports System.Data
Imports System.Data.SqlClient

Module CommandParameters
    Sub Main()

        'set up rudimentary data
        Dim fname As String = "Zachariah"
        Dim lname As String = "Zinn"

        'create connection
        Dim conn As SqlConnection = New SqlConnection _
        ("Data Source=.\sqlexpress;" & _
         "Integrated Security=True;" & _
         "database=northwind")

        'define scalar query
        Dim sqlqry As String = "select count(*)from employees"

        'define insert statement
        Dim sqlins As String = "insert into employees " & _
        "(firstname,lastname)values(@fname,@lname)"

        'define delete statement
        Dim sqldel As String = "delete from employees " & _
        "where firstname = @fname " & _
        "and lastname = @lname"

        'create commands
        Dim cmdqry As SqlCommand = New SqlCommand(sqlqry, conn)
        Dim cmdnon As SqlCommand = New SqlCommand(sqlins, conn)
        cmdnon.Prepare()

        'add parameters to the command for statements
        cmdnon.Parameters.Add("@fname", SqlDbType.NVarChar, 10)
        cmdnon.Parameters.Add("@lname", SqlDbType.NVarChar, 20)

        Try
            'Open connection
            conn.Open()

            'execute query to get number of employees
            Console.WriteLine("Before INSERT: Number of employees {0}" _
            , cmdqry.ExecuteScalar())
```

```
        'execute nonquery to insert an employee
        cmdnon.Parameters("@fname").Value = fname
        cmdnon.Parameters("@lname").Value = lname
        Console.WriteLine("Executing statement {0}" _
        , cmdnon.CommandText)

        cmdnon.ExecuteNonQuery()

        Console.WriteLine("After INSERT: Number of employees {0}" _
        , cmdqry.ExecuteScalar())

        'execute nonquery to delete an employee
        cmdnon.CommandText = sqldel
        Console.WriteLine("Executing statement {0}" _
         , cmdnon.CommandText)
        cmdnon.ExecuteNonQuery()
        Console.WriteLine("After DELETE: Number of employees {0}" _
        , cmdqry.ExecuteScalar())

    Catch ex As SqlException
        Console.WriteLine(ex)

    Finally
        ' Close connection
        conn.Close()
        Console.WriteLine("Connection closed.")
    End Try
  End Sub
End Module
```

3. Make CommandParameters the startup project, and then run it by pressing Ctrl+F5. You should see the results in Figure 11-7.

Figure 11-7. *Using command parameters*

How It Works

First, you set up your sample data:

```
'set up rudimentary data
Dim fname As String = "Zachariah"
Dim lname As String = "Zinn"
```

You then add two parameters, @fname and @lname, to the Parameters collection property of the command you want to parameterize:

```
'create commands
Dim cmdqry As SqlCommand = New SqlCommand(sqlqry, conn)
Dim cmdnon As SqlCommand = New SqlCommand(sqlins, conn)
cmdnon.Prepare()

'add parameters to the command for statements
cmdnon.Parameters.Add("@fname", SqlDbType.NVarChar, 10)
cmdnon.Parameters.Add("@lname", SqlDbType.NVarChar, 20)
```

Note that you provide the parameter names as strings and then specify the data types of the columns you expect to use them with. The SqlDbType enumeration contains a member for every SQL Server data type except cursor and table, which can't be directly used by Visual Basic .NET programs. The Add method is overloaded. Since nvarchar requires you to specify its maximum length, you include that as the third argument.

Finally, you set the parameter values before executing the command:

```
'execute nonquery to insert an employee
cmdnon.Parameters("@fname").Value = fname
cmdnon.Parameters("@lname").Value = lname
```

■**Note** You use the same command, cmdnon, to execute both the INSERT and DELETE statements. The parameter values don't change, even though the SQL in CommandText does. The Parameters collection is the source of parameter values for whatever SQL is in CommandText. The SQL does not have to use all or even any of the parameters, but it cannot use any parameters not in the command's Parameters collection.

Notice in Figure 11-7 that when you display the SQL in CommandText, you see the parameter names rather than their values. Values are substituted for parameters when the SQL is submitted to the database server, not when the values are assigned to the members of the Parameters collection.

Summary

In this chapter, we covered what an ADO.NET command is and how to create a command object. We also discussed associating a command with a connection, setting command text, and using ExecuteScalar(), ExecuteReader(), and ExecuteNonQuery() statements.

In the next chapter, you'll look at data readers.

CHAPTER 12

■■■

Using Data Readers

In Chapter 11, you used data readers to retrieve data from a multirow result set. In this chapter, we'll look at data readers in more detail. You'll see how they're used and their importance in ADO.NET programming.

In this chapter, we'll cover the following:

- Understanding data readers in general

- Getting data about data

- Getting data about tables

- Using multiple result sets with a data reader

Understanding Data Readers in General

The third component of a data provider, in addition to connections and commands, is the *data reader*. Once you've connected to a database and queried it, you need some way to access the result set. This is where the data reader comes in.

Note If you're from an ADO background, an ADO.NET data reader is like an ADO forward-only/read-only client-side record set, but it's not a COM object.

Data readers are objects that implement the System.Data.IDataReader interface. A data reader is a fast, unbuffered, forward-only, read-only *connected* stream that retrieves data on a per-row basis. It reads one row at a time as it loops through a result set.

You can't directly instantiate a data reader; instead, you create one with the ExecuteReader method of a command. For example, assuming cmd is a SqlClient command object for a query, here's how to create a SqlClient data reader:

```
Dim rdr As SqlDataReader=cmd.ExecuterReader
```

You can now use this data reader to access the query's result set.

Tip One point that we'll discuss further in the next chapter is choosing a data reader versus a dataset. The general rule is to always use a data reader for simply retrieving data. If all you need to do is display data, all you need to use in most cases is a data reader.

We'll demonstrate basic data reader usage with a few examples. The first example is the most basic; it simply uses a data reader to loop through a result set.

Let's say you've successfully established a connection with the database, a query has been executed, and everything seems to be going fine—what now? The next sensible thing to do would be to retrieve the rows and process them.

Try It Out: Looping Through a Result Set

The following console application shows how to use a SqlDataReader to loop through a result set and retrieve rows.

1. Create a new Visual Basic Console Application project named Chapter12. When Solution Explorer opens, save the solution.

2. Rename the Chapter12 project to DataLooper. Rename the Module1.vb file to DataLooper.vb, and replace the generated code with the code in Listing 12-1.

Listing 12-1. DataLooper.vb

```vb
Imports System
Imports System.Data
Imports System.Data.SqlClient

Module DataLooper
    Sub Main()

        Dim connstring As String = _
        ("Data Source=.\sqlexpress;" & _
         "Integrated Security=True;" & _
         "database=northwind")

        'create command (with both text and connection)
        Dim sql As String = "select contactname from customers"

        'create connection
        Dim conn As SqlConnection = New SqlConnection(connstring)

        Try
            'Open connection
            conn.Open()

            Dim cmd As SqlCommand = New SqlCommand(sql, conn)
```

```vb
                    'create data reader
                    Dim rdr As SqlDataReader = cmd.ExecuteReader
                    'loop through result set
                    While (rdr.Read)
                        'print one row at a time
                        Console.WriteLine("{0}", _
                        rdr.GetValue(0))
                    End While
            'close data reader
                    rdr.Close()
            Catch e As Exception
                Console.WriteLine("Error Occurred:" & e.ToString)

            Finally
                ' Close connection
                conn.Close()
            End Try
        End Sub
End Module
```

3. Run the DataLooper by pressing Ctrl+F5. You should see the results in Figure 12-1.

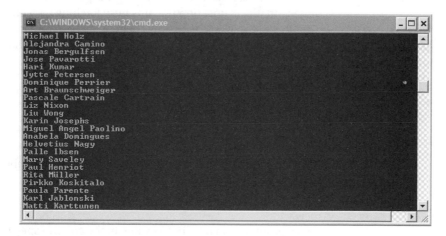

Figure 12-1. *Looping through a result set*

How It Works

SqlDataReader is an abstract class and can't be instantiated explicitly. For this reason, you obtain an instance of a SqlDataReader by executing the ExecuteReader method of SqlCommand:

```vb
'create data reader
Dim rdr As SqlDataReader = cmd.ExecuteReader
```

ExecuteReader method doesn't just create a data reader; it sends the SQL to the connection for execution, so when it returns you can loop through each row of the result set and retrieve values column by column. To do this, you call the Read method of SqlDataReader, which returns true if a row is available and advances the *cursor* (the internal pointer to the next row in the result set) or returns false if another row isn't available. Since the Read method advances the cursor to the next available row, you have to call it for all the rows in the result set, so you call it as the condition in a while loop:

```
'loop through result set
While (rdr.Read)
    'print one row at a time
    Console.WriteLine("{0}", _
    rdr.GetValue(0))
End While
```

Once you call the Read method, the next row is returned as a collection and stored in the SqlDataReader object itself. To access data from a specific column, you can use a number of methods (we'll cover these in the next section), but for this application you use the ordinal indexer lookup method, giving the column number to the reader to retrieve values (just as you'd specify an index for an array). Since in this case you choose a single column from the Customers table while querying the database, only the "zeroth" indexer is accessible, so you hard-code the index as rdr.GetValue(0).

To use the *connection* for another purpose or to run another query on the database, it's important to call the Close method of SqlDataReader to close the reader explicitly. Once a reader is attached to an active connection, the connection remains busy fetching data for the reader and remains unavailable for other use until the reader has been detached from it. That's why you close the reader in the try block rather than in the finally block (even though this simple program doesn't need to use the connection for another purpose):

```
'close data reader
rdr.Close()
```

Using Ordinal Indexers

You use an ordinal indexer to retrieve column data from the result set. Let's learn more about ordinal indexers. The code

```
rdr.GetValue(0)
```

is a reference to the data reader's Item property and returns the value in the column specified for the current row. The value is returned as an object.

Try It Out: Using Ordinal Indexers

In this example, you'll build a console application that uses an ordinal indexer.

1. Add a new Visual Basic Console Application project named OrdinalIndexer to your Chapter12 solution. Rename Module1.vb to OrdinalIndexer.vb.

2. Replace the code in OrdinalIndexer.vb with the code in Listing 12-2.

Listing 12-2. OrdinalIndexer.vb

```vb
Imports System
Imports System.Data
Imports System.Data.SqlClient

Module OrdinalIndexer
    Sub Main()

        Dim connstring As String = _
        ("Data Source=.\sqlexpress;" & _
         "Integrated Security=True;" & _
         "database=northwind")

        'create command (with both text and connection)
        Dim sql As String = "select companyname,contactname " & _
        "from customers " & _
        "where contactname like 'M%'"

        'create connection
        Dim conn As SqlConnection = New SqlConnection(connstring)

        Try
            'Open connection
            conn.Open()

            Dim cmd As SqlCommand = New SqlCommand(sql, conn)

            'create data reader
            Dim rdr As SqlDataReader = cmd.ExecuteReader

            'print headings
            Console.WriteLine("{0}    {1}", _
                "Company Name".PadRight(25), _
                "Contact Name".PadRight(20))

            Console.WriteLine("{0}    {1}", _
                "============".PadRight(25), _
                "============".PadRight(20))

            'loop through result set
            While (rdr.Read)
                Console.WriteLine(" {0} | {1}", _
                rdr(0).ToString().PadLeft(25), _
                rdr(1).ToString().PadLeft(20))
            End While
```

```
                        'close data reader
                        rdr.Close()
                Catch e As Exception
                        Console.WriteLine("Error Occurred:" & e.ToString)

                Finally
                        ' Close connection
                        conn.Close()
                End Try
        End Sub
End Module
```

3. Make OrdinalIndexer the startup project, and run it by pressing Ctrl+F5. You should
see the results in Figure 12-2.

Figure 12-2. *Displaying multiple columns*

How It Works

You query the Customers table for the columns CompanyName and ContactName, where
contact names begin with the letter "M."

```
        'create command (with both text and connection)
        Dim sql As String = "select companyname,contactname " & _
        "from customers " & _
"where contactname like 'M%'"
```

Since two columns are selected by your query, the returned data also comprises a collection of rows from only these two columns, thus allowing access to only two possible ordinal
indexers, 0 and 1.

You read each row in a while loop, fetching values of the two columns with their indexers.
Since the returned value is an object, you need to explicitly convert the value to a string so that
you can use the PadLeft method to format the output in such a way that all the characters will
be right-aligned; spaces for padding are added on the left for a specified total length:

```
    'loop through result set
    While (rdr.Read)
        Console.WriteLine(" {0} | {1}", _
        rdr(0).ToString().PadLeft(25), _
        rdr(1).ToString().PadLeft(20))
    End While
```

After processing all rows in the result set, you explicitly close the reader to free the connection:

```
'close data reader
rdr.Close()
```

Using Column Name Indexers

Most of the time we don't keep track of column numbers and prefer retrieving values by their respective column names, simply because it's much easier to remember them by their names, which also makes the code more self-documenting.

You use column name indexing by specifying column names instead of ordinal index numbers. This has its advantages. For example, a table may be changed by the addition or deletion of one or more columns, upsetting column ordering and raising exceptions in older code that uses ordinal indexers. Using column name indexers would avoid this issue, but ordinal indexers are faster, since they directly reference columns rather than look them up by name.

The following code snippet retrieves the same columns (CompanyName and ContactName) that the last example did, using column name indexers:

```
'loop through result set
While (rdr.Read)
  Console.WriteLine(" {0} | {1}", _
  rdr("companyname").ToString().PadLeft(25), _
  rdr("contactname").ToString().PadLeft(20))
End While
```

Replace the ordinal indexers in OrdinalIndexer.cs with column name indexers, rerun the project, and you'll get the same results as in Figure 12-2.

The next section discusses a better approach for most cases.

Using Typed Accessor Methods

When a data reader returns a value from a data source, the resulting value is retrieved and stored locally in a .NET type rather than the original data source type. This in-place type conversion feature is a trade-off between consistency and speed, so to give some control over the data being retrieved, the data reader exposes typed accessor methods that you can use if you know the specific type of the value being returned.

Typed accessor methods all begin with Get, take an ordinal index for data retrieval, and are type safe; Visual Basic .NET won't allow you to get away with unsafe casts. These methods turn out to be faster than both the ordinal and the column name indexer methods. Being faster than column name indexing seems only logical, as the typed accessor methods take ordinals for referencing; however, we need to explain how it's faster than ordinal indexing. This is because even though both techniques take in a column number, the conventional ordinal indexing method needs to look up the data source data type of the result and then go through a type conversion. This overhead of looking up the schema is avoided with typed accessors.

.NET types and typed accessor methods are available for almost all data types supported by SQL Server and OLE DB databases.

Table 12-1 should give you a brief idea of when to use typed accessors and with what data type. It lists SQL Server data types, their corresponding .NET types, .NET typed accessors, and special SQL Server–specific typed accessors designed particularly for returning objects of type System.Data.SqlTypes.

Table 12-1. *SQL Server Typed Accessors*

SQL Server Data Types	.NET Type	.NET Typed Accessor
bigint	Int64	GetInt64
binary	Byte[]	GetBytes
bit	Boolean	GetBoolean
char	String or Char[]	GetString or GetChars
datetime	DateTime	GetDateTime
decimal	Decimal	GetDecimal
float	Double	GetDouble
image or long varbinary	Byte[]	GetBytes
int	Int32	GetInt32
money	Decimal	GetDecimal
nchar	String or Char[]	GetString or GetChars
ntext	String or Char[]	GetString or GetChars
numeric	Decimal	GetDecimal
nvarchar	String or Char[]	GetString or GetChars
real	Single	GetFloat
smalldatetime	DateTime	GetDateTime
smallint	Int16	GetInt16
smallmoney	Decimal	GetDecimal
sql_variant	Object	GetValue
long varchar	String or Char[]	GetString or GetChars
timestamp	Byte[]	GetBytes
tinyint	Byte	GetByte
uniqueidentifier	Guid	GetGuid
varbinary	Byte[]	GetBytes
varchar	String or Char[]	GetString or GetChars

Table 12-2 contains some available OLE DB data types, their corresponding .NET types, and their .NET typed accessors.

Table 12-2. *OLE DB Typed Accessors*

OLE DB Type	.NET Type	.NET Typed Accessor
DBTYPE_I8	Int64	GetInt64
DBTYPE_BYTES	Byte[]	GetBytes
DBTYPE_BOOL	Boolean	GetBoolean
DBTYPE_BSTR	String	GetString
DBTYPE_STR	String	GetString
DBTYPE_CY	Decimal	GetDecimal
DBTYPE_DATE	DateTime	GetDateTime
DBTYPE_DBDATE	DateTime	GetDateTime
DBTYPE_DBTIME	DateTime	GetDateTime
DBTYPE_DBTIMESTAMP	DateTime	GetDateTime
DBTYPE_DECIMAL	Decimal	GetDecimal
DBTYPE_R8	Double	GetDouble
DBTYPE_ERROR	ExternalException	GetValue
DBTYPE_FILETIME	DateTime	GetDateTime
DBTYPE_GUID	Guid	GetGuid
DBTYPE_I4	Int32	GetInt32
DBTYPE_LONGVARCHAR	String	GetString
DBTYPE_NUMERIC	Decimal	GetDecimal
DBTYPE_R4	Single	GetFloat
DBTYPE_I2	Int16	GetInt16
DBTYPE_I1	Byte	GetByte
DBTYPE_UI8	UInt64	GetValue
DBTYPE_UI4	UInt32	GetValue
DBTYPE_UI2	UInt16	GetValue
DBTYPE_VARCHAR	String	GetString
DBTYPE_VARIANT	Object	GetValue
DBTYPE_WVARCHAR	String	GetString
DBTYPE_WSRT	String	GetString

To see typed accessors in action, you'll build a console application that uses them. For this example, you'll use the Products table from the Northwind database.

Table 12-3 shows the data design of the table. For the data types given in this table, use Table 12-1 to look up their corresponding typed accessor methods so you can use them correctly in your application.

Table 12-3. *Northwind Products Table Data Types*

Column Name	Data Type	Length	Allow Nulls?
ProductID (unique)	int	4	No
ProductName	nvarchar	40	No
SupplierID	int	4	Yes
CategoryID	int	4	Yes
QuantityPerUnit	nvarchar	20	Yes
UnitPrice	money	8	Yes
UnitsInStock	smallint	2	Yes
UnitsOnOrder	smallint	2	Yes
ReorderLevel	smallint	2	Yes
Discontinued	bit	1	No

Try It Out: Using Typed Accessor Methods

Here, you'll build a console application that uses typed accessors.

1. Add a new Visual Basic Console Application project named TypedAccessors to your Chapter12 solution. Rename Module1.vb to TypedAccessors.vb.

2. Replace the code in TypedAccessors.vb with the code in Listing 12-3.

Listing 12-3. TypedAccessors.vb

```
Imports System
Imports System.Data
Imports System.Data.SqlClient

Module TypedAccessors
    Sub Main()

        Dim connstring As String = _
        ("Data Source=.\sqlexpress;" & _
         "Integrated Security=True;" & _
         "database=northwind")

        'create command (with both text and connection)
        Dim sql As String = "select productname, " & _
        "unitprice,unitsinstock,discontinued " & _
        "from products"

        'create connection
        Dim conn As SqlConnection = New SqlConnection(connstring)
```

```vb
        Try
            'Open connection
            conn.Open()

            'create command
            Dim cmd As SqlCommand = New SqlCommand(sql, conn)

            'create data reader
            Dim rdr As SqlDataReader = cmd.ExecuteReader

            'loop through result set
            While (rdr.Read)
                Console.WriteLine("{0} {1} {2} {3}", _
                rdr.GetString(0).PadRight(35), _
                rdr.GetDecimal(1), _
                rdr.GetInt16(2), _
                rdr.GetBoolean(3))
            End While

            'close data reader
            rdr.Close()
        Catch e As Exception
            Console.WriteLine("Error Occurred:" & e.ToString)

        Finally
            ' Close connection
            conn.Close()
        End Try
    End Sub
End Module
```

3. Make TypedAccessors the startup project, and run it by pressing Ctrl+F5. You should see the results in Figure 12-3. (Only the first 20 rows are displayed in the figure.)

Figure 12-3. *Using typed accessors*

How It Works

You query the Products table for ProductName, UnitPrice, UnitsInStock, and Discontinued:

```
Dim sql As String = "select productname, " & _
"unitprice,unitsinstock,discontinued " & _
"from products"
```

The reason we have you choose these columns is to deal with different kinds of data types and show how to use relevant typed accessors to obtain the correct results.

```
'loop through result set
While (rdr.Read)
    Console.WriteLine("{0} {1} {2} {3}", _
    rdr.GetString(0).PadRight(35), _
    rdr.GetDecimal(1), _
    rdr.GetInt16(2), _
    rdr.GetBoolean(3))
End While
```

Looking at Table 12-1, you can see that you can access nvarchar, money, smallint, and bit data types in SQL Server with the GetString, GetDecimal, GetInt16, and GetBoolean accessor methods, respectively.

This technique is fast and completely type safe. By this, we mean that if implicit conversions from native data types to .NET types fail, an exception is thrown for invalid casts. For instance, if you try using the GetString method on a bit data type instead of using the GetBoolean method, a "Specified cast is not valid" exception will be thrown.

Getting Data About Data

So far, all you've done is retrieve data from a data source. Once you have a populated data reader in your hands, you can do a lot more. There are a number of useful methods for retrieving schema information or retrieving information directly related to a result set. Table 12-4 describes some of the metadata methods and properties of a data reader.

Table 12-4. *Data Reader Metadata Properties and Methods*

Method or Property Name	Description
Depth	A property that gets the depth of nesting for the current row
FieldCount	A property that holds the number of columns in the current row
GetDataTypeName	A method that accepts an index and returns a string containing the name of the column data type
GetFieldType	A method that accepts an index and returns the .NET Framework type of the object
GetName	A method that accepts an index and returns the name of the specified column

Method or Property Name	Description
GetOrdinal	A method that accepts a column name and returns the column index
GetSchemaTable	A method that returns column metadata
HasRows	A property that indicates whether the data reader has any rows
RecordsAffected	A property that gets the number of rows changed, inserted, or deleted

Try It Out: Getting Information About a Result Set with a Data Reader

In this exercise, you'll use some of these methods and properties.

1. Add a new Visual Basic Console Application project named ResultSetInfo to your Chapter12 solution. Rename Module1.vb to ResultSetInfo.vb.

2. Replace the code in ResultSetInfo.vb with the code in Listing 12-4.

Listing 12-4. ResultSetInfo.vb

```
Imports System
Imports System.Data
Imports System.Data.SqlClient

Module ResultSetInfo
    Sub Main()

        Dim connstring As String = _
        ("Data Source=.\sqlexpress;" & _
         "Integrated Security=True;" & _
         "database=northwind")

        'create command (with both text and connection)
        Dim sql As String = "select contactname,contacttitle " & _
        "from customers where " & _
        "contactname like 'M%'"

        'create connection
        Dim conn As SqlConnection = New SqlConnection(connstring)

        Try
            'Open connection
            conn.Open()

            'create command
            Dim cmd As SqlCommand = New SqlCommand(sql, conn)
```

```vbnet
        'create data reader
        Dim rdr As SqlDataReader = cmd.ExecuteReader

        'get column names
        Console.WriteLine("Column Name:{0} {1}", _
        rdr.GetName(0).PadRight(20), _
        rdr.GetName(1))

        'get column data types
        Console.WriteLine("Data Type:{0} {1}", _
        rdr.GetDataTypeName(0).PadRight(20), _
        rdr.GetDataTypeName(1))

        Console.WriteLine()

        'loop through result set
        While (rdr.Read)
            'get column values for all rows
            Console.WriteLine("{0} {1}", _
            rdr.GetString(0).ToString().PadRight(25), _
            rdr.GetString(1))
        End While

        'get number of columns
        Console.WriteLine()
        Console.WriteLine("Number of columns in a row: {0}", _
        rdr.FieldCount)

        'get info about each column
        Console.WriteLine("'{0}' is at index {1} " & _
        "and its type is: {2}", _
          rdr.GetName(0), _
          rdr.GetOrdinal("contactname"), _
          rdr.GetFieldType(0))

        Console.WriteLine("'{0}' is at index {1} " & _
        "and its type is: {2}", _
          rdr.GetName(1), _
          rdr.GetOrdinal("contacttitle"), _
          rdr.GetFieldType(1))

        'close data reader
        rdr.Close()
    Catch e As Exception
        Console.WriteLine("Error Occurred:" & e.ToString)
```

```
        Finally
            ' Close connection
            conn.Close()
        End Try
    End Sub
End Module
```

3. Make ResultSetInfo the startup project, and run it by pressing Ctrl+F5. You should see the results in Figure 12-4.

Figure 12-4. *Displaying result set metadata*

How It Works

The GetName method gets a column name by its index. This method returns information *about* the result set, so it can be called before the first call to Read():

```
'get column names
Console.WriteLine("Column Name:{0} {1}", _
rdr.GetName(0).PadRight(20), _
rdr.GetName(1))
```

The GetDataTypeName method returns the database data type of a column. It too can be called before the first call to the Read method:

```
'get column data types
Console.WriteLine("Data Type:{0} {1}", _
rdr.GetDataTypeName(0).PadRight(20), _
rdr.GetDataTypeName(1))
```

The FieldCount property of the data reader contains the number of columns in the result set. This is useful for looping through columns without knowing their names or other attributes.

```
'get number of columns
Console.WriteLine()
Console.WriteLine("Number of columns in a row: {0}", ➥
_ rdr.FieldCount)
```

Finally, you see how the `GetOrdinal` and `GetFieldType` methods are used. The former returns a column index based on its name; the latter returns the Visual Basic type. These are the countertypes of `GetName()` and `GetDataTypeName()`, respectively.

```
'get info about each column
Console.WriteLine("'{0}' is at index {1} " & _
"and its type is: {2}", _
  rdr.GetName(0), _
  rdr.GetOrdinal("contactname"), _
  rdr.GetFieldType(0))
```

So much for obtaining information about result sets. You'll now learn how to get information about schemas.

Getting Data About Tables

The term *schema* has several meanings in regard to relational databases. Here, we use it to refer to the design of a data structure, particularly a database table. A table consists of rows and columns, and each column can have a different data type. The columns and their attributes (data type, length, and so on) make up the table's schema.

To retrieve schema information easily, you can call the `GetSchemaTable` method on a data reader. As the name suggests, this method returns a `System.Data.DataTable` object, which is a representation (schema) of the table queried and contains a collection of rows and columns in the form of `DataRow` and `DataColumn` objects. These rows and columns are returned as collection objects by the properties `Rows` and `Columns` of the `DataTable` class.

However, here's where a slight confusion usually occurs. Data column objects aren't column values; rather, they are column definitions that represent and control the behavior of individual columns. They can be looped through by using a column name indexer, and they can tell you a lot about the dataset.

Try It Out: Getting Schema Information

Here you'll see a practical demonstration of the `GetSchemaTable` method.

1. Add a new Visual Basic Console Application project named SchemaTable to your Chapter12 solution. Rename `Module1.vb` to `SchemaTable.vb`.

2. Replace the code in `SchemaTable.vb` with the code in Listing 12-5.

Listing 12-5. SchemaTable.vb

```vb
Imports System
Imports System.Data
Imports System.Data.SqlClient

Module SchemaTable
    Sub Main()

        Dim connstring As String = _
        ("Data Source=.\sqlexpress;" & _
         "Integrated Security=True;" & _
         "database=northwind")

        'create command (with both text and connection)
        Dim sql As String = "select * from employees"

        'create connection
        Dim conn As SqlConnection = New SqlConnection(connstring)

        Try
            'Open connection
            conn.Open()

            'create command
            Dim cmd As SqlCommand = New SqlCommand(sql, conn)

            'create data reader
            Dim rdr As SqlDataReader = cmd.ExecuteReader

            'store Employees schema in a data table
            Dim schema As DataTable = rdr.GetSchemaTable

            Dim row As DataRow
            For Each row In schema.Rows
                Dim col As DataColumn
                For Each col In schema.Columns
                    Console.WriteLine _
                    ((col.ColumnName + " = " + row(col).ToString))
                Next col
                Console.WriteLine("----------------")
            Next row

            'close data reader
            rdr.Close()
        Catch e As Exception
            Console.WriteLine("Error Occurred:" & e.ToString)
```

```
        Finally
            ' Close connection
            conn.Close()
        End Try
    End Sub
End Module
```

3. Make SchemaTable the startup project, and run it by pressing Ctrl+F5. You should see the results in Figure 12-5. (Only the information for the table and the first column are displayed in the figure.)

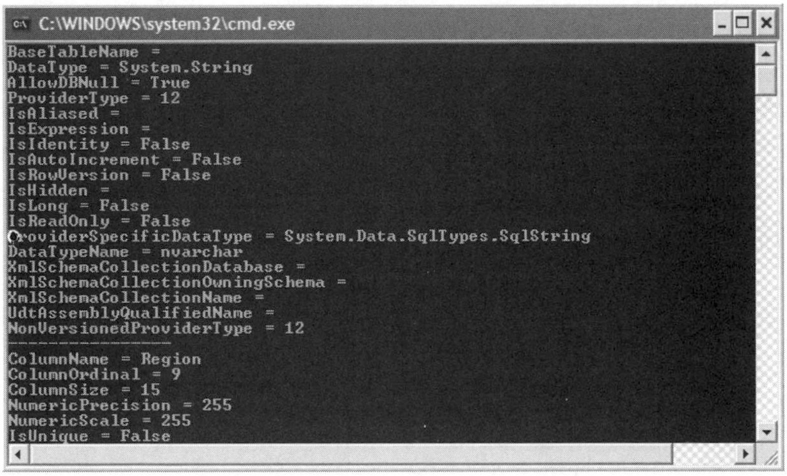

Figure 12-5. *Displaying schema metadata*

How It Works

This code is a bit different from what you've written earlier. When the call to the GetSchemaTable method is made, a populated instance of a data table is returned:

```
'store Employees schema in a data table
Dim schema As DataTable = rdr.GetSchemaTable
```

You can use a data table to represent a complete table in a database, either in the form of a table that represents its schema or in the form of a table that holds all its original data for offline use.

In this example, once you grab hold of a schema table, you retrieve a collection of rows through the Rows property of DataTable and a collection of columns through the Columns property of DataTable. (You can use the Rows property to add a new row into the table altogether or remove one, and you can use the Columns property for adding or deleting an existing column—we'll cover this in Chapter 13.) Each row returned by the table describes one column in the original table, so for each of these rows, you traverse through the column's schema information one by one, using a nested For Each loop:

```
'display info from each row in the data table.
'each row describes a column in the database table.
For Each row In schema.Rows
  Dim col As DataColumn
    For Each col In schema.Columns
    Console.WriteLine _
    ((col.ColumnName + " = " + row(col).ToString))
    Next col
      Console.WriteLine("----------------")
Next row
```

Notice how you use the ColumnName property of the DataColumn object to retrieve the current schema column name in the loop, and then you retrieve the value related to that column's definition by using the familiar indexer-style method that uses a DataRow object. DataRow has a number of overloaded indexers, and this is only one of several ways of doing it.

Using Multiple Result Sets with a Data Reader

Sometimes you may want to get a job done quickly and also want to query the database with two or more queries at the same time. And, you wouldn't want the overall application performance to suffer in any way either by instantiating more than one command or data reader or by exhaustively using the same objects over and over again, adding to the code as you go.

So, is there a way you can get a single data reader to loop through multiple result sets? Yes, data readers have a method, NextResult(), that advances the reader to the next result set.

Try It Out: Handling Multiple Result Sets

In this example, you'll use NextResult() to process multiple result sets.

1. Add a new Visual Basic Console Application project named MultipleResults to your Chapter12 solution. Rename Module1.vb to MultipleResults.vb.

2. Replace the code in MultipleResults.vb with the code in Listing 12-6.

Listing 12-6. MultipleResults.vb

```
Imports System
Imports System.Data
Imports System.Data.SqlClient

Module MultipleResults
    Sub Main()

        Dim connstring As String = _
        ("Data Source=.\sqlexpress;" & _
         "Integrated Security=True;" & _
         "database=northwind")
```

```vb
        'query1
        Dim sql1 As String = "select companyname,contactname " & _
        "from customers where " & _
        "companyname like 'A%'"

        'query2
        Dim sql2 As String = "select firstname," & _
        "lastname from employees"

        'combine queries
        Dim sql As String = sql1 + sql2

        'create connection
        Dim conn As SqlConnection = New SqlConnection(connstring)

        Try
            'Open connection
            conn.Open()

            'create command
            Dim cmd As SqlCommand = New SqlCommand(sql, conn)

            'create data reader
            Dim rdr As SqlDataReader = cmd.ExecuteReader

            Do
                While rdr.Read()
                    ' Print one row at a time
                    Console.WriteLine("{0} : {1}", rdr(0), rdr(1))
                End While
                Console.WriteLine("".PadLeft(60, "=".ToString))
            Loop While rdr.NextResult()

        Catch e As Exception
            Console.WriteLine("Error Occurred:" & e.ToString)

        Finally
            ' Close connection
            conn.Close()
        End Try
    End Sub
End Module
```

3. Make MultipleResults the startup project, and run it by pressing Ctrl+F5. You should see the results in Figure 12-6.

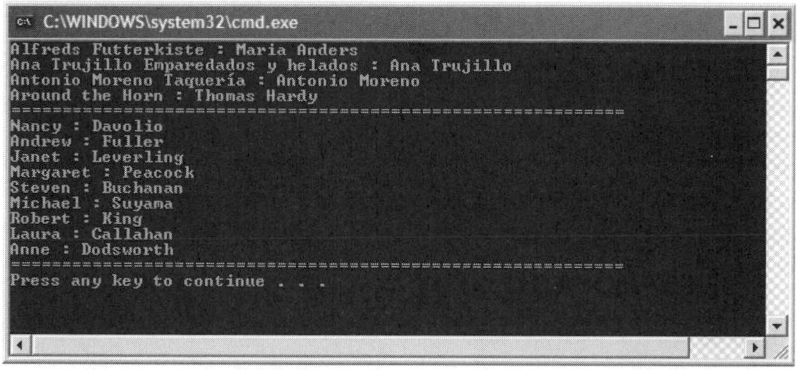

Figure 12-6. *Handling multiple result sets*

How It Works

This program is essentially the same as the first, `DataLooper.cs` (Listing 12-1). Here, you define two separate queries and then combine them:

```
'query1
Dim sql1 As String = "select companyname,contactname " & _
"from customers where " & _
"companyname like 'A%'"

'query2
Dim sql2 As String = "select firstname," & _
"lastname from employees"

'combine queries
Dim sql As String = sql1 + sql2
```

The only other change is that you loop through result sets. You nest the loop that retrieves rows inside one that loops through result sets:

```
Do
    While rdr.Read()
        ' Print one row at a time
        Console.WriteLine("{0} : {1}", rdr(0), rdr(1))
    End While
    Console.WriteLine("".PadLeft(60, "=".ToString))
Loop While rdr.NextResult()
```

We have you choose only two character-string columns per query to simplify things. Extending this to handle result tables with different numbers of columns and column data types is straightforward.

Summary

In this chapter, you used data readers to perform a variety of common tasks, from simply looping through single result sets to handling multiple result sets. You learned how to retrieve values for columns by column name and index and learned about methods available for handling values of different data types. You also learned how to get information about result sets and get schema information.

In the next chapter, we'll cover a really interesting aspect of ADO.NET: handling database data while disconnected from the database.

CHAPTER 13

■■■

Using Datasets and Data Adapters

In Chapter 12, you saw how to use data readers to access database data in a connected, forward-only, read-only fashion. Often, this is all you want to do, and a data reader suits your purposes perfectly.

In this chapter, you'll look at a new object for accessing data, the dataset. Unlike data readers, which are objects of data provider–specific classes that implement the `System.Data.IDataReader` interface, datasets are objects of the class `System.Data.DataSet`, a distinct ADO.NET component used by all data providers. Datasets are completely independent of and can be used either connected to or disconnected from data sources. Their fundamental purpose is to provide a relational view of data stored in an in-memory cache.

■Note In yet another somewhat confusing bit of terminology, the class is named `DataSet`, but the generic term is spelled dataset (when one expects data set). Why Microsoft does this is unclear, especially since data set is the more common usage outside ADO.NET. Nonetheless, we'll follow the .NET convention and call `Dataset` objects datasets.

So, if a dataset doesn't have to be connected to a database, how do you populate it with data and save its data back to the database? This is where *data adapters* come in. Think of data adapters as bridges between datasets and data sources. Without a data adapter, a dataset can't access any kind of data source. The data adapter takes care of all connection details for the dataset, populates it with data, and updates the data source.

In this chapter, we'll cover the following:

- Understanding the object model

- Working with datasets and data adapters

- Propagating changes to a data source

- Concurrency

- Using datasets and XML

- Using data tables without datasets

- Understanding typed and untyped datasets

Understanding the Object Model

We'll start this chapter with a quick presentation of all the new objects you'll need to understand in order to work with datasets and data adapters. You'll start by looking at the difference between datasets and data readers, and then move on to look in more detail at how data is structured within a dataset and how a dataset works in collaboration with a data adapter.

Datasets vs. Data Readers

If you simply want to read and display data, then you need to use only a data reader, as you saw in the previous chapter, particularly if you're working with large quantities of data. In situations where you need to loop through thousands or millions of rows, you want a fast sequential reader (reading rows from the result set one at a time), and the data reader does this job in an efficient way.

If you need to manipulate the data in any way and then update the database, you should use a dataset. A data adapter fills a dataset by using a data reader; additional resources are needed to save data for disconnected use. You should think about whether you really need a dataset; otherwise, you'll just be wasting resources. Unless you need to update the data source or use other dataset features such as reading and writing to XML files, exporting database schemas, and creating XML views of a database, use a data reader.

A Brief Introduction to Datasets

The notion of a dataset in ADO.NET is a big step in the world of multitiered database application development. When retrieving or modifying large amounts of data, maintaining an open connection to a data source while waiting for users to make requests is an enormous waste of precious resources.

Datasets help tremendously here, because they enable you to store and modify large amounts of data in a local cache, view the data as tables, and process the data in an *offline* mode (in other words, disconnected from the database).

Let's look at an example. Imagine you're trying to connect to a remote database server over the Internet for detailed information about some business transactions. You search on a particular date for all available transactions, and the results are displayed. Behind the scenes, your application creates a connection with the data source, joins a couple of tables, and retrieves the results. Suppose you now want to edit this information and add or remove details. Whatever the reason, your application will go through the same cycle over and over again: creating a new connection, joining tables, and retrieving data. Not only is there overhead in creating a new connection each time, but you may be doing a lot of other redundant work, especially if you're dealing with the same data. Wouldn't it be better if you could connect to the data source once, store the data locally in a structure that resembles a relational database, close the connection, modify the local data, and then propagate the changes to the data source when the time is right?

This is exactly what the dataset is designed to do. A dataset stores relational data as collections of *data tables*. You met data tables briefly in the previous chapter when a `System.Data.DataTable` object was to hold schema information. In that instance, however, the data table contained only schema information, but in a dataset, the data tables contain both metadata describing the structure of the data and the data itself.

Figure 13-1 shows the dataset architecture.

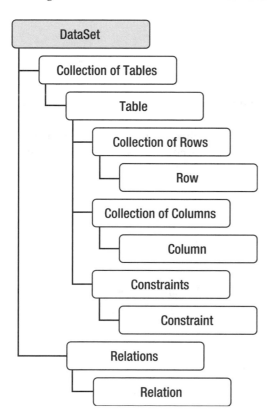

Figure 13-1. *Dataset architecture*

The architecture mirrors the logical design of a relational database. You'll see how to use data tables, data rows, and data columns in this chapter.

A Brief Introduction to Data Adapters

When you first instantiate a dataset, it contains no data. You obtain a populated dataset by passing it to a data adapter, which takes care of connection details and is a component of a data provider. A dataset isn't part of a data provider. It's like a bucket, ready to be filled with water, but it needs an external pipe to let the water in. In other words, the dataset needs a data adapter to populate it with data and to support access to the data source.

Each data provider has its own data adapter in the same way that it has its own connection, command, and data reader. Figure 13-2 depicts the interactions between the dataset, data adapter, and data source.

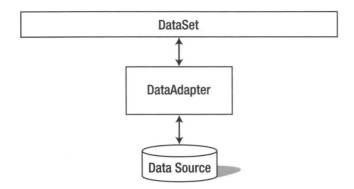

Figure 13-2. *Dataset, data adapter, and data source interaction*

The data adapter constructor is overloaded. You can use any of the following to get a new data adapter. We're using the SQL Server data provider, but the constructors for the other data providers are analogous.

```
Dim da As SqlDataAdapter=New SqlAdapter
Dim da As SqlDataAdapter=New SqlAdapter(cmd)
Dim da As SqlDataAdapter=New SqlAdapter(sql,conn)
Dim da As SqlDataAdapter=New SqlAdapter(sql,connstring)
```

So, you can create a data adapter in four ways:

- You can use its parameterless constructor (assigning SQL and the connection later).

- You can pass its constructor a command (here, cmd is a SqlCommand object).

- You can pass a SQL string and a connection.

- You can pass a SQL string and a connection string.

You'll see all this working in action shortly. For now, we'll move on and show how to use data tables, data columns, and data rows. You'll use these in upcoming sections.

A Brief Introduction to Data Tables, Data Columns, and Data Rows

A data table is an instance of the class System.Data.DataTable. It's conceptually analogous to a relational table. As shown in Figure 13-1, a data table has collections of data rows and data columns. You can access these nested collections via the Rows and Columns properties of the data table.

A data table can represent a stand-alone independent table, either inside a dataset— as you'll see in this chapter—or as an object created by another method, as you saw in the previous chapter when a data table was returned by calling the GetSchemaTable method on a data reader.

A data column represents the schema of a column within a data table and can then be used to set or get column properties. For example, you could use it to set the default value of a column by assigning a value to the DefaultValue property of the data column.

You obtain the collection of data columns using the data table's `Columns` property, whose indexer accepts either a column name or a zero-based index, for example (where dt is a data table):

```
Dim col As DataColumn=dt.Columns("ContactName")
Dim col As DataColumn=dt.Column(2)
```

A data row represents the data in a row. You can programmatically add, update, or delete rows in a data table. To access rows in a data table, you use its `Rows` property, whose indexer accepts a zero-based index, for example (where dt is a data table):

```
Dim row As DataRow=dt.Rows(2)
```

That's enough theory for now. It's time to do some coding and see how these objects work together in practice!

Working with Datasets and Data Adapters

The dataset constructor is overloaded:

```
Dim ds As DataSet=New DataSet
Dim ds As DataSet=New DataSet("MyDataSet")
```

If you use the parameterless constructor, the dataset name defaults to `NewDataSet`. If you need more than one dataset, it's good practice to use the other constructor and name it explicitly. However, you can always change the dataset name by setting its `DataSetName` property.

You can populate a dataset in several ways, including the following:

- Using a data adapter

- Reading from an XML document

In this chapter, we'll use data adapters. However, in the "Using Datasets and XML" section, you'll take a quick peek at the converse of the second method, and you'll write from a dataset to an XML document.

Try It Out: Populating a Dataset with a Data Adapter

In this example, you'll create a dataset, populate it with a data adapter, and then display its contents.

1. Create a new Visual Basic Console Application project named Chapter13. When Solution Explorer opens, save the solution.

2. Rename the Chapter13 project to PopDataset. Rename the `Module1.vb` file to `PopDataset.vb`, and replace the generated code with the code in Listing 13-1.

Listing 13-1. PopDataSet.vb

```vb
Imports System
Imports System.Data
Imports System.Data.SqlClient

Module PopDataSet
    Sub Main()

        Dim connstring As String = _
        ("Data Source=.\sqlexpress;" & _
         "Integrated Security=True;" & _
         "database=northwind")

        'create command (with both text and connection)
        Dim sql As String = "select productname,unitprice " & _
        "from products where unitprice < 20"

        'create connection
        Dim conn As SqlConnection = New SqlConnection(connstring)

        Try
            'Open connection
            conn.Open()

            Dim cmd As SqlCommand = New SqlCommand(sql, conn)

            'create data adapter
            Dim da As SqlDataAdapter = New SqlDataAdapter(sql,conn)

            'create dataset
            Dim ds As DataSet = New DataSet

            'fill dataset
            da.Fill(ds, "products")

            'get data table
            Dim dt As DataTable = ds.Tables("products")

            'display data
            Dim row As DataRow
            For Each row In dt.Rows
                Dim col As DataColumn
                For Each col In dt.Columns
                    Console.WriteLine(row(col))
                Next col
                Console.WriteLine("".PadLeft(20, "="c))
            Next row
```

```
        Catch e As Exception
            Console.WriteLine("Error Occurred:" & e.ToString)

        Finally
            ' Close connection
            conn.Close()
        End Try
    End Sub
End Module
```

3. Run PopDataset by pressing Ctrl+F5. You should see the results in Figure 13-3. (Only the last eight rows are displayed.)

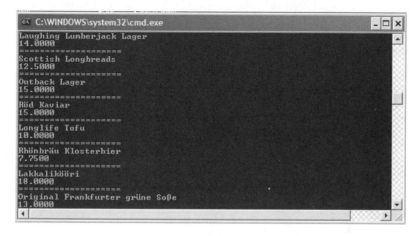

Figure 13-3. *Populating a dataset*

How It Works

After defining a query and opening a connection, you create and initialize a data adapter:

```
'create data adapter
Dim da As SqlDataAdapter = New SqlDataAdapter(sql,conn)
```

and then create a dataset:

```
'create dataset
Dim ds As DataSet = New DataSet
```

At this stage, all you have is an empty dataset. The key line is where you use the Fill method on the data adapter to execute the query, retrieve the data, and populate the dataset:

```
'fill dataset
da.Fill(ds, "products")
```

The Fill method uses a data reader internally to access the table schema and data and then use them to populate the dataset.

Note that this method isn't just used for filling datasets. It has a number of overloads and can also be used for filling an individual data table without a dataset, if needed.

If you don't provide a name for the table to the `Fill` method, it will automatically be named `TableN`, where `N` starts as an empty string (the first table name is simply `Table`) and increments every time a new table is inserted into the dataset. It's better practice to explicitly name data tables, but here it doesn't matter.

If the same query is run more than once, on the dataset that already contains data, `Fill()` updates the data, skipping the process of redefining the table based on the schema.

It's worth mentioning here that the following code would have produced the same result. Instead of passing the SQL and connection to the data adapter's constructor, you could have set its `SelectCommand` property with a command that you create with the appropriate SQL and connection:

```
'create data adapter
Dim da As SqlDataAdapter = New SqlDataAdapter
da.SelectCommand=New SqlCommand(sql,conn)
```

With a populated dataset at your disposal, you can now access the data in individual data tables. (This dataset contains only one data table.)

```
'get data table
Dim dt As DataTable = ds.Tables("products")
```

Finally, you use nested `For Each` loops to access the columns in each row and output their data values to the screen:

```
'display data
 Dim row As DataRow
 For Each row In dt.Rows
   Dim col As DataColumn
    For Each col In dt.Columns
     Console.WriteLine(row(col))
    Next col
    Console.WriteLine("".PadLeft(20, "="c))
 Next row
```

Filtering and Sorting in a Dataset

In the previous example, you saw how to extract data from a dataset. However, if you're working with datasets, chances are that you're going to want to do more with the data than merely display it. Often, you'll want to dynamically filter or sort the data. In the following example, you'll see how you can use data rows to do this.

Try It Out: Dynamically Filtering and Sorting Data in a Dataset

We'll get all the rows and columns from the Customers table, filter the result for only German customers, and sort it by company. We'll use a separate query to find products, and fill two data tables in the same dataset.

1. Add a new Visual Basic Console Application project named FilterSort to your Chapter13 solution. Rename Module1.vb to FilterSort.vb.

2. Replace the code in FilterSort.vb with the code in Listing 13-2.

Listing 13-2. FilterSort.vb

```
Imports System
Imports System.Data
Imports System.Data.SqlClient

Module FilterSort
    Sub Main()

        Dim connstring As String = _
        ("Data Source=.\sqlexpress;" & _
         "Integrated Security=True;" & _
         "database=northwind")

        'query 1
        Dim sql1 As String = "select * from customers"

        'query 2
        Dim sql2 As String = " select * from products " & _
                             "where unitprice < 10"

        'combine queries
        Dim sql As String = sql1 + sql2

        'create connection
        Dim conn As SqlConnection = New SqlConnection(connstring)

        Try
            'Open connection
            conn.Open()

            'create data adapter
            Dim da As SqlDataAdapter = New SqlDataAdapter
            da.SelectCommand = New SqlCommand(sql, conn)

            'create and fill dataset
            Dim ds As DataSet = New DataSet
            da.Fill(ds, "customers")

            ' get the data tables collection
            Dim dtc As DataTableCollection = ds.Tables
```

```vb
        ' display data from first data table
        '
        ' display output header
        Console.WriteLine("Results from Customers table:")
        Console.WriteLine(("CompanyName".PadRight(20) +
        "ContactName".PadLeft(23) + ControlChars.Lf))

        ' set display filter
        Dim fl As String = "country = 'Germany'"

        ' set sort
        Dim srt As String = "companyname asc"

        ' display filtered and sorted data
        Dim row As DataRow
        For Each row In dtc("customers").Select(fl, srt)
            Console.WriteLine("{0}" + ControlChars.Tab + "{1}",
            row("CompanyName").ToString(). _
            PadRight(25), row("ContactName"))
        Next row

        ' display data from second data table
        '
        ' display output header
        Console.WriteLine(ControlChars.Lf + "----------------")
        Console.WriteLine("Results from Products table:")
        Console.WriteLine(("ProductName".PadRight(20) + _
        "UnitPrice".PadLeft(21) + ControlChars.Lf))

        ' display data
        'Dim row As DataRow
        For Each row In dtc(1).Rows
            Console.WriteLine("{0}" + ControlChars.Tab + "{1}",
            row("productname").ToString(). _
            PadRight(25), row("unitprice"))
        Next row

    Catch e As Exception
        Console.WriteLine("Error Occurred:" & e.ToString)

    Finally
        ' Close connection
        conn.Close()
    End Try
End Sub
End Module
```

3. Make FilterSort the startup project, and run it by pressing Ctrl+F5. You should see the results in Figure 13-4.

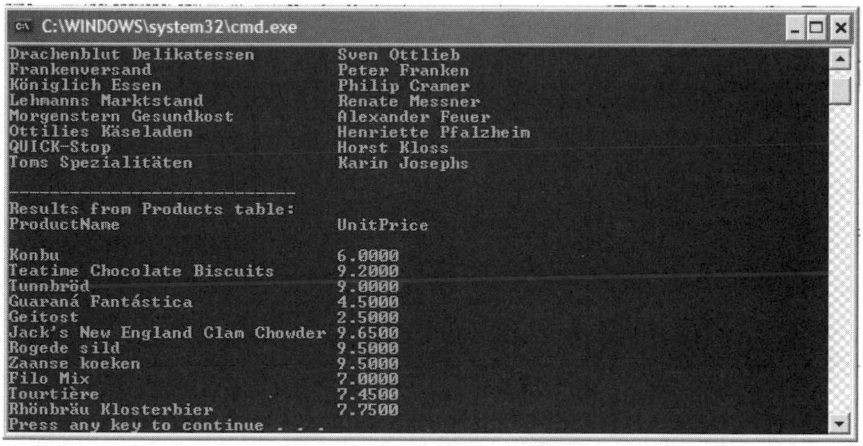

Figure 13-4. *Filtering and sorting a data table*

How It Works

You code and combine two queries for execution on the same connection:

```
'query 1
 Dim sql1 As String = "select * from customers"

'query 2
 Dim sql2 As String = " select * from products " & _
                      "where unitprice < 10"

'combine queries
 Dim sql As String = sql1 + sql2

'create connection
 Dim conn As SqlConnection = New SqlConnection(connstring)
```

You create a data adapter, assigning to its SelectCommand property a command that encapsulates the query and connection (for internal use by the data adapter's Fill method):

```
'create data adapter
 Dim da As SqlDataAdapter = New SqlDataAdapter
 da.SelectCommand = New SqlCommand(sql, conn)
```

You then create and fill a dataset:

```
'create and fill dataset
 Dim ds As DataSet = New DataSet
 da.Fill(ds, "customers")
```

Each query returns a separate result set, and each result set is stored in a separate data table (in the order in which the queries were specified). The first table is explicitly named customers; the second is given the default name customers1.

You get the data table collection from the dataset Tables property for ease of reference later:

```
// get the data tables collection
DataTableCollection dtc = ds.Tables;
```

As part of displaying the first data table, you declare two strings:

```
// set display filter
string fl = "country = 'Germany'";

// set sort
string srt = "companyname asc";
```

The first string is a *filter expression* that specifies row selection criteria. It's syntactically the same as a SQL WHERE clause predicate. You want only rows where the Country column equals "Germany". The second string specifies your sort criteria and is syntactically the same as a SQL ORDER BY clause, giving a data column name and sort sequence.

You use a For Each loop to display the rows selected from the data table, passing the filter and sort strings to the Select method of the data table. This particular data table is the one named Customers in the data table collection.

```
// display filtered and sorted data
For Each row In dtc(1).Rows
    Console.WriteLine("{0}" + ControlChars.Tab + "{1}",
    row("productname").ToString().PadRight(25), row("unitprice"))
Next row
```

You obtain a reference to a single data table from the data table collection (the dtc object) using the table name that you specify when creating the dataset. The overloaded Select method does an internal search on the data table, filters out rows not satisfying the selection criterion, sorts the result as prescribed, and finally returns an array of data rows. You access each column in the row, using the column name in the indexer.

It's important to note that you can achieve the same result—much more efficiently—if you simply use a different query for the customer data:

```
select
    *
from
    customers
where
    country = 'Germany'
order by
    companyname
```

This would be ideal in terms of performance, but it'd be feasible only if the data you needed were limited to these specific rows in this particular sequence. However, if you were building a more elaborate system, it might be better to pull all the data once from the database (as you do here) and then filter and sort it in different ways. ADO.NET's rich suite of methods for manipulating datasets and their components gives you a broad range of techniques for meeting specific needs in an optimal way.

Tip In general, try to exploit SQL, rather than code Visual Basic .NET procedures, to get the data you need from the database. Database servers are optimized to perform selections and sorts, as well as other things. Queries can be far more sophisticated and powerful than the ones you've been playing with in this book. By carefully (and creatively) coding queries to return *exactly* what you need, you not only minimize resource demands (on memory, network bandwidth, and so on), but also reduce the code you must write to manipulate and format result set data.

The loop through the second data table is interesting mainly for its first line, which uses an ordinal index:

```
For Each row In dtc(1).Rows
```

Since you don't rename the second data table (you could do so with its TableName property), it is better to use the index rather than the name (customers1), since a change to the name in the Fill() call would require you to change it here, an unlikely thing to remember to do, if the case ever arises.

Comparing FilterSort to PopDataSet

In the first example, PopDataSet (Listing 13-1), you saw how simple it is to get data into a dataset. The second example, FilterSort (Listing 13-2), was just a variation, demonstrating how multiple result sets are handled and how to filter and sort data tables. However, the two programs have one major difference. Did you notice it?

FilterSort doesn't explicitly open a connection! In fact, it's the first (but won't be the last) program you've written that doesn't. Why doesn't it?

The answer is simple but *very* important. The Fill method *automatically* opens a connection if it's not open when Fill() is called. It then closes the connection after filling the dataset. However, if a connection is open when Fill() is called, it uses that connection and *doesn't* close it afterward.

So, although datasets are completely independent of databases (and connections), just because you're using a dataset doesn't mean you're running disconnected from a database. If you want to run disconnected, use datasets, but don't open connections before filling them (or, if a connection is open, close it first). Datasets in themselves don't imply either connected or disconnected operations.

You leave the standard conn.Close(); in the finally block. Since Close() can be called without error on a closed connection, it presents no problems if called unnecessarily, but it definitely guarantees that the connection will be closed, whatever may happen in the try block.

■Note If you want to prove this for yourself, simply open the connection in `FilterSort` before calling `Fill()` and then display the value of the connection's `State` property. It will be `Open`. Comment out the `Open()` call, and run it again. `State` will be closed.

Using Data Views

In the previous example, you saw how to dynamically filter and sort data in a data table using the `Select` method. However, ADO.NET has another approach for doing much the same thing and more: *data views*. A data view (an instance of class `System.Data.DataView`) enables you to create dynamic views of the data stored in an underlying data table, reflecting all the changes made to its content and its ordering. This differs from the `Select` method, which returns an array of data rows whose contents reflect the changes to data values but not the data ordering.

■Note A data view is a dynamic representation of the contents of a data table. Like a SQL view, it doesn't actually hold data.

Try It Out: Refining Data with a Data View

We won't cover all aspects of data views here, as they're beyond the scope of this book. However, to show how they can be used, we'll present a short example that uses a data view to dynamically sort and filter an underlying data table.

1. Add a new Visual Basic Console Application project named DataViews to your Chapter13 solution. Rename `Module1.vb` to `DataViews.vb`.

2. Replace the code in `DataViews.vb` with the code in Listing 13-3.

   Listing 13-3. `DataViews.vb`

   ```
   Imports System
   Imports System.Data
   Imports System.Data.SqlClient

   Module DataViews
       Sub Main()

           Dim connstring As String = _
           ("Data Source=.\sqlexpress;" & _
            "Integrated Security=True;" & _
            "database=northwind")
   ```

```vbnet
                    'query
                    Dim sql As String = "select contactname,country from
                    customers"

                    'create connection
                    Dim conn As SqlConnection = New SqlConnection(connstring)

                    Try
                        'create data adapter
                        Dim da As SqlDataAdapter = New SqlDataAdapter
                        da.SelectCommand = New SqlCommand(sql, conn)

                        'create and fill dataset
                        Dim ds As DataSet = New DataSet
                        da.Fill(ds, "customers")

                        ' get data table reference
                        Dim dt As DataTable = ds.Tables("customers")

                        ' create data view
                    Dim dv As New DataView(dt, "country = 'Germany'", "country", _
                    DataViewRowState.CurrentRows)

                        ' display data from data view
                        Dim drv As DataRowView
                        For Each drv In dv
                            Dim i As Integer
                            For i = 0 To dv.Table.Columns.Count - 1
                                Console.Write((drv(i) + ControlChars.Tab))
                            Next i
                            Console.WriteLine()
                        Next drv

                    Catch e As Exception
                        Console.WriteLine("Error Occurred:" & e.ToString)

                    Finally
                        ' Close connection
                        conn.Close()
                    End Try
                End Sub
            End Module
```

3. Make DataViews the startup project, and run it by pressing Ctrl+F5. You should see the results in Figure 13-5.

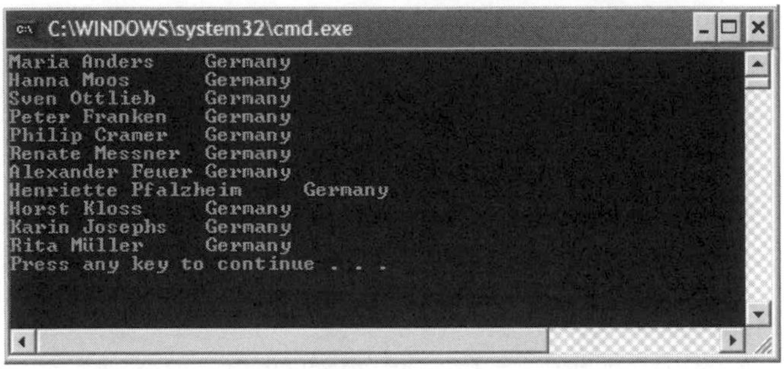

Figure 13-5. *Using a data view*

How It Works

This program is basically the same as the other examples, so we'll focus on its use of a data view. You create a new data view and initialize it by passing four parameters to its constructor:

```
' create data view
Dim dv As New DataView(dt, "country = 'Germany'", "country", _
DataViewRowState.CurrentRows)
```

The first parameter is a data table, the second is a filter for the contents of the data table, the third is the sort column, and the fourth specifies the types of rows to include in the data view.

System.Data.DataViewRowState is an enumeration of states that rows can have in a data view's underlying data table. Table 13-1 summarizes the states.

Table 13-1. *Data View Row States*

DataViewRowState **Members**	**Description**
Added	A new row
CurrentRows	Current rows including unchanged, new, and modified ones
Deleted	A deleted row
ModifiedCurrent	The current version of a modified row
ModifiedOriginal	The original version of a modified row
None	None of the rows
OriginalRows	Original rows, including unchanged and deleted rows
Unchanged	A row that hasn't been modified

Every time a row is added, modified, or deleted, its row state changes to the appropriate one in Table 13-1. This is useful if you're interested in retrieving, sorting, or filtering specific rows based on their state (for example, all new rows in the data table or all rows that have been modified).

You then loop through the rows in the data view:

```
' display data from data view
Dim drv As DataRowView
   For Each drv In dv
     Dim i As Integer
       For i = 0 To dv.Table.Columns.Count - 1
         Console.Write((drv(i) + ControlChars.Tab))
       Next i
     Console.WriteLine()
   Next drv
```

Just as a data row represents a single row in a data table, a *data row view* (perhaps it would have been better to call it a *data view row*) represents a single row in a data view. You retrieve the filtered and the sorted column data for each data row view and output it to the console.

As this simple example suggests, data views offer a powerful and flexible means of dynamically changing what data one works within a data table.

Modifying Data in a Dataset

In the following sections, you'll work through a practical example showing a number of ways to update data in data tables programmatically. Note that here you'll just modify the data in the dataset but not update the data in the database. You'll see in the "Propagating Changes to a Data Source" section how to persist the original data source changes made to a dataset.

■**Note** Changes you make to a dataset aren't automatically propagated to a database. To save the changes in a database, you need to connect to the database again and explicitly perform the necessary updates.

Try It Out: Modifying a Data Table in a Dataset

Let's update a row and add a row in a data table.

1. Add a new Visual Basic Console Application project named ModifyDataTable to your Chapter13 solution. Rename `Module1.vb` to `ModifyDataTable.vb`.

2. Replace the code in `ModifyDataTable.vb` with the code in Listing 13-4.

Listing 13-4. ModifyDataTable.vb

```vb
Imports System
Imports System.Data
Imports System.Data.SqlClient

Module ModifyDataTable
    Sub Main()

        Dim connstring As String = _
        ("Data Source=.\sqlexpress;" & _
         "Integrated Security=True;" & _
         "database=northwind")

        'create command (with both text and connection)
        Dim sql As String = "select * from employees " & _
        "where country = 'UK'"

        'create connection
        Dim conn As SqlConnection = New SqlConnection(connstring)
        Try
            ' create data adapter
            Dim da As New SqlDataAdapter()
            da.SelectCommand = New SqlCommand(sql, conn)

            ' create and fill dataset
            Dim ds As New DataSet()
            da.Fill(ds, "employees")

            ' get data table reference
            Dim dt As DataTable = ds.Tables("employees")

            ' FirstName column should be nullable
            dt.Columns("firstname").AllowDBNull = True

            ' modify city in first row
            dt.Rows(0)("city") = "Wilmington"

            ' add a row
            Dim newRow As DataRow = dt.NewRow()
            newRow("firstname") = "Roy"
            newRow("lastname") = "Beatty"
            newRow("titleofcourtesy") = "Sir"
            newRow("city") = "Birmingham"
            newRow("country") = "UK"
            dt.Rows.Add(newRow)
```

```
                    ' display rows
                    Dim row As DataRow
                    For Each row In dt.Rows
                        Console.WriteLine("{0} {1} {2}",
                        row("firstname").ToString().PadRight(15), row("lastname"). _
                        ToString().PadLeft(25), row("city"))
                    Next row

                    ' code for updating the database would come here

                Catch e As Exception
                    Console.WriteLine(("Error: " + e.ToString))
                Finally
                    ' close connection
                    conn.Close()
                End Try
            End Sub
    End Module
```

3. Make ModifyDataTable the startup project, and run it by pressing Ctrl+F5. You should see the results in Figure 13-6.

Figure 13-6. *Modifying a data table*

How It Works

As before, you use a single data table in a dataset:

```
' get data table reference
Dim dt As DataTable = ds.Tables("employees")
```

Next, you can see an example of how you can change the schema information. You select the FirstName column, whose `AllowNull` property is set to `false` in the database, and you change it—just for the purposes of demonstration—to `true`:

```
' FirstName column should be nullable
dt.Columns("firstname").AllowDBNull = True
```

Note that you can use an ordinal index (for example, `dt.Columns[1]`) if you know what the index for the column is, but using * to select all columns makes this less reliable since the position of a column may change if the database table schema changes.

You can modify a row using the same technique. You simply select the appropriate row and set its columns to whatever values you want, consistent with the column data types, of course. The following line shows the City column of the first row of the dataset being changed to Wilmington:

```
' modify city in first row
dt.Rows(0)("city") = "Wilmington"
```

Next you add a new row to the data table:

```
' add a row
Dim newRow As DataRow = dt.NewRow()
newRow("firstname") = "Roy"
newRow("lastname") = "Beatty"
newRow("titleofcourtesy") = "Sir"
newRow("city") = "Birmingham"
newRow("country") = "UK"
dt.Rows.Add(newRow)
```

The NewRow method creates a data row (a System.Data.DataRow instance). You use the data row's indexer to assign values to its columns. Finally, you add the new row to the data table, calling the Add method on the data table's Rows property, which references the rows collection.

Note that you don't provide a value for EmployeeID since it's an IDENTITY column. If you were to persist the changes to the database, SQL Server would automatically provide a value for it.

Updating data sources requires learning more about data adapter methods and properties. Let's take a look at these now.

Propagating Changes to a Data Source

You've seen how a data adapter populates a dataset's data tables. What you haven't looked at yet is how a data adapter updates and synchronizes a data source with data from a dataset. It has three properties that support this (analogous to its SelectCommand property, which supports queries):

- UpdateCommand

- InsertCommand

- DeleteCommand

We'll describe each of these properties briefly and then put them to work.

UpdateCommand Property

The UpdateCommand property of the data adapter holds the command used to update the data source when the data adapter's Update method is called.

For example, to update the City column in the Employees table with the data from a data table, one approach is to write code such as the following (where da is the data adapter, dt is the data table, conn is the connection, and ds is the dataset):

```
' create command to update Employees City column
da.UpdateCommand = New SqlCommand("update employees " + _
 "set " + "   city = " + "'" + dt.Rows(0)("city") + "' " + _
 "where employeeid = " + "'" + dt.Rows(0)("employeeid") + "' ", conn)

' update Employees table
da.Update(ds, "employees")
```

This isn't very pretty—or useful. Basically, you code an UPDATE statement and embed two data column values for the first row in a data table in it. It's valid SQL, but that's its only virtue and it's not much of one, since it updates only one database row, the row in Employees corresponding to the first data row in the employees data table.

Another approach works for any number of rows. Recall from the CommandParameters program in Chapter 11 how you used command parameters for INSERT statements. You can use them in any query or data manipulation statement. Let's recode the preceding code with command parameters.

Try It Out: Propagating Dataset Changes to a Data Source

Here you'll change the city in the first row of the Employees table and persist the change in the database.

1. Add a new Visual Basic Console Application project named PersistChanges to your Chapter13 solution. Rename Module1.vb to PersistChanges.vb.

2. Replace the code in PersistChanges.vb with the code in Listing 13-5. (This is a variation on ModifyDataTable.vb in Listing 13-4, with the nullability and insertion logic removed since they're irrelevant here.)

Listing 13-5. PersistChanges.vb

```
Imports System
Imports System.Data
Imports System.Data.SqlClient

Module PersistChanges
    Sub Main()
        Dim connstring As String = _
        ("Data Source=.\sqlexpress;" & _
         "Integrated Security=True;" & _
         "database=northwind")

        'query
        Dim qry As String = "select * from employees " & _
        "where country = 'UK'"
```

```vb
'SQL to update employees
Dim upd As String = "update employees " & _
"set city = @city " & _
"where employeeid = @employeeid"

'create connection
Dim conn As SqlConnection = New SqlConnection(connstring)
Try
    ' create data adapter
    Dim da As New SqlDataAdapter()
    da.SelectCommand = New SqlCommand(qry, conn)

    ' create and fill dataset
    Dim ds As New DataSet()
    da.Fill(ds, "employees")

    ' get data table reference
    Dim dt As DataTable = ds.Tables("employees")

    ' modify city in first row
    dt.Rows(0)("city") = "Wilmington"

    ' display rows
    Dim row As DataRow
    For Each row In dt.Rows
        Console.WriteLine("{0} {1} {2}", _
        row("firstname").ToString().PadRight(15), _
        row("lastname").ToString().PadLeft(25), _
        row("city"))
    Next row

    ' update Employees
    '
    ' create command
    Dim cmd As New SqlCommand(upd, conn)
    '
    ' map parameters
    '
    ' City
    cmd.Parameters.Add("@city", SqlDbType.NVarChar, 15, "city")
    '
    ' EmployeeID
    Dim parm As SqlParameter = cmd.Parameters.Add _
    ("@employeeid", SqlDbType.Int, 4, "employeeid")
    parm.SourceVersion = DataRowVersion.Original
    '
```

```
                    ' Update database
                    da.UpdateCommand = cmd
                    da.Update(ds, "employees")
                Catch e As Exception
                    Console.WriteLine(("Error: " + e.ToString))
                Finally
                    ' close connection
                    conn.Close()
                End Try
        End Sub
    End Module
```

3. Make PersistChanges the startup project, and run it by pressing Ctrl+F5. You should see the result in Figure 13-7.

Figure 13-7. *Modifying a row*

How It Works

You add an UPDATE statement and change the name of the original query string variable from sql to upd in order to clearly distinguish it from this statement:

```
'SQL to update employees
Dim upd As String = "update employees " & _
"set city = @city " & _
"where employeeid = @employeeid"
```

You replace the update comment in the try block with quite a bit of code. Let's look at it piece by piece. Creating a command is nothing new, but notice that you use the update SQL variable (upd), not the query one (sql):

```
' update Employees
'
' create command
Dim cmd As New SqlCommand(upd, conn)
```

Then you configure the command parameters. The @city parameter is mapped to a data column named city. Note that you don't specify the data table, but you must be sure the type and length are compatible with this column in whatever data table you eventually use:

```
' City
cmd.Parameters.Add("@city", SqlDbType.NVarChar, 15,
"city")
```

Next, you configure the @employeeid parameter, mapping it to a data column named employeeid. Unlike @city, which by default takes values from the current version of the data table, you want to make sure that @employeeid gets values from the version *before* any changes. Although it doesn't matter here, since you don't change any employee IDs, it's a good habit to specify the original version for primary keys, so if they do change, the correct rows are accessed in the database table. Note also that you save the reference returned by the Add method so you can set its SourceVersion property. Since you don't need to do anything else with @city, you don't have to save a reference to it.

```
' EmployeeID
  Dim parm As SqlParameter = cmd.Parameters.Add _
 ("@employeeid", SqlDbType.Int, 4, "employeeid")
  parm.SourceVersion = DataRowVersion.Original
```

Finally, you set the data adapter's UpdateCommand property with the command to update the Employees table so it will be the SQL the data adapter executes when you call its Update method. You then call Update on the data adapter to propagate the change to the database. Here you have only one change, but since the SQL is parameterized, the data adapter will look for all changed rows in the employees data table and submit updates for all of them to the database.

```
' Update database
  da.UpdateCommand = cmd
  da.Update(ds, "employees")
```

Figure 13-7 shows the change to the city, and if you check with Database Explorer or SSMSE, you'll see the update has been propagated to the database. The city for employee Steven Buchanan is now Wilmington, not London.

InsertCommand Property

The data adapter uses the InsertCommand property for inserting rows into a table. Upon calling the Update method, all rows added to the data table will be searched for and propagated to the database.

Try It Out: Propagating New Dataset Rows to a Data Source

Let's propagate a new row to the database, in another variation on ModifyDataTable.vb in Listing 13-4.

1. Add a new Visual Basic Console Application project named PersistAdds to your Chapter13 solution. Rename Module1.vb to PersistAdds.vb.

2. Replace the code in PersistAdds.vb with the code in Listing 13-6.

Listing 13-6. PersistAdds.vb

```
Imports System
Imports System.Data
Imports System.Data.SqlClient
Module PersistAdds
    Sub Main()
        Dim connstring As String = _
            ("Data Source=.\sqlexpress;" & _
             "Integrated Security=True;" & _
             "database=northwind")

        'query
        Dim qry As String = "select * from employees " & _
        "where country = 'UK'"

        'SQL to insert employees
        Dim ins As String = "insert into employees " & _
        "(firstname,lastname,titleofcourtesy,city,country)" & _
        "values(@firstname,@lastname,@titleofcourtesy,@city,@country)"

        'create connection
        Dim conn As SqlConnection = New SqlConnection(connstring)
        Try
            ' create data adapter
            Dim da As New SqlDataAdapter()
            da.SelectCommand = New SqlCommand(qry, conn)

            ' create and fill dataset
            Dim ds As New DataSet()
            da.Fill(ds, "employees")

            ' get data table reference
            Dim dt As DataTable = ds.Tables("employees")

            ' add a row
            Dim newRow As DataRow = dt.NewRow()
            newRow("firstname") = "Roy"
            newRow("lastname") = "Beatty"
            newRow("titleofcourtesy") = "Sir"
            newRow("city") = "Birmingham"
            newRow("country") = "UK"
            dt.Rows.Add(newRow)
```

```
            ' display rows
            Dim row As DataRow
            For Each row In dt.Rows
                Console.WriteLine("{0} {1} {2}", _
                row("firstname").ToString().PadRight(15), _
                row("lastname").ToString().PadLeft(25),row("city"))
            Next row

            ' insert employees
            '
            ' create command
            Dim cmd As New SqlCommand(ins, conn)
            '
            ' map parameters
            cmd.Parameters.Add("@firstname", _
            SqlDbType.NVarChar, 10, "firstname")
            cmd.Parameters.Add("@lastname", _
            SqlDbType.NVarChar, 20, "lastname")
            cmd.Parameters.Add("@titleofcourtesy", _
            SqlDbType.NVarChar, 25, "titleofcourtesy")
            cmd.Parameters.Add("@city", _
            SqlDbType.NVarChar, 15, "city")
            cmd.Parameters.Add("@country", _
            SqlDbType.NVarChar, 15, "country")
            '
            ' insert employees
            da.InsertCommand = cmd
            da.Update(ds, "employees")
        Catch e As Exception
            Console.WriteLine(("Error: " + e.ToString))
        Finally
            ' close connection
            conn.Close()
        End Try
    End Sub
End Module
```

3. Make PersistAdds the startup project, and run it by pressing Ctrl+F5. You should see the results in Figure 13-8.

Figure 13-8. *Adding a row*

How It Works

You add an INSERT statement and change the name of the original query string variable from sql to ins in order to clearly distinguish it from this statement:

```
'SQL to insert employees
Dim ins As String = "insert into employees " & _
"(firstname,lastname,titleofcourtesy,city,country)" & _
"values(@firstname,@lastname,@titleofcourtesy,@city,@country)"
```

You replace the update comment in the try block with quite a bit of code. Let's look at it piece by piece. Creating a command is nothing new, but notice that you use the insert SQL variable (ins), not the query one (sql):

```
' insert employees
'
' create command
Dim cmd As New SqlCommand(ins, conn)
```

Then you configure the command parameters. The five columns for which you'll provide values are each mapped to a named command parameter. You don't supply the primary key value since it's generated by SQL Server, and the other columns are nullable, so you don't have to provide values for them. Note that all the values are current values, so you don't have to specify the SourceVersion property.

```
' map parameters
cmd.Parameters.Add("@firstname", _
SqlDbType.NVarChar, 10, "firstname")
cmd.Parameters.Add("@lastname", _
SqlDbType.NVarChar, 20, "lastname")
cmd.Parameters.Add("@titleofcourtesy", _
SqlDbType.NVarChar, 25, "titleofcourtesy")
cmd.Parameters.Add("@city", _
SqlDbType.NVarChar, 15, "city")
cmd.Parameters.Add("@country", _
SqlDbType.NVarChar, 15, "country")
```

Finally, you set the data adapter's InsertCommand property with the command to insert into the Employees table so it will be the SQL the data adapter executes when you call its Update method. You then call Update on the data adapter to propagate the change to the database. Here you add only one row, but since the SQL is parameterized, the data adapter will look for all new rows in the employees data table and submit inserts for all of them to the database:

```
' insert employees
da.InsertCommand = cmd
da.Update(ds, "employees")
```

Figure 13-8 shows the new row, and if you check with Database Explorer or SSMSE, you'll see the row has been propagated to the database. Roy Beatty is now in the Employees table.

DeleteCommand Property

You use the DeleteCommand property to execute SQL DELETE statements.

Try It Out: Propagating New Dataset Rows to a Data Source

In this example, you'll again modify ModifyDataTable.vb (Listing 13-4) to delete a row from the database.

1. Add a new Visual Basic Console Application project named PersistDeletes to your Chapter13 solution. Rename Module1.vb to PersistDeletes.vb.

2. Replace the code in PersistDeletes.vb with the code in Listing 13-7.

Listing 13-7. PersistDeletes.vb

```vb
Imports System
Imports System.Data
Imports System.Data.SqlClient

Module PersistDeletes
    Sub Main()

        Dim connstring As String = _
        ("Data Source=.\sqlexpress;" & _
        "Integrated Security=True;" & _
        "database=northwind")

        'query
        Dim qry As String = "select * from employees " & _
        "where country = 'UK'"

        'SQL to delete employees
        Dim del As String = "delete from employees " & _
        "where employeeid = @employeeid"

        'create connection
        Dim conn As SqlConnection = New SqlConnection(connstring)

        Try
            'create data adapter
            Dim da As SqlDataAdapter = New SqlDataAdapter
            da.SelectCommand = New SqlCommand(qry, conn)

            'create and fill dataset
            Dim ds As DataSet = New DataSet
            da.Fill(ds, "employees")

            'get data table reference
            Dim dt As DataTable = ds.Tables("employees")
```

```
        'delete employees
        '
        'create command
        Dim cmd As SqlCommand = New SqlCommand(del, conn)
        '
        'map parameters
        cmd.Parameters.Add("@employeeid", _
        SqlDbType.Int, 4, "employeeid")
        '
        'select employees
        Dim filt As String = "firstname = 'Roy'" & _
        "and lastname = 'Beatty'"

        ' delete employees
        Dim row As DataRow
        For Each row In dt.Select(filt) '
            row.Delete()
        Next row
        da.DeleteCommand = cmd
        da.Update(ds, "employees")

        ' display rows
        For Each row In dt.Rows
            Console.WriteLine("{0} {1} {2}", _
            row("firstname").ToString().PadRight(15), _
            row("lastname").ToString().PadLeft(25),row("city"))
        Next row
    Catch e As Exception
        Console.WriteLine(("Error: " + e.ToString))
    Finally
        ' close connection
        conn.Close()
    End Try
    End Sub
End Module
```

3. Make PersistDeletes the startup project, and run it by pressing Ctrl+F5. You should see the output in Figure 13-9.

Figure 13-9. *Deleting a row*

How It Works

You add a DELETE statement (and change the name of the original query string variable from sql to del in order to clearly distinguish it from this statement):

```
'SQL to delete employees
 Dim del As String = "delete from employees " & _
 "where employeeid = @employeeid"
```

You insert the DELETE code ahead of the display. After creating a command and mapping a parameter:

```
'delete employees
'
'create command
 Dim cmd As SqlCommand = New SqlCommand(del, conn)
'
'map parameters
 cmd.Parameters.Add("@employeeid", _
 SqlDbType.Int, 4, "employeeid")
```

you select the row to delete and delete it. Actually, you select all rows for employees named Roy Beatty, since you don't know (or care about) their employee IDs. Although you expect only one row to be selected, you use a loop to delete all the rows. (If you were to run the PersistAdds program multiple times, you'd have more than one row that matches this selection criteria.)

```
'select employees
 Dim filt As String = "firstname = 'Roy'" & _
 "and lastname = 'Beatty'"

'delete employees
 Dim row As DataRow
 For Each row In dt.Select(filt) '
     row.Delete()
 Next row
```

Finally, you set the data adapter's DeleteCommand property with the command to delete from the Employees table so it will be the SQL the data adapter executes when you call its Update method. You then call Update() on the data adapter to propagate the changes to the database:

```
da.DeleteCommand = cmd
da.Update(ds, "employees")
```

Whether you delete one row or several, your SQL is parameterized, and the data adapter will look for all deleted rows in the employees data table and submit deletes for all of them to the Employees database table.

If you check with Database Explorer or SSMSE, you'll see the row has been removed from the database. Roy Beatty is no longer in the Employees table.

Command Builders

Although it's straightforward, it's a bit of a hassle to code SQL statements for the `UpdateCommand`, `InsertCommand`, and `DeleteCommand` properties, so each data provider has its own *command builder*. If a data table corresponds to a single database table, you can use a command builder to automatically generate the appropriate `UpdateCommand`, `InsertCommand`, and `DeleteCommand` properties for a data adapter. This is all done transparently when a call is made to the data adapter's `Update` method.

To be able to dynamically generate `INSERT`, `DELETE`, and `UPDATE` statements, the command builder uses the data adapter's `SelectCommand` property to extract metadata for the database table. If any changes are made to the `SelectCommand` property after invoking the `Update` method, you should call the `RefreshSchema` method on the command builder to refresh the metadata accordingly.

To create a command builder, you create an instance of the data provider's command builder class, passing a data adapter to its constructor. For example, the following code creates a SQL Server command builder:

```
Dim da As SqlDataAdapter=New SqlDataAdapter
Dim cb As SqlCommandsBuilder=New SqlCommandBuilder
```

■Note For a command builder to work, the `SelectCommand` data adapter property must contain a query that returns either a primary key or a unique key for the database table. If none is present, an `InvalidOperation` exception is generated, and the commands aren't generated.

Try It Out: Using SqlCommandBuilder

Here, you'll convert `PersistAdds.vb` in Listing 13-6 to use a command builder.

1. Add a new Visual Basic Console Application project named PersistAddsBuilder to your Chapter13 solution. Rename `Module1.vb` to `PersistAddsBuilder.vb`.

2. Replace the code in `PersistAddsBuilder.vb` with the code in Listing 13-8.

   Listing 13-8. `PersistAddsBuilder.vb`

```
Imports System
Imports System.Data
Imports System.Data.SqlClient
Module PersistAddsBuilder
    Sub Main()
        Dim connstring As String = _
        ("Data Source=.\sqlexpress;" & _
        "Integrated Security=True;" & _
        "database=northwind")
```

```vb
'query
Dim qry As String = "select * from employees " & _
"where country = 'UK'"

'create connection
Dim conn As SqlConnection = New SqlConnection(connstring)
Try
    ' create data adapter
    Dim da As New SqlDataAdapter()
    da.SelectCommand = New SqlCommand(qry, conn)

    'create command builder
    Dim cb As SqlCommandBuilder = New SqlCommandBuilder(da)

    ' create and fill dataset
    Dim ds As New DataSet()
    da.Fill(ds, "employees")

    ' get data table reference
    Dim dt As DataTable = ds.Tables("employees")

    ' add a row
    Dim newRow As DataRow = dt.NewRow()
    newRow("firstname") = "Roy"
    newRow("lastname") = "Beatty"
    newRow("titleofcourtesy") = "Sir"
    newRow("city") = "Birmingham"
    newRow("country") = "UK"
    dt.Rows.Add(newRow)

    ' display rows
    Dim row As DataRow
    For Each row In dt.Rows
        Console.WriteLine("{0} {1} {2}", _
        row("firstname").ToString().PadRight(15), _
        row("lastname").ToString().PadLeft(25),row("city"))
    Next row

    ' insert employees
    da.Update(ds, "employees")

Catch e As Exception
    Console.WriteLine(("Error: " + e.ToString))
Finally
    ' close connection
    conn.Close()
```

```
            End Try
        End Sub
    End Module
```

3. Make PersistAddsBuilder the startup project, and run it by pressing Ctrl+F5. You should see the results in Figure 13-10. Roy Beatty is back in the Employees table.

Figure 13-10. *Adding a row using a command builder*

How It Works

The most interesting thing to note isn't the line (yes, just one plus a comment) you add as much as what you replace. The single statement

```
'create command builder
 Dim cb As SqlCommandBuilder = New SqlCommandBuilder(da)
```

makes all the following code unnecessary:

```
'SQL to insert employees
Dim ins As String = "insert into employees " & _
"(firstname,lastname,titleofcourtesy,city,country)" & _
        "values(@firstname,@lastname,@titleofcourtesy,@city,@country)"

' create command
Dim cmd As New SqlCommand(ins, conn)
' map parameters
cmd.Parameters.Add("@firstname", _
SqlDbType.NVarChar, 10, "firstname")
cmd.Parameters.Add("@lastname", _
SqlDbType.NVarChar, 20, "lastname")
cmd.Parameters.Add("@titleofcourtesy", _
SqlDbType.NVarChar, 25, "titleofcourtesy")
cmd.Parameters.Add("@city", _
SqlDbType.NVarChar, 15, "city")
cmd.Parameters.Add("@country", _
SqlDbType.NVarChar, 15, "country")

' insert employees
da.InsertCommand = cmd
```

Obviously, using command builders is preferable to manually coding SQL; however, remember that they work only on single tables and that the underlying database table must have a primary or unique key. Also, the data adapter `SelectCommand` property must have a query that includes the key columns.

■**Note** Though all five of the data providers in the .NET Framework Class Library have command builder classes, no class or interface exists in the `System.Data` namespace that defines them. So, if you want to learn more about command builders, the best place to start is the description for the builder in which you're interested. The `System.Data.DataSet` class and the `System.Data.IDataAdapter` interface define the underlying components that command builders interact with, and their documentation provides the informal specification for the constraints on command builders.

Concurrency

You've seen that updating a database with datasets and data adapters is relatively straightforward. However, we've oversimplified things; you've been assuming that no other changes have been made to the database while you've been working with disconnected datasets.

Imagine two separate users trying to make conflicting changes to the same row in a dataset and then trying to propagate these changes to the database. What happens? How does the database resolve the conflicts? Which row gets updated first, or second, or at all? The answer is unclear. As with so many real-world database issues, it all depends on a variety of factors. However, ADO.NET provides a fundamental level of concurrency control that's designed to prevent update anomalies. The details are beyond the scope of this book, but the following is a good conceptual start.

Basically, a dataset marks all added, modified, and deleted rows. If a row is propagated to the database but has been modified by someone else since the dataset was filled, the data manipulation operation for the row is ignored. This technique is known as *optimistic concurrency* and is essentially the job of the data adapter. When the `Update` method is called, the data adapter attempts to reconcile all changes. This works well in an environment where users seldom contend for the same data.

This type of concurrency is different from what's known as *pessimistic concurrency*, which *locks* rows upon modification (or sometimes even on retrieval) to avoid conflicts. Most database managers use some form of locking to guarantee data integrity.

Disconnected processing with optimistic concurrency is essential to successful multi-tier systems. How to employ it most effectively given the pessimistic concurrency of DBMSs is a thorny problem. Don't worry about it now, but keep in mind that many issues exist, and the more complex your application, the more likely you'll have to become an expert in concurrency.

Using Datasets and XML

XML is the fundamental medium for data transfer in .NET. In fact, XML is a major foundation for ADO.NET. Datasets organize data internally in XML format and have a variety of methods for reading and writing in XML. For example:

- You can import and export the structure of a dataset as an XML schema using `System.Data.DataSet`'s `ReadXmlSchema` and `WriteXmlSchema` methods.

- You can read the data (and, optionally, the schema) of a dataset from and write it to an XML file with `ReadXml()` and `WriteXml()`. This can be useful when exchanging data with another application or making a local copy of a dataset.

- You can bind a dataset to an XML document (an instance of `System.Xml.XmlDataDocument`). The dataset and data document are *synchronized*, so either ADO.NET or XML operations can be used to modify it.

Let's look at one of these in action: copying a dataset to an XML file.

■**Note** If you're unfamiliar with XML, don't worry. ADO.NET doesn't require any detailed knowledge of it. Of course, the more you know, the better you can understand what's happening transparently.

Try It Out: Extracting a Dataset to an XML File

You can preserve the contents and schema of a dataset in one XML file using the dataset's `WriteXml` method or in separate files using `WriteXml()` and `WriteXmlSchema()`. `WriteXml()` is overloaded, and in this example we'll show a version that extracts both data and schema.

1. Add a new Visual Basic Console Application project named WriteXML to your Chapter13 solution. Rename `Module1.vb` to `WriteXML.vb`.

2. Replace the code in `WriteXML.vb` with the code in Listing 13-9.

   Listing 13-9. `WriteXML.vb`

```vb
Imports System
Imports System.Data
Imports System.Data.SqlClient

Module WriteXML
  Sub Main()

    Dim connstring As String = _
    ("Data Source=.\sqlexpress;" & _
    "Integrated Security=True;" & _
    "database=northwind")
```

```
'create command (with both text and connection)
Dim sql As String = "Select productname,unitprice " & _
"from products"

'create connection
Dim conn As SqlConnection = New SqlConnection(connstring)

 Try

   'create data adapter
   Dim da As SqlDataAdapter = New SqlDataAdapter
   da.SelectCommand = New SqlCommand(sql, conn)

     'Open connection
     conn.Open()

     'create and fill dataset
      Dim ds As DataSet = New DataSet
      da.Fill(ds, "products")

     'extract dataset to XML file
     ds.WriteXml("C:\Documents and Settings\Toshiba User\" & _
     "My Documents\Visual Studio
      2008\Projects\Chapter13\productstable.xml")
     Console.WriteLine("The XML file is Created")

     Catch e As Exception
         Console.WriteLine("Error Occurred:" & e.ToString)

     Finally
         ' Close connection
         conn.Close()
  End Try
   End Sub
End Module
```

3. Make WriteXML the startup project, and run it by pressing Ctrl+F5. You should see the output in Figure 13-11.

Figure 13-11. *Extracting a data table as XML*

4. Not much seems to have happened, but that's because you wrote to a file rather than to the screen. Open `productstable.xml` to see the XML. (One way in Visual Studio is to use File ➤ Open File.) Figure 13-12 shows the XML extracted for the first five product rows.

```
<?xml version="1.0" standalone="yes"?>
<NewDataSet>
  <products>
    <productname>Chai</productname>
    <unitprice>18.0000</unitprice>
  </products>
  <products>
    <productname>Chang</productname>
    <unitprice>19.0000</unitprice>
  </products>
  <products>
    <productname>Aniseed Syrup</productname>
    <unitprice>10.0000</unitprice>
  </products>
  <products>
    <productname>Chef Anton's Cajun Seasoning</productname>
    <unitprice>22.0000</unitprice>
  </products>
  <products>
    <productname>Chef Anton's Gumbo Mix</productname>
    <unitprice>21.3500</unitprice>
  </products>
```

Figure 13-12. *Data table extracted as XML*

■Tip By default, extracted XML documents are plain text files. You can open the `productstable.xml` file in any editor, or even use the `type` or `more` commands to view it from the command line.

How It Works

You replace a console display loop with a method call to write the XML file:

```
'extract dataset to XML file
ds.WriteXml("C:\Documents and Settings\Toshiba User\" & _
"My Documents\Visual Studio
2008\Projects\Chapter13\productstable.xml")
```

You give the full path for the XML file to place it in the solution directory. Were you to give only the file name, it would have been placed in the `bin\Release` subdirectory under the `WriteXML` project directory.

Note that the XML has simply mapped the dataset as a hierarchy. The first XML element, `<NewDataSet>`, is the dataset name (defaulting to `NewDataSet` since you don't specify one). The next element, `<products>`, uses the data table name (you have only one data table since you use only one query to populate the dataset), and it's nested inside the dataset element. The data column elements, `<productname>` and `<unitprice>`, are nested inside this element.

The data for each column appears (as plain text) between the *start tag* (for example, <productname>) and the *end tag* (for example, </productname>) for each column element. Note that the <products> elements represent individual rows, not the whole table. So, the column elements are contained within the start tag <products> and end tag </products> for each row.

If you scroll to the bottom of the XML file, you'll find the end tag </NewDataSet> for the dataset.

Using Data Tables Without Datasets

As we mentioned in our first example, "Populating a Dataset with a Data Adapter," data tables can be used without datasets. Most of the time this involves calling the same methods on data tables that you use for datasets. We'll give one example. You should then be able to analogize from it for other processing.

■**Note** Datasets and data tables can also be used without data adapters. Such uses are beyond the scope of this book.

Try It Out: Populating a Data Table with a Data Adapter

This example is based on our first example, PopDataSet.vb (Listing 13-1). You'll create a data table, populate it with a data adapter, and then display its contents.

1. Add a new Visual Basic Console Application project named PopDataTable to your Chapter13 solution. Rename Module1.vb to PopDataTable.vb.

2. Replace the code in PopDataTable.vb with the code in Listing 13-10. The lines changed from Listing 13-1 are highlighted in bold.

   Listing 13-10. PopDataTable.vb

   ```
   Imports System
   Imports System.Data
   Imports System.Data.SqlClient

   Module PopDataTable
       Sub Main()

           Dim connstring As String = _
           ("Data Source=.\sqlexpress;" & _
            "Integrated Security=True;" & _
            "database=northwind")
   ```

```vb
'create command (with both text and connection)
Dim sql As String = "select productname,unitprice " & _
"from products where unitprice < 20"

'create connection
Dim conn As SqlConnection = New SqlConnection(connstring)

Try
 'Open connection
 conn.Open()

'create data adapter
Dim da As SqlDataAdapter = New SqlDataAdapter(sql, conn)

    'create data table
    Dim dt As DataTable = New DataTable

    'fill data table
    da.Fill(dt)

    'display data
    Dim row As DataRow
    For Each row In dt.Rows
        Dim col As DataColumn
        For Each col In dt.Columns
            Console.WriteLine(row(col))
        Next col
        Console.WriteLine("".PadLeft(20, "="c))
    Next row

Catch e As Exception
    Console.WriteLine("Error Occurred:" & e.ToString)

Finally
    ' Close connection
    conn.Close()
End Try
    End Sub
End Module
```

3. Run PopDataTable by pressing Ctrl+F5. You should see the same results as in Figure 13-3 earlier for PopDataSet.vb.

How It Works

Instead of creating a dataset:

```
' create dataset
Dim ds As New DataSet()
```

you create a data table:

```
'create data table
Dim dt As DataTable = New DataTable
```

And instead of filling a dataset:

```
'fill dataset
da.Fill(ds, "products")
```

you fill a data table:

```
'fill data table
 da.Fill(dt)
```

Since a data table can hold only one table, notice that the Fill method doesn't accept the data table name as an argument. And, since you don't have to find a particular data table in a dataset, there is no need for

```
'get data table
Dim dt As DataTable = ds.Tables("products")
```

Otherwise, the code needs no changes.

■**Tip** Unless you really need to organize data tables in datasets so you can define relationships between them, using one or more data tables instead of one (or more) datasets is easier to code and takes up fewer runtime resources.

Understanding Typed and Untyped Datasets

Datasets can be *typed* or *untyped*. The datasets you've used so far have all been untyped. They were instances of System.Data.DataSet. An untyped dataset has no built-in schema. The schema is only implicit. It grows as you add tables and columns to the dataset, but these objects are exposed as collections rather than as XML schema elements. However, as we mentioned in passing in the previous section, you can explicitly export a schema for an untyped dataset with WriteXmlSchema (or WriteXml).

A typed dataset is one that's derived from System.Data.DataSet and uses an XML Schema (typically in an .xsd file) in declaring the dataset class. Information from the schema (tables, columns, and so on) is extracted, generated as Visual Basic code, and compiled, so the new dataset class is an actual .NET type with appropriate objects and properties.

Either typed or untyped datasets are equally valid, but typed datasets are more efficient and can make code somewhat simpler. For example, using an untyped dataset, you'd need to write this:

```
Console.WriteLine(ds.Tables(0).Rows(0)("CompanyName"))
```

to get the value for the CompanyName column of the Customers table, assuming that the data table was the first in the dataset. With a typed dataset, you can access its data tables and data columns as class members. You could replace the previous code with this:

```
Console.WriteLine(ds.Customers(0).CompanyName)
```

making the code more intuitive. In addition, the Visual Studio code editor has IntelliSense support for typed datasets.

Typed datasets are more efficient than untyped datasets because typed datasets have a defined schema, and when they're populated with data, runtime type identification and conversion aren't necessary, since this has been taken care of at compile time. Untyped datasets have a lot more work to do every time a result set is loaded.

However, typed datasets aren't always the best choice. If you're dealing with data that isn't basically well defined, whose definition dynamically changes, or is only of temporary interest, the flexibility of untyped datasets can outweigh the benefits of typed ones.

This chapter is already long enough. Since we're not concerned with efficiency in our small sample programs, we won't use typed datasets and we don't need to cover creating them here.

Our emphasis in this book is explaining how Visual Basic .NET works with ADO.NET by showing you how to code fundamental operations. If you can code them yourself, you'll have insight into what Visual Basic .NET does when it generates things for you, as in the next chapter on using Windows Forms. This is invaluable for understanding how to configure generated components and debugging applications that use them.

Although you can code an .xsd file yourself (or export an XSL schema for an untyped dataset with System.Data.DataSet.WriteXmlSchema() and modify it) and then use the xsd.exe utility to create a class for a typed dataset, it's a lot of work, is subject to error, and is something you'll rarely (if ever) want or need to do.

Summary

In this chapter, we covered the basics of datasets and data adapters. A dataset is a relational representation of data that has a collection of data tables, and each data table has collections of data rows and data columns. A data adapter is an object that controls how data is loaded into a dataset (or data table) and how changes to the dataset data are propagated back to the data source.

We presented basic techniques for filling and accessing datasets, demonstrated how to filter and sort data tables, and noted that though datasets are database-independent objects, disconnected operation isn't the default mode.

We discussed how to propagate data modifications back to databases with parameterized SQL and the data adapter's UpdateCommand, InsertCommand, and DeleteCommand properties, and how command builders simplify this for single-table updates.

We briefly mentioned the important issue of concurrency and then introduced XML, the fundamental technology behind ADO.NET.

We provided an example of populating a data table without a dataset, and you should be able to analogize this for all the other operations on datasets that we covered. Finally, we discussed typed and untyped datasets

Now that you've seen the basics of using ADO.NET, we'll move from console applications to Windows applications.

Building Windows Forms Applications

This chapter introduces you to the concepts related to Windows Forms, which will give you an understanding about Windows Forms and developing Windows Forms Applications using Visual Basic 2008.

In this chapter, we'll cover the following:

- Understanding Windows Forms

- User interface design principles

- Best practices for user interface design

- Working with Windows Forms

- Understanding the Design and Code views

- Sorting properties in the Properties window

- Setting properties of solutions, projects, and Windows Forms

- Working with controls

- Setting dock and anchor properties

- Adding a new form to the project

- Implementing an MDI form

Understanding Windows Forms

Windows Forms, also known as WinForms, is the name given to the graphical user interface (GUI) application programming interface (API) included as a part of Microsoft's .NET Framework, providing access to the native Microsoft Windows interface elements by wrapping the existing Windows API in managed code.

WinForms are basic building blocks of the user interface. They work as containers to host controls that allow you to present an application. WinForms is the most commonly used interface for an application's development, although other types of applications are also available, such as console applications and services. But WinForms offer the best possible way to interact with the user and accepts user input in the form of key presses or mouse clicks.

User Interface Design Principles

The best mechanism for interacting with any application is often a user interface. Therefore, it becomes important to have an efficient design that is easy to use. When designing the user interface, your primary consideration should be the people who will use the application. They are your target audience, and knowing your target audience makes it easier for you to design a user interface that helps users learn and use your application. A poorly designed user interface, on the other hand, can lead to frustration and inefficiency if it causes the target audience to avoid or even discard your application.

Forms are the primary element of a Microsoft Windows application. As such, they provide the foundation for each level of user interaction. Various controls, menus, and so on can be added to forms to supply specific functionality. In addition to being functional, your user interface should be attractive and inviting to the user.

Best Practices for User Interface Design

The user interface provides a mechanism for users to interact with your application. Therefore, an efficient design that is easy to use is of paramount importance. The following are some guidelines for designing user-friendly, elegant, and simple user interfaces.

Simplicity

Simplicity is an important aspect of a user interface. A visually "busy" or overly complex user interface makes it harder and more time-consuming to learn the application. A user interface should allow a user to quickly complete all interactions required by the program, but it should expose only the functionality needed at each stage of the application.

When designing your user interface, you should keep program flow and execution in mind, so that users of your application will find it easy to use. Controls that display related data should be grouped together on the form. ListBox, ComboBox, and CheckBox controls can be used to display data and allow users to choose between preset options. The use of a tab order (the order by which users can cycle through controls on a form by pressing the Tab key) allows users to rapidly navigate fields.

Trying to reproduce a real-world object is a common mistake when designing user interfaces. For instance, if you want to create a form that takes the place of a paper form, it is natural to attempt to reproduce the paper form in the application. This approach might be appropriate for some applications, but for others, it might limit the application and provide no real user benefit, because reproducing a paper form can limit the functionality of your application. When designing an application, think about your unique situation and try to use the computer's capabilities to enhance the user experience for your target audience.

Default values are another way to simplify your user interface. For example, if you expect 90 percent of the users of an application to select Washington in a State field, make Washington the default choice for that field.

Information from your target audience is paramount when designing a user interface. The best information to use when designing a user interface is input from the target audience. Tailor your interface to make frequent tasks easy to perform.

Position of Controls

The location of controls on your user interface should reflect their relative importance and frequency of use. For example, if you have a form that is used to input both required information and optional information, the controls for the required information are more important and should receive greater prominence. In Western cultures, user interfaces are typically designed to be read left-to-right and top-to-bottom. The most important or frequently used controls are most easily accessed at the top of a form. Controls that will be used after a user completes an action on a form, such as a Submit button, should follow the logical flow of information and be placed at the bottom of the form.

It is also necessary to consider the relatedness of information. Related information should be displayed in controls that are grouped together. For example, if you have a form that displays information about a customer, a purchase order, or an employee, you can group each set of controls on a Tab control that allows a user to easily move back and forth between displays.

Aesthetics is also an important consideration in the placement of controls. You should try to avoid forms that display more information than can be understood at a glance. Whenever possible, controls should be adequately spaced to create visual appeal and ease of accessibility.

Consistency

Your user interface should exhibit a consistent design across each form in your application. An inconsistent design can make your application seem disorganized or chaotic, hindering adoption by your target audience. Don't ask users to adapt to new visual elements as they navigate from form to form.

Consistency is created through the use of colors, fonts, size, and types of control employed throughout the application. Before any actual application development takes place, you should decide on a visual scheme that will remain consistent throughout the application. For web applications, CSS (Cascading Style Sheets) offers the best mechanism to ensuring a consistent look and feel throughout your web application.

Aesthetics

Whenever possible, a user interface should be inviting and pleasant. Although clarity and simplicity should not be sacrificed for the sake of attractiveness, you should endeavor to create an application that will not dissuade users from using it.

Color

Judicious use of color helps make your user interface attractive to the target audience and inviting to use. It is easy to overuse color, however. Loud, vibrant colors might appeal to some users, but others might have a negative reaction. When designing a background color scheme for your application, the safest course is to use muted colors with broad appeal.

Always research any special meanings associated with color that might affect user response to your application. If you are designing an application for a company, you might consider using the company's corporate color scheme in your application. When designing for international audiences, be aware that certain colors might have cultural significance. Maintain consistency, and do not overdo the color.

Always think about how color might affect usability. For example, gray text on a white background can be difficult to read and thus impairs usability. Also, be aware of usability issues related to color blindness. Some people, for example, are unable to distinguish between red and green. Therefore, red text on a green background is invisible to such users. Do not rely on color alone to convey information. Contrast can also attract attention to important elements of your application.

Fonts

Usability should determine the fonts you choose for your application. For usability, avoid fonts that are difficult to read or highly embellished. Stick to simple, easy-to-read fonts such as Palatino or Times New Roman. Also, as with other design elements, fonts should be applied consistently throughout the application. Use cursive or decorative fonts only for visual effects, such as on a title page if appropriate, and never to convey important information.

Images and Icons

Pictures and icons add visual interest to your application, but careful design is essential to their use. Images that appear "busy" or distract the user will hinder use of your application. Icons can convey information, but again, careful consideration of end-user response is required before deciding on their use. For example, you might consider using a red octagon similar to a US stop sign to indicate that users might not want to proceed beyond that point in the application. Whenever possible, icons should be kept to simple shapes that are easily rendered in a 16-by-16-pixel square.

Working with Windows Forms

To work with Windows Forms, you need to create a Windows Forms Application project using Visual Studio 2008. To do so, click Start ➤ Programs ➤ Microsoft Visual Studio 2008, and from the list shown choose Microsoft Visual Studio 2008. This will open the Visual Studio start page. Click File ➤ New ➤ Project. Now you will see the New Project dialog box from which you can choose the template for Windows Forms Application, as shown in Figure 14-1.

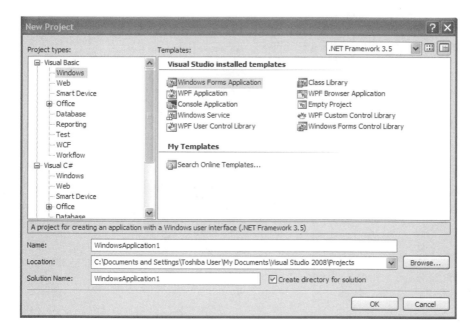

Figure 14-1. *Choosing the Windows Forms Application project template*

By default, the project is named as WindowsApplication1 (the next would be WindowsApplication2, and so on). You can enter another name for your project in the Name text box when you choose the project template, or you can rename your project later.

Once you have chosen the desired template, click OK. This will open the Visual Studio integrated development environment (IDE), so called because it has all the development-related tools, windows, dialog boxes, options, and so forth embedded (or integrated) inside one common window, which makes the development process easier.

In the IDE, you will see that a Windows Form named Form1.vb has been added as you open the project, and on the right-hand side you can also see the Solution Explorer window. You also need to know about one more window called the Properties window. If the Properties window is not available below the Solution Explorer window, you can open it by clicking View ➤ Properties Window or pressing F4. Now the development environment will look as shown in Figure 14-2.

Because this is a Windows Forms Application project, you will be working with controls or tools that allow you to achieve functionality in the form of a GUI. You can pick the controls from the Toolbox, shown on the left-hand side of the Windows Form, in the development environment. If you hover your mouse pointer on the Toolbox tab, the Toolbox window will open for you, as shown in Figure 14-3, and you can pick controls from there and drop them on the surface of the Windows Form.

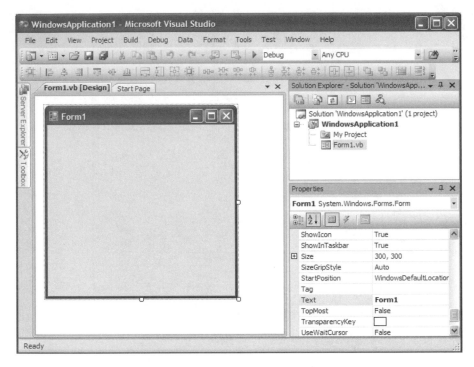

Figure 14-2. *IDE with Solution Explorer and the Properties window*

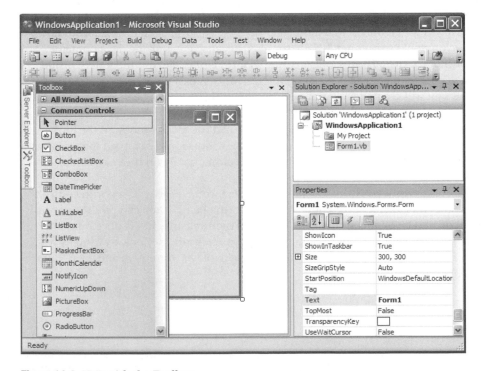

Figure 14-3. *IDE with the Toolbox*

Understanding the Design and Code Views

You mainly deal with two views in the Visual Studio IDE: Design view and Code view. When you open the Visual Studio IDE, by default it displays the Design view, as shown in Figure 14-3. Design view allows you to drag controls and drop them onto the form. You can use the Properties window to set the properties of objects and forms or other files shown in Solution Explorer. Solution Explorer also allows you to rename the project, forms, or even other files included in the project. You can rename these objects by selecting them, right-clicking, and selecting Rename from the context menu.

Basically, Design view gives you a visual way to work with the controls, objects, project files, and so forth. On the other hand, you'll want to use the other view available in the Visual Studio IDE, Code view, when you are working with code to implement the functionality behind the visual controls sitting on the surface of your Windows Forms.

To switch from Design view to Code view, click View ➤ Code or right-click the Windows Form in Design view and select View Code. Either method will open the code editor for you as shown in Figure 14-4.

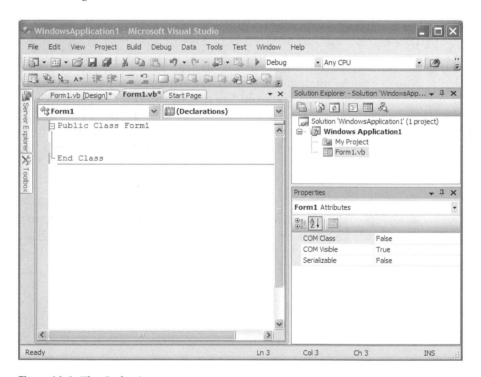

Figure 14-4. *The Code view*

The code editor window displays all the code functionality. In Figure 14-4, note the Form1.vb tab (in which you see Code view) is beside the Form1.vb [Design] tab, which is actually the Design mode of the Windows Form Form1; these tabs allow you to switch between all the GUI elements of Design view and the related code in Code view that helps you to achieve functionality. Interestingly, if you were to try accessing the Toolbox while in Code view, you would see that there are no controls in the Toolbox. But when you switch back to Design view, you'll find the Toolbox is fully loaded with the controls.

To switch back to Design view, right-click the form in Code view and select View Designer; you will see that now you are back to Design mode and can continue working with the visual elements, or controls.

You can also use Solution Explorer to switch between Design and Code view by selecting your desired Windows Form (in case you have multiple Windows Forms open), right-clicking, and choosing either View Code or View Designer. This will open either the Code or Design view of the selected Windows Form.

Sorting Properties in the Properties Window

Each object such as a form, control, and so on has a lot of properties you may need to set while working with any application. To help you navigate the many properties listed in the Properties window, you can sort them either by category or alphabetically. Let's look at each of these sorting options.

Categorized View

The Categorized view organizes properties in the form of sets of properties, and each set has a name to describe that collection of properties; for example, there are categories named Appearance, Behavior, Data, Design, Focus, and so on. You can switch to the Categorized view by clicking the icon on the very left of the toolbar shown in the top of the Properties window.

In Figure-14-5, which shows the Categorized view, under the Appearance category, you will see all properties listed that define the look and feel of the object (in this case, a form). Note the other categories also shown in Figure 14-5.

■**Note** We have intentionally kept other categories in the collapsed mode in Figure 14-5, just to show you all the categories. When you switch to the Categorized view, you will see that all the categories are expanded by default.

Figure 14-5. *Categorized view of properties*

Alphabetical View

The Alphabetical view organizes properties in ascending order by name from "a" to "z." You can switch to the Alphabetical view by clicking the icon located at the second position from the left of the toolbar shown in the top of the Properties window.

In Figure 14-6, which shows this view, all the properties listed are organized alphabetically. In our experience, working with the Alphabetical view, rather than the Categorized view, makes life much easier. An example will help to show why. Say you are seeking the Font property. In the Categorized view, you have to know under which category this property is located to find it. However, if you have properties organized in the Alphabetical view, you can easily locate this property because it begins with the letter F, so you know whether you need to go back or forward to find this property for your control.

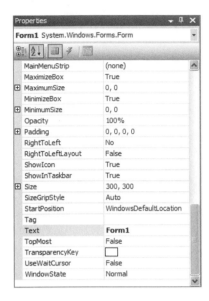

Figure 14-6. *Alphabetical view of properties*

Setting Properties of Solutions, Projects, and Windows Forms

Before you begin putting controls on the Windows Form, you need to learn how to modify some property values of the solution, project, and the form you created earlier (shown previously in Figure 14-2).

Select the WindowsApplication1 solution, go to the Properties window, and set its Name property value to Chapter14.

Select the WindowsApplication1 project in Solution Explorer, go to the Properties window, and modify the Project File property value, which defines the file name of the project, to appear as WinApp.vbproj.

Now change the name of Windows Form: select Form1.vb in Solution Explorer, in the Properties window modify the File Name property from Form1.vb to WinApp.vb, and click Yes in the dialog box that appears.

Now double-click WinApp.vb, located in the Solution Explorer window. Once WinApp.vb is selected, you will see that the list of properties has changed in the Properties window. Select the Text property and modify its value from Form1 to Windows Application. The Text property defines the name shown on the title bar of the form.

After setting the properties for your solution, project, and Windows Form, the IDE will look as shown in Figure 14-7.

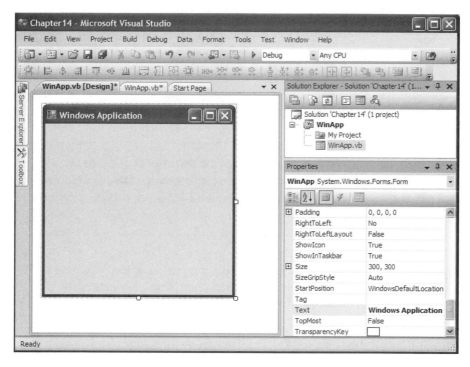

Figure 14-7. *IDE after setting the properties for your solution, project, and Windows Form*

Working with Controls

Now that you have your Windows Forms Application in place, you can start working with the controls.

The basic element of any windows application is the control, which plays a key role by providing the visual meaning to the code functionality embedded in an application.

Based on our years of combined experience, we can confidently say the most commonly used controls are Label, Button, TextBox, RadioButton, ListBox, and ComboBox. Applications cannot exist without these controls. Next, you'll see how you can incorporate these controls in your application.

Try It Out: Working with the TextBox and Button Controls

In this exercise, you'll create a Windows Forms Application having three labels, two text boxes, and a button. The application will accept your name as input and then flash a "Welcome" message.

1. Go to the project named WinApp located under the solution named Chapter14, which you created earlier (refer to Figure 14-7). Ensure that you are in Design view.

2. Drag a Label control onto the form, and position it at the top and the center. Select the label named label1, navigate to the Properties window, and set its Text property to Welcome. Select the Font property, click the ellipsis button, and specify the size of the Label control as 16 points from the Size drop-down list.

■Tip You can also double-click any control in the Toolbox to add it to the form. The difference between dragging a control and double-clicking is that while dragging, you can position the control as you desire on the form. But if you just double-click a control, it will be added to the top-left corner; so if you prefer it in a different location, you still have to drag it there.

---

3. Drag two more Label controls onto the form, and put them below the "Welcome" text, a little toward the left of the form. Select the label named label2, navigate to the Properties window, and set its Text property to First Name. Select the label named label3, and set its Text property in the Properties window to Last Name.

4. Drag two TextBox controls onto the form, and put the TextBox named textBox1 in front of the First Name label and the TextBox named textBox2 in front of the Last Name label.

5. Select textBox1, go to the Properties window, and set its Name property to txtFname. Select textBox2, and in the Properties window set its Name property to txtLname.

6. Drag a Button control onto the form and place it below the Label and TextBox controls. Select the Button control, go to the Properties window, change the Name property to btnSubmit, and then set its Text property to Submit.

Now you have your GUI design of the application ready; it should resemble the form shown in Figure 14-8.

Figure 14-8. *GUI design of the Windows Application form*

It's time to add functionality and switch the Code view. You are going to read in the First Name and Last Name values supplied by the user and flash a message on a click of the Submit button, which means you need to put all the functionality behind the Submit button's click event, which will eventually read the values from the TextBoxes. To achieve this, continue with these steps:

7. Double-click the Submit button. This will take you to Code view, and you will see that the btnSubmit_Click event template has been added to the code editor window, as shown in Figure 14-9.

8. Now add the following code inside this btnSubmit_Click event to achieve the desired functionality:

```
MessageBox.Show("Hello" & " " & txtFname.Text & " " & txtLname.Text & " " & _
"Welcome to the Windows Application","Welcome")
```

9. Once you have added the code, click Build ➤ Build Solution, and ensure that the project gets build successfully.

Figure 14-9. *Code view of your Windows Forms Application project*

10. Now it's time to run and test the application. To do so, press Ctrl+F5. Visual Studio 2008 will load the application.

11. Enter values in the First Name and Last Name text boxes, and then click the Submit button; you will see a message similar to the one shown in Figure 14-10.

12. Click OK, and then close the Windows Application form.

Figure 14-10. *Running the Windows Application form*

How It Works

Visual Studio comes with a lot of features to help developers while writing code. One of these features is that you can just double-click the GUI element for which you want to add the code, and you will be taken to the code associated with the GUI element in Code view. For example, when you double-click the Submit button in Design view, you are taken to the Code view, and the btnSubmit_Click event template automatically gets generated.

To achieve the functionality for this control, you add the following code:

```
MessageBox.Show("Hello" & " " & txtFname.Text & " " & txtLname.Text & " " & _
"Welcome to the Windows Application", "Welcome")
```

MessageBox.Show is a VB.NET method that pops up a message box. To display a "Welcome" message with the first name and last name specified by the user in the message box, you apply a string concatenation approach while writing the code.

In the code segment, you hard-code the message "Hello Welcome to the Windows Application" but with the first name and last name of the user appearing after the word "Hello" and concatenated with the rest of the message, "Welcome to the Windows Application".

For readability, you also add single space characters (" ") concatenated by instances of the + operator in between the words and values you are reading from the Text property of the txtFnam and txtLname. If you do not include the single space character (" ") during string concatenation, the words will be run into each other, and the message displayed in the message box will be difficult to read.

Setting Dock and Anchor Properties

Prior to Visual Studio 2005, resizing Windows Forms would require you to reposition and/or resize controls on those forms. For instance, if you had some controls on the left side of a form, and you tried to resize the form by stretching it toward the right side or bring it back toward the left, the controls wouldn't readjust themselves according to the width of the resized form. Developers were bound to write code to shift controls accordingly to account for the user resizing the form. This technique was very code heavy and not so easy to implement.

With Visual Studio 2005 came two new properties, Anchor and Dock, which are so easy to set at design time itself. The same Dock and Anchor properties are available with Visual Studio 2008, and they solve the problem with the behavior of controls that users face while resizing forms.

Dock Property

The Dock property allows you to attach a control to one of the edges of its parent. The term "parent" applies to Windows Forms, because Windows Forms contain the controls that you drag and drop on them. By default, the Dock property of any control is set to None.

For example, a control docked to the top edge of a form will always be connected to the top edge of the form, and it will automatically resize in the left and right directions when its parent is resized.

The Dock property for a control can be set by using the provided graphical interface in the Properties window as shown in Figure 14-11.

Figure 14-11. *Setting the Dock property*

Anchor Property

When a user resizes a form, the controls maintain a constant distance from the edges of its parent form with the help of the Anchor property. The default value for the Anchor property for any control is set to Top, Left, which means that this control will maintain a constant distance from the top and left edges of the form. The Anchor property can be set by using the provided graphical interface in the Properties window, as shown in Figure 14-12.

Due to the default setting of Anchor property to Top, Left, if you try to resize a form by stretching it toward the right side, you will see that its controls are still positioned on the left rather than shifting to the center of the form to adjust to the size of the form after resizing is done.

If opposite edges, for example, Left and Right, are both set in the Anchor property, the control will stretch when the form is resized. However, if neither of the opposite edges is set in the Anchor property, the control will float when the parent is resized.

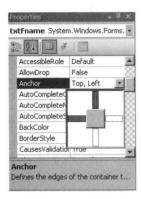

Figure 14-12. *Setting the Anchor property*

Try It Out: Working with the Dock and Anchor Properties

In this exercise, you will use the existing Windows Forms Application named WinApp, which you created previously in the chapter. You will see how to modify this application in such a way that when you resize the form, its controls behave accordingly and keep the application presentable for the user.

1. Go to Solution Explorer and open the WinApp project. Open the WinApp form in Design mode.

2. Select the form by clicking its title bar; you will see handles around form's border, which allow you to resize the form's height and width.

3. Place the cursor on the handle of the right-hand border, and when mouse pointer becomes double-headed, click and stretch the form toward the right-hand side. You will see that form's width increases, but the controls are still attached to the left corner of the form.

4. Similarly, grab the handle located on the bottom of the form and try to increase the height of the form. You will notice that the controls are still attached to the top side of the form.

   Have a look at Figure 14-13, which shows a resized (height and width) form and the position of the controls. The controls appear in the top-left corner because their Dock property values are None and Anchor property values are Top, Left.

Figure 14-13. *Resized form and position of controls*

Now you will try to set the Dock and Anchor properties for the controls and then retest the application.

5. Select the Label control having a Text value of Welcome, and go to the Properties window. Select the AutoSize property and set its value to False (default value is True).

6. Resize the width of the Label control to the width of the form, and adjust the Label control to the top border of the form. Set this control's TextAlign property to Top, Center.

7. Set the Dock property for the Label control from None to Top, which means you want the label to always be affixed with the top border of the form.

8. Now select all the remaining controls (two Labels, two TextBoxes, and one Button) either by scrolling over all of them while holding down the left mouse button or selecting each with a click while pressing down either the Shift or Ctrl key.

9. Once you have selected all the controls, go to the Properties window. You will see listed all the properties common to the controls you have selected on the form.

10. Select the Anchor property; modify its value from the default Top, Left to Top, Left, and Right. This will allow you to adjust the controls accordingly as soon as you resize the form. The controls will also grow in size accordingly to adjust to the width of the form, as you can see in Figure 14-14.

Figure 14-14. *The effect of the Anchor property setting Top, Left, Right on a resized form*

■**Note** The Anchor property has very interesting behaviors; you can try setting this property in various combinations and see their effects when you resize your form.

---

11. Return the form to its previous size so you can see the effects of setting another Anchor property.

12. Select all the controls again as you did in Step 8. Set the Anchor property to Top only and try resizing the form now. You will notice that the controls are floating in the middle of the form when you resize it, as you can see in Figure 14-15.

Figure 14-15. *The effect of the Anchor property setting Top on a resized form*

13. Save the changes in your project by clicking File ➤ Save All.

How It Works

When you resize the form, it will behave according to the settings of the Dock and Anchor properties.

In the first instance, you set the Dock property of the Label control to Top, which allows this Label control to be affixed to the top border of the form and span the entire width of the form. Setting the Anchor property of the remaining controls to Top, Left, and Right shifts the controls in such a manner that they will maintain a constant distance from the left and right borders of the form.

Adding a New Form to the Project

You'll obviously need multiple Windows Forms in any given project. By default, every project opens with only one Windows Form, but you are free to add more.

Try It Out: Adding a New Form to the Windows Project

In this exercise, you will add another Windows Form to your project. You will also work with a ListBox control and see how to add items to that control.

1. Navigate to Solution Explorer and select the WinApp project, right-click, and click Add ➤ Windows Form. This will add a new Windows Form in your project.

2. In the Add New Item dialog box displayed, change the form's name from Form1.vb to AddNames.vb. Click Add. The new form with the name AddNames will be added to your project.

3. Ensure that the newly added form AddNames is open in Design view. Drag a Label control onto the form and change its Text property to Enter Name.

4. Drag a TextBox control onto the AddNames form, and modify its Name property to txtName.

5. Drag a ListBox control onto the AddNames form, and modify its Name property to lstName.

6. Add a Button control to the AddNames form and modify its Name property to btnAdd and its Text property to Add.

   Now you are done with the design part of the AddNames form; your form should look like the one shown in Figure 14-16.

Figure 14-16. *GUI design of the AddNames form*

You want the user to add a name into the TextBox and click the Add button, after which that name will be added to the ListBox. To do so, you need to write the code functionality behind the click event of the Add button.

7. Double-click the Add button and write the following code, which will read the name entered into the TextBox and add it to the ListBox, inside the btnAdd_Click event.

```
lstName.Items.Add(txtName.Text)
txtName.Clear()
```

8. Go to the Build menu and select Build Solution. You should see a message indicating a successful build.

Keep your current project open, as you'll need it immediately for the next exercise. (Don't worry; we'll explain how this and the next exercise work afterward.)

Try It Out: Setting the Startup Form

Setting the startup form in a VB .NET project is a little tricky, so we wanted to break it out into its own exercise. To set a startup form, follow these steps:

1. In Solution Explorer select the WinApp project, right-click the project, and select the Properties option. You will be on the Application page by default. There you will see a list box named Startup Form; by default it will have the name of the first form you created, WinApp. Open the Startup Form drop-down list and choose AddNames, as shown in Figure 14-17. This will ensure that when you run the project it will open the AddNames form rather than the WinApp form.

2. Run the project by pressing Ctrl+F5. When the AddNames form appears, enter your name in the provided text box and click the Add button. Your name will be added in the list box, as shown in Figure 14-18.

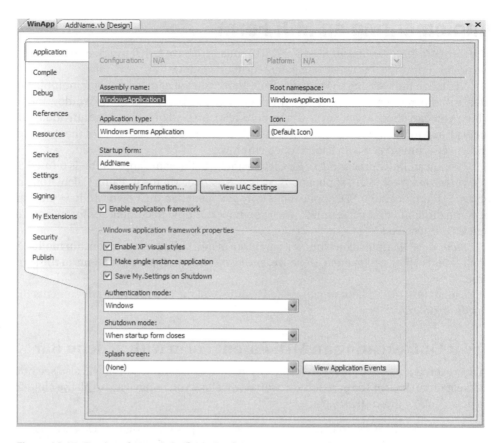

Figure 14-17. *Setting the startup form in the Properties window*

Figure 14-18. *Running the AddNames Windows Forms Application*

Implementing an MDI Form

The term *Multiple Document Interface* (MDI) means to have a GUI interface that allows multiple documents or forms under one parent form or window.

Visualize the working style of Microsoft Word: you are allowed to open multiple documents in one parent window, and all the documents will get listed in the Window menu, from which you can choose whichever you want to read, instead of having the individual documents open in their own windows, which makes it difficult to handle all of the documents and covers your screen with a lot of open windows.

Having an individual window for each instance of the same application is termed *Single Document Interface* (SDI); applications such as Notepad, Microsoft Paint, Calculator, and so on are SDI applications. SDI applications only get opened in their own windows and can become difficult to manage, unlike when you have multiple documents or forms open inside one MDI interface.

Hence, MDI applications follow a parent form and child form relationship model. MDI applications allow you to open, organize, and work with multiple documents at the same time.

The parent (MDI) form organizes and arranges all the child forms or documents that are currently open.

Try It Out: Creating an MDI Parent Form with a Menu Bar

In this exercise, you will create an MDI form in the WinApp project. You will also see how to create a menu bar for the parent form, which will allow you to navigate to all the child forms. To do so, follow these steps:

1. Navigate to Solution Explorer, select the WinApp project, right-click, and select Add ➤ Windows Form. Change the Name value from Form1.vb to ParentForm.vb, and click Add.

2. Select the newly added ParentForm in Design mode, and navigate to the Properties window. Set the IsMdiContainer property value to True (the default value is False). Notice that the background color of the form has changed to dark gray.

3. Modify the size of the ParentForm so that it can accommodate the two forms you created earlier, WinApp and AddNames, inside it.

4. Add a menu to the ParentForm by dragging a MenuStrip (a control that serves the purpose of a menu bar) onto the ParentForm. In the top-left corner, you should now see a drop-down sporting the text Type Here. Enter **Open Forms** in the drop-down. This will be your main top-level menu.

5. Now under the Open Forms menu, add a submenu by entering the text **Win App**.

6. Under the Win App submenu, enter **Add Names**.

7. Now click the top menu, Open Forms, and on the right side of it, type **Help**.

8. Under the Help menu, enter **Exit**.

9. Now it's time to attach code to the submenus you have added under the main menu Open Forms. First, you'll add code for the submenu Win App, which basically will open the WinApp form. In Design mode, double-click the Win App submenu, which will take you to the code editor. Under the click event, add the following code:

```
Dim wa As WinApp = New WinApp
 wa.Show()
```

10. Now you need to associate functionality with the Add Names submenu: double-click this submenu, and under the click event add the following code:

```
Dim an As AddNames = New AddNames
 an.Show()
```

11. To associate functionality with the Exit submenu located under the Help main menu, double-click Exit, and under the click event add the following code:

```
Application.Exit()
```

Again, keep your current project open, as you'll need it immediately for the next exercise. (Don't worry; we'll explain how this and the next exercise work afterward.)

Try It Out: Creating an MDI Child Form and Running an MDI Application

In this exercise, you will associate all the forms you created earlier as MDI child forms to the main MDI parent form you created in the previous task.

1. In the project you modified in the previous exercise, you'll first make the WinApp form an MDI child form. To do so, you need to set the MdiParent property to the name of the MDI parent form, but in the code editor. You have already added functionality in the previous task (opening the WinApp form); just before the line where you are calling the Show method, add the following code:

```
wa.MdiParent=Me
```

After adding this line, the code will appear as follows:

```
 Dim wa As WinApp = New WinApp
 wa.MdiParent = Me
wa.Show()
```

■**Note** Me is a VB language keyword that represents the current instance of the class. In this case, it refers to the ParentForm. Because you are writing this code inside ParentForm, you can use the Me keyword for the same.

2. Now you will make the AddNames form an MDI child form. To do so, you need to set the MdiParent property to the name of the MDI parent form, but in the code editor. Add the following code as you have done in the previous step:

```
an.MdiParent=Me
```

After adding this line, the code will appear as follows:

```
Dim an As AddNames = New AddNames
an.MdiParent = Me
an.Show()
```

3. Now you have all the code functionality in place, and you are almost set to run the application. But first, you have to bring all the controls to the MDI form, ParentForm in this case, and so you need to set ParentForm as the startup object. To do so, select the WinApp project, right-click, and select Properties. Set the Startup Form drop-down to ParentForm(see Figure 14-17 earlier in the chapter for reference).

4. Now build the solution, and run the application by pressing F5; the MDI application will open and should appear as shown in Figure 14-19.

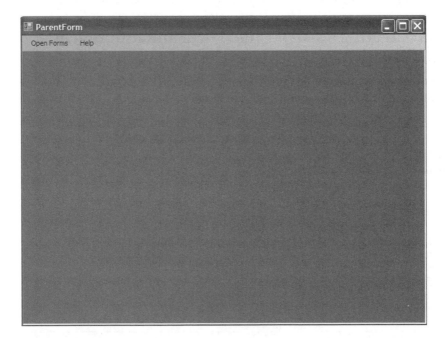

Figure 14-19. *Running an MDI form application*

5. Click Open Forms ➤ Win App; the WinApp form should open. Again, open the main menu and click Add Names. Both the forms should now be open inside your main MDI parent form application, as shown in Figure 14-20.

Figure 14-20. *Opening child forms inside an MDI form application*

6. Because both the forms are open inside one MDI parent, it becomes easier to work with them. Switch back and forth between these forms by clicking their title bars.

7. Once you are done with the forms, close the application by selecting Help ➤ Exit.

How It Works

Let's talk about the "Creating an MDI Parent Form with a Menu Bar" task first. You use the following code:

```
Dim wa As WinApp = New WinApp
wa.Show()
```

This creates an instance of the WinApp form and opens it for you.

The following code creates an instance of the AddNames form and opens it for you:

```
Dim an As AddNames = New AddNames
an.Show()
```

You close the application with the following code:

```
Application.Exit()
```

In the "Creating an MDI Child Form and Running an MDI Application" task, you add the lines shown in bold:

```
Dim wa As WinApp = New WinApp
wa.MdiParent = Me
wa.Show()

Dim an As AddNames = New AddNames
an.MdiParent = Me
an.Show()
```

The wa.MdiParent = Me line tells the child form which form is its parent. As you want all the child forms to appear inside ParentForm, and you write the code inside the MDI parent form, you can use the Me keyword to represent the current object.

Summary

In this chapter, you learned about Windows Forms and the design principles associated with graphical user interface design. You also learned the importance of commonly ignored features, such as font styles and colors, and their impact on applications and effect on large numbers of users. You also worked with properties that solve the resizing problem of Windows Forms. You looked at the importance of MDI applications, and then you created an MDI application with menu controls.

In the next chapter, you will see how to build an ASP.NET application.

CHAPTER 15

■■■

Building ASP.NET Applications

This chapter focuses on the concepts behind web application development and the key components that play an important role in the web environment. It also shows you how to work with some new features of ASP.NET during the development of a web application.

In this chapter, we'll cover the following:

- Understanding web functionality

- Introduction to ASP.NET and web pages

- Understanding the Visual Studio 2008 web site types

- Layout of an ASP.NET web site

- Using Master Pages

Understanding Web Functionality

A *web application*, also often referred to as a web site, is one that you want to run over the Internet or an intranet. The technique .NET came up with to build web applications is by using web forms, which work in the ASP.NET environment and accept code functionality from the Visual Basic language.

Before you dive into web forms and learn how to develop a web application, you need to understand what components drive this entire web world and how these components serve various applications running over it.

Basically, there are three key players that make all web applications functional: the web server, the web browser, and Hypertext Transfer Protocol (HTTP). Let's have a look at their communication process:

1. The web browser initiates a request to the web server for a resource.

2. HTTP sends a GET request to the web server, and the web server processes that request.

3. The web server initiates a response; HTTP sends the response to the web browser.

4. The web browser processes the response and displays the result on the web page.

5. The user inputs data or performs some action that forces data to be sent again to the web server.

6. HTTP will POST the data back to the web server, and the web server processes that data.

7. HTTP sends the response to the web browser.

8. The web browser processes the response and displays the result on the web page.

Now that you have a general understanding of the communication process, let's have a closer look at each of the key components.

The Web Server

The web server is responsible for receiving and handling all requests coming from browsers through HTTP. After receiving a request, the web server will process that request and send the response back to the browser. Right after this, usually the web server will close its connection with the database and release all resources, opened files, network connections, and so forth, which become part of the request to be processed on the web server.

The web server does all this cleaning of data, resources, and so on in order to be stateless. The term *state* refers to the data that gets stored between the request sent to the server and the response delivered to the browser.

Today's web sites run as applications and consist of many web pages, and data on one web page is often responsible for the output that will be displayed on the next web page; in this situation, being stateless defeats the whole purpose of such web sites, and so maintaining state becomes important.

To be stateful, the web server will keep connections and resources alive for a period of time by anticipating that there will be an additional request from the web browser.

The Web Browser and HTTP

The web browser is the client-side application that displays web pages. The web browser works with HTTP to send a request to the web server, and then the web server responds to the web browser or web client's request with the data the user wants to see or work with.

HTTP is a communication protocol that is used to request web pages from the web server and then to send the response back to the web browser.

Introduction to ASP.NET and Web Pages

ASP.NET is available to all .NET developers, as it comes with Microsoft .NET Framework. ASP.NET provides a web development model to build web applications by using any .NET-compliant language. ASP.NET code is compiled rather than interpreted, and it supports the basic features of .NET Framework such as strong typing, performance optimizations, and so on. After the code has been compiled, the .NET CLR will further compile the ASP.NET code to native code, which provides improved performance.

Web pages serve the purpose of a user interface for your web application. ASP.NET adds programmability to the web page. ASP.NET implements application logic using code, which will be sent for execution on the server side. ASP.NET web pages have the following traits:

- They are based on Microsoft ASP.NET technology, in which code that runs on the server dynamically generates web page output to the browser or client device.

- They are compatible with any language supported by the .NET common language runtime, including Microsoft Visual Basic, Microsoft Visual C#, Microsoft J#, and Microsoft JScript .NET.

- They are built on the Microsoft .NET Framework. This provides all the benefits of the framework, including a managed environment, type safety, and inheritance.

The web page consists of application code that serves requests by users; to do so, ASP.NET compiles the code into the assemblies. *Assemblies* are files that contain metadata about the application and have the file extension `.dll`. After the code is compiled, it is translated into a language-independent and CPU-independent format called *Microsoft Intermediate Language* (MSIL), also known as *Intermediate Language* (IL). While running the web site, MSIL runs in the context of the .NET Framework and gets translated into CPU-specific instructions for the processor on the PC running the web application.

Understanding the Visual Studio 2008 Web Site Types

Visual Studio 2008 offers various ways of creating a web project or web site. Though web sites are only meant for the Internet or intranets, Visual Studio 2008 has three types, based on location, that can serve as a foundation for any web site that web developers are working on. The purpose of having these options is that they simplify the system requirements on the developer's machine.

If you have ever worked with classic ASP applications (not ASP.NET), recall the days of Visual Studio 6.0, when developers were required to use Internet Information Services (IIS) to work with and test an ASP web application. This issue has been resolved with the evolution of Visual Studio; now you can develop a web site without having IIS installed on your machine.

■Note Internet Information Services (formerly called Internet Information Server) is a set of Internet-based services where all web applications can reside and run. IIS provides complete web administration facility to the web applications hosted inside it.

A new Web Site project can be built in the Visual Studio 2008 IDE by accessing File ➤ New ➤ Web Site.

Let's have look at the types of web sites offered by Visual Studio 2008.

File System Web Site

A file system–based web site is stored on the computer like any other folder structure. The main feature of this type of web site is that it uses a lightweight ASP.NET development server that is part of Visual Studio 2008, and so it does not necessarily require IIS to be available on the developer's local machine.

Figure 15-1 shows the New Web Site dialog box with the web site Location option set to File System; notice also the path of the folder where this web site will be stored.

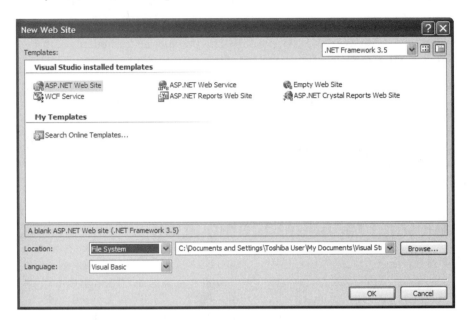

Figure 15-1. *Specifying a file system web site*

FTP Web Site

A web site based on the File Transfer Protocol (FTP) helps you to manage and transfer files between a local machine and a remote web site. The FTP web site offers a Windows Explorer– like interface and exposes the folder structure where files, documents, and so on are kept for sharing purposes.

You can access the FTP site to share, transfer, or download files from a remote FTP site to your local computer, or you can upload files to the remote FTP site.

Figure 15-2 shows the New Web Site dialog box with the web site Location option set to FTP.

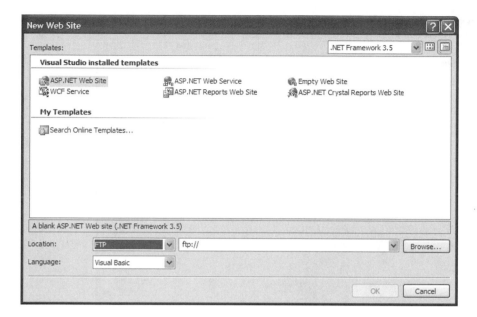

Figure 15-2. *Specifying an FTP web site*

■Note Building FTP sites requires a user's credentials to be passed. Usually there is no anonymous FTP site; you should specify the FTP address using the `ftp://user:pwd@ftpaddress:port` syntax.

HTTP Web Site

A web site based on HTTP is preferable for building entirely commercial web-based products. The HTTP web site requires IIS on the local machine of the developer, as it is configured as an application in the virtual directory of IIS. The IIS server brings a lot of administrative power to web applications sitting inside IIS.

Figure 15-3 shows the New Web Site dialog box with the web site Location option set to HTTP.

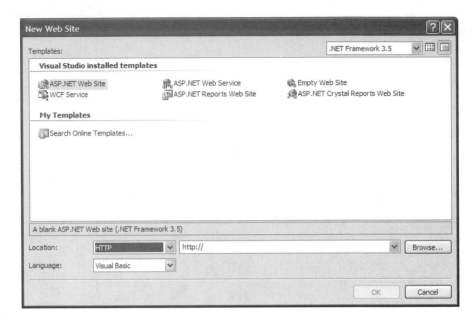

Figure 15-3. *Specifying an HTTP web site*

Layout of an ASP.NET Web Site

Let's open a new web site and explore its layout. Open the Visual Studio 2008 IDE, and select File ➤ New ➤ Web Site. In the New Web Site dialog box, select ASP.NET Web Site as the project template, and then choose HTTP as the location and Visual Basic as the language. In the text box adjacent to the Location drop-down list box, modify the path from `http://` to `http://localhost/Chapter15`, which indicates that you are going to create a web site under IIS with the name Chapter15. Click OK.

Now navigate to Solution Explorer so you can see what components make up a Web Site project. After you create the project, it will open as shown in Figure 15-4.

So that you understand the function of the components for a Web Site project, we'll discuss each component shown under Solution Explorer in the Chapter15 Web Site project next.

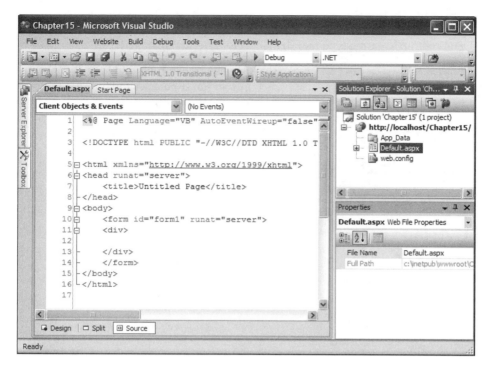

Figure 15-4. *Layout of an ASP.NET web site*

Web Pages

Web pages, also known as web forms, provide an interface for user interaction. By default, each Web Site project comes with one Default.aspx page, or form, and can have as many other web pages with different names as you like to achieve the functionality you desire. The name Default.aspx has special meaning for IIS; the Default.aspx page will be loaded automatically when someone accesses the web site URL.

The Default.aspx page can be used as the home page for your web site, or you can insert some hyperlinks on this page and write code behind those hyperlinks to redirect users to other pages. By default, Default.aspx is added to the list of default content pages under IIS. Besides those pages that are already listed, you can add any other pages to be treated as default pages for your web site. You can even remove the default setting of IIS, which allows a user's web browser to recognize Default.aspx as the default page to be loaded while that user is accessing the web site, so it becomes unnecessary to pass the name of the page while the web site is being accessed.

For this example, you need to provide the URL as http://localhost/Chapter15, which will load the Default.aspx page. However, if there is any other page available with a name other than Default.aspx, you need to pass that name along with the URL: for example, http://localhost/Chapter15/MyPage.aspx. Also note that the URLs are not case sensitive.

You can access IIS by either of the following methods:

- Click Start ➤ Run and then type **InetMgr** (short for Internet manager).

- Click Start ➤ Settings ➤ Control Panel. Select Administrative Tools and then click the Internet Information Services (IIS) Manager option. You should see the Internet Information Services (IIS) Manager window as shown in Figure 15-5.

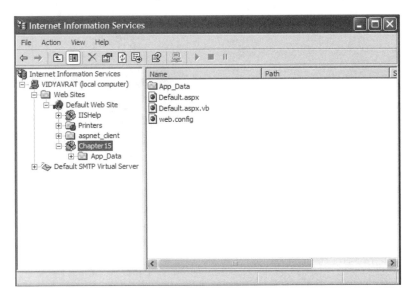

Figure 15-5. *Internet Information Services (IIS) Manager window*

■**Note** Under Internet Information Services, the default pages are established as properties of your web site.

Now right-click your Chapter15 Web Site project and select the Properties option. In the Chapter15 Properties window, shown in Figure 15-6, switch to the Documents tab page, and you will see that the Default.aspx page is available in the list of default content pages. IIS works as a web server, which is why you see listed other page types that work as default pages for other types of web sites that could have been built using other technologies (for example, ASP could be used and for that purpose Default.asp is also listed). If required, you can click the Add button to add another page of your web site to be recognized as a default page. You can also remove a page listed as a default page by selecting the particular page and clicking the Remove button. By default, you will see that the option Enable default content page is active; you can disable this functionality by removing the check mark.

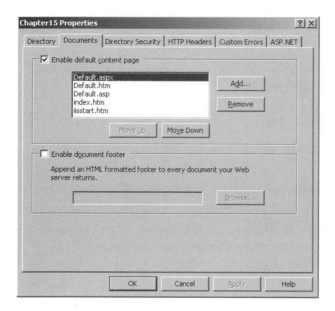

Figure 15-6. *Chapter15 Properties window*

Application Folders

ASP.NET comes with some predefined folders into which you can insert data files, style sheets, resource files (used in a global scope in the application), and so on and achieve functionality throughout the project.

The App_Data folder is the default folder, which is added automatically when you create an ASP.NET Web Site project.

To add other available folders, right-click the project, select the Add ASP.NET Folder option, and then choose the folder that is appropriate for the type of web application you are building.

The web.config File

The web.config file is an important file of a web project. This file helps the developer by providing a central location where all the settings required for various actions like database connections, debugging mode, and so on can be set, and these settings will be applied and accessible throughout the project.

■**Note** The web.config file is not automatically added to the ASP.NET Web Site project if you select File System as the storage location. The web.config file is also not added if you choose the location of a folder with the File System option selected while saving the project.

Another feature of the web.config file is that it is simple to read and write to, just like a Notepad file, because it comes in XML format.

The web.config file has a lot of predefined tags that help you organize the configuration settings for your web application. The most important thing to remember is that all tags need to be embedded inside the parent tags <Configuration></Configuration>.

Try It Out: Working with a Web Form

In this exercise, you will add a web form with basic controls, and then you will attach the required functionality to the controls.

1. Navigate to Solution Explorer, select the Chapter15 project, right-click it, and select Add New Item.

2. In the Add New Item dialog box, modify the form name to appear as Input.aspx and ensure that the Language drop-down list shows Visual Basic as the language to be used. Click Add to add the Input.aspx form to your project.

3. Right-click the Input.aspx web form and select the View Designer option; this will open the Input.aspx page in Design view, where you can drag and drop controls onto the web page.

4. Drag a Label control (named Label1) onto the form, and modify its Text property to Enter Name.

5. Drag a TextBox control (named TextBox1) onto the form. Drag a Button control (named Button1) onto the form and modify its Text property to Submit. All three controls should appear in one line.

6. Now add another Label control (named Label2) below the three controls you added previously, and set its Text property to blank (i.e., no text is assigned).

7. To attach the code behind the Button control, double-click the Button control.

8. Source view opens, taking you inside the Input.aspx.vb tab page, where you will see the blank template for the Button1_Click event. Add the following code to the click event of the button:

```
Label2.Text = "Hello" & " " & TextBox1.Text & " " + "You are Welcome!"
```

9. Begin testing the application by selecting Input.aspx, right-clicking, and choosing the View in Browser option.

10. The Input.aspx form will appear in the browser. Enter a name in the provided text box and click the Submit button. You should receive output similar to that shown in Figure 15-7.

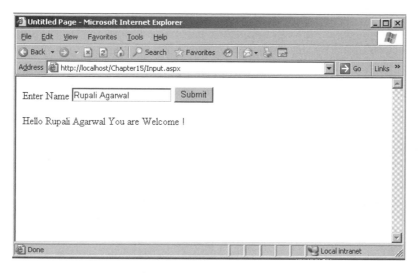

Figure 15-7. *Testing the web form application*

Try It Out: Working with Split View

In this exercise, you will see how to modify the properties of ASP control elements such as asp:Label, asp:TextBox, and so on. You will also see how Split view, a brand-new feature of Visual Studio 2008, works.

1. Navigate back to the IDE, right-click the `Input.aspx` form, and select the View Markup option. This view will take you to Source view, where you will see the HTML tags defined for the controls that you dragged and dropped on the `Input.aspx` web form earlier. This view allows you to set properties for ASP.NET elements such as asp:Label, asp:TextBox, and asp:Button to be specific to your application.

2. Next you'll set the color for Label1 so it will appear in some color other than black as in the previous exercise. To do so, go to the line where all the properties for asp:Label1 are defined, place the cursor after the Text property defined for Label1, and type **ForeColor=Red**. As you start typing the property name, because of the IntelliSense feature, you'll see the complete property name and many other color names listed, so you can use this feature to choose any color as well.

   You have modified asp:Label1 in source view, so to see your change in effect, you need to switch back to Design view. When you have a lot of changes, it can be a tedious process to see how each change made to the various controls and their respective properties looks.

   To avoid this tedious switching between Source and Design view, Visual Studio 2008 has come up with a brand-new feature called Split view. This feature allows you to work with both Source and Design view displayed so you can immediately see how changes done in the code affect the controls.

3. Click the Split button located on the bottom of the IDE between the Design and Source buttons. You should now be able to see the code in Source view and the controls in Design view in one common window, as shown in Figure 15-8.

4. Modify the ForeColor property of Label1 to Blue and set the Font Size property of Label2 to XX-Large. When you make these changes, you will see a pop-up message stating that Design view is out of sync with the Source view, as shown in Figure 15-9.

5. Click the pop-up message to synchronize Source view and Design view. This causes the changes made to the code to be reflected in Design view (see Figure 15-10).

6. Now right-click Input.aspx and select the View in Browser option to see the output.

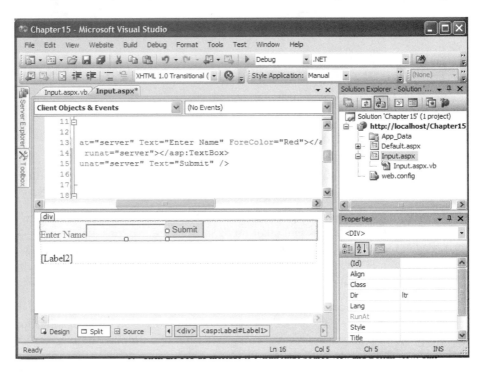

Figure 15-8. *Split view of your Web Site project*

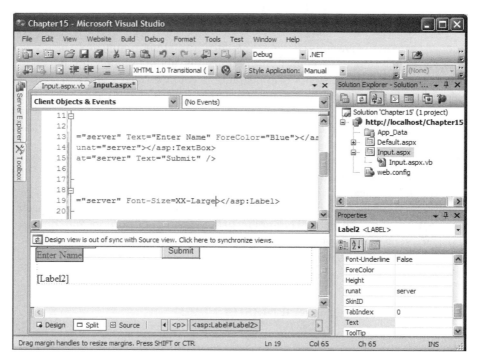

Figure 15-9. *Synchronization pop-up message of Split view*

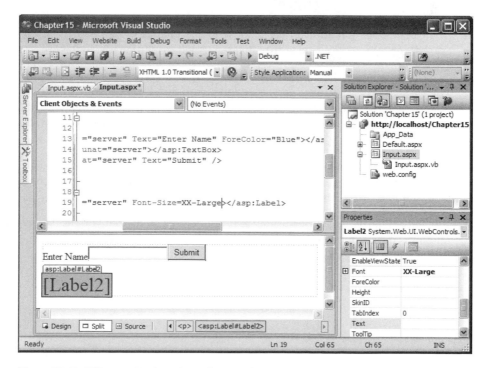

Figure 15-10. *Effect on Design view after synchronization*

Using Master Pages

As touched upon in the previous chapter, aesthetics are an important feature of any web application. As a developer, you may be more concerned about functionality, but at the same time you can't overlook consistency of appearance in your web pages. This can seem to be a complex task, as any web application consists of up to dozens of web pages or web forms; and if you try to apply a common look and feel to an individual web page, you can imagine how tedious a task it would become for you, and whoever else is working on your application, to ensure that all web pages have a consistent look and feel.

ASP.NET has a solution to this important need for consistency among all the web pages in your web application, and this feature is known as *Master Pages*.

In your web application, you will define one Master Page with the look and feel you want that all other web pages must inherit. The Master Page also contains a content page embedded inside it. The look and feel will be applied to the Master Page portion, and the content of child pages will be merged inside the content page area. The content page is represented in the form of a ContentPlaceHolder control, which is added automatically whenever you create a Master Page.

Try It Out: Working with a Master Page

In this exercise, you will see how to create a Master Page. You will also see how to set a Master Page for an existing or newly created child page.

1. Navigate back to the IDE, right-click the Chapter15 project, and select the Add New Item option.

2. In the dialog box that appears, select Master Page, change its name to Ch15MasterPage.master, and ensure that the Language setting is Visual Basic. Click Add.

3. The Ch15MasterPage.master page is added in Solution Explorer, and Source view opens. Switch to Design view; you will see that a ContentPlaceHolder control is added to the Master Page, as shown in Figure 15-11. This is the default template of any Master Page.

   Note in Figure 15-11 that the area outside the ContentPlaceHolder is where you can apply all the settings to be part of the Master Page, and the area inside the Content-PlaceHolder is where the content of other pages will appear.

4. You will add an image to the Master Page, but before you do that you need to add a folder to contain image files. Right-click the project, click New Folder, and name it Images. To add images to this folder, right-click it and select Add Existing Item. Select the item you want to add, and then click Add. The image will be added to this folder and made available for use anywhere in this project.

Figure 15-11. *Template of a Master Page*

Note For the purposes of this example, we are using an image named `Pearl HR.JPG`, which is also provided with the code in the `Images` folder. You can use any other picture from your machine.

---

5. Drag an Image control to just above the ContentPlaceHolder1. Just to ensure that you have added the Image control correctly above the ContentPlaceHolder1, switch to Source view and look at the `asp:Image` tag, which should be above the `asp:ContentPlaceHolder` tag as shown in Figure 15-12.

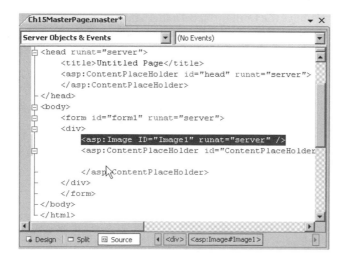

Figure 15-12. *Analyzing position of controls in Source view of a Master Page*

6. Switch to Design view, select the image, and open the Properties window. Click the ellipsis button beside the ImageUrl property. This will take you to the Select Image dialog box, as shown in Figure 15-13. Select the Pearl HR.JPG image located under the Images folder and click OK.

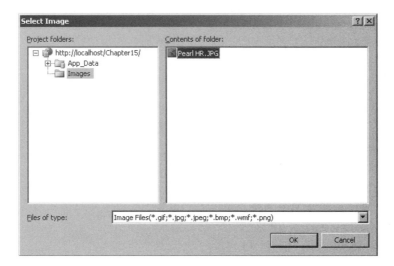

Figure 15-13. *Selecting an image*

7. The image added to the Master Page may not be the size you want it to be, in which case you should set its Size and Width properties in the Properties window. The Pearl HR.JPG image used in this exercise was added at its full size, so we have set its Height and Width properties to 53px and 153px, respectively, to appear as a logo having the proper dimensions on the page.

8. Now drag a Label control above the ContentPlaceHolder and to the right of the Image control. Open the Properties window, set this Label control's Text property to the text you want (for example, we have set it to Pearl HR Solution), and then set its Font Size to XX-Large. Now your Master Page is ready (see Figure 15-14).

Figure 15-14. *Master Page with controls*

9. Now you will set the Master Page for some child web pages so they can inherit the layout of the Master Page. Go to Solution Explorer, open the Input.aspx page in Design view, open the Properties window, and click the ellipsis button beside the MasterPageFile property. This will take you to the Select a Master Page dialog box. Select Ch15MasterPage.master, and click OK.

10. Switch to Source view of the Input.aspx page. You need to modify it by removing all the lines except the control tags and embedding these lines inside the <asp:Content> </asp:Content> tags (see Figure 15-15).

```
1  <%@ Page Language="VB" AutoEventWireup="false"
2  CodeFile="Input.aspx.vb" Inherits="Input"
3  MasterPageFile="~/Ch15MasterPage.master" %>
4
5  <asp:Content ID="Content1" ContentPlaceHolderID="ContentPlaceHolder1"
6  Runat="Server"><br />
7      <asp:Label ID="Label1" runat="server" Text="Enter Name"
8      ForeColor=Blue  ></asp:Label>
9      <asp:TextBox ID="TextBox1" runat="server"></asp:TextBox>
10     <asp:Button ID="Button1" runat="server" onclick="Button1_Click"
11     Text="Submit" />
12     <p>
13         <asp:Label ID="Label2" runat="server" Font-Size=XX-Large></asp:Label>
14     </p>
15     </asp:Content>
16
```

Figure 15-15. *Child form displaying Master Page settings with controls*

11. After modifying the code, switch back to Design view. You will see the page in Design mode as shown in Figure 15-16.

12. Now open `Input.aspx` in your browser. You should see output similar to what is shown in Figure 15-17.

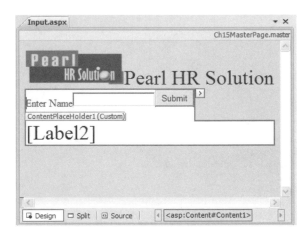

Figure 15-16. *Design view showing child page with Master Page applied*

Figure 15-17. *Runtime version of child page with Master Page applied*

13. Close the browser window.

14. As you have created a Master Page, it will be accessible to any newly created pages. Right-click the project in Solution Explorer, click Add New Item, select Web Form, and ensure that the Select Master Page option is checked. Click OK. This will open the Select a Master Page dialog box. Select the listed Master Page. This will create a new web page based on the Master Page that you have selected (see Figure 15-18).

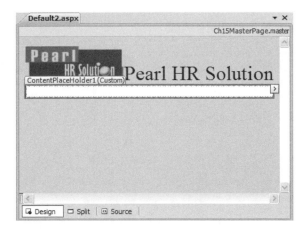

Figure 15-18. *New web form added with a Master Page applied*

The controls that you want to include on the newly added web form must be placed inside only the ContentPlaceHolder. In Figure 15-18, note also the text Ch15MasterPage.master in the top-right corner of ContentPlaceHolder. If you click this text, you will be taken to the Master Page. You can make changes there, and they will be reflected on the child pages.

Summary

In this chapter, you learned about the web technology ASP.NET. You also learned about the various types of web sites you can create in Visual Studio 2008. You saw how to work with the Split view feature to save you time in development. You now also have an understanding of the importance of Master Pages, and how to create them and allocate Master Pages to existing web pages and newly created web pages.

In the next chapter, you will see how to handle exceptions.

Handling Exceptions

Up to now, we've been rather relaxed in our handling of database exceptions. Robust database applications demand more careful attention to this important issue. Structured exception handling is both elegant and robust. In database programming, errors come from three sources: application programs, ADO.NET, and database servers. We assume you're familiar with handling application exceptions in VB .NET with Try statements, so we'll focus on the last two sources.

In this chapter, we'll cover the following:

- Handling ADO.NET exceptions

- Handling database exceptions

Handling ADO.NET Exceptions

First, we'll show you how to handle exceptions thrown by ADO.NET. These exceptions arise when ADO.NET is trying to communicate with SQL Server, before the database server responds. We'll use a Windows application, since it makes generating and viewing error situations and messages more convenient. To expediently generate an exception, you'll try to execute a stored procedure without specifying the CommandText property. You'll do this first without handling the exception, and then you'll modify things to handle it.

Try It Out: Handling an ADO.NET Exception (Part 1)

To handle an ADO.NET exception, follow these steps:

1. Create a new Windows Forms Application project named Chapter16. When Solution Explorer opens, save the solution.

2. Rename the Chapter16 project to AdoNetExceptions.

3. Change the Text property of Form1 to ADO.NET Exceptions.

4. Add a Tab control to the form. By default, the Tab control will include two tab pages. Change the Text property of tabPage1 to ADO.NET and the second tab page's Text property to Database.

5. Add a button to the tab page titled ADO .NET Exceptions, and change its Text property to ADO.NET Exception-1. Add a label to the right of this button, and for its Text property type **Incorrect ADO.NET code will cause an exception**.

6. Add a second button to the tab page, and change its Text property to ADO.NET Exception-2. Add a label to the right of this button, and for its Text property type **Accessing a nonexistent column will cause exception**.

The layout should now look like Figure 16-1.

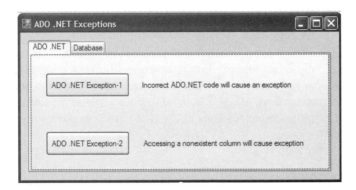

Figure 16-1. *ADO.NET tab page*

7. Add the following Imports directive for the SQL Server data provider namespace to Form1.vb:

Imports System.Data.SqlClient

8. Insert the code in Listing 16-1 into the click event handler for button1. This will provide the first exception.

Listing 16-1. button1_Click()

```
Dim conn As SqlConnection = New SqlConnection _
("Data Source=.\sqlexpress;" & _
 "Integrated Security=True;" & _
 "database=northwind")

'create command
Dim cmd As SqlCommand = conn.CreateCommand

'Specify that a stored procedure is to be executed
cmd.CommandType = CommandType.StoredProcedure

'Deliberately fail to specify the procedure
'cmd.CommandText = "sp_Select_All_Employees"
```

```
'Open connection
conn.Open()

'Create data reader
Dim dr As SqlDataReader = cmd.ExecuteReader

'Close reader
dr.Close()

If conn.State = ConnectionState.Open Then
    MessageBox.Show("Closing the connection")
    conn.Close()
End If
```

9. Run the program by pressing Ctrl+F5. Click the ADO.NET Exception-1 button, and you'll see the message box in Figure 16-2. Click Quit.

Figure 16-2. *Unhandled exception message*

10. Modify the button1_Click event handler with the bold code in Listing 16-2.

Listing 16-2. *Modifications to* button1_Click()

```
Dim conn As SqlConnection = New SqlConnection _
 ("Data Source=.\sqlexpress;" & _
  "Integrated Security=True;" & _
  "database=northwind")

'create command
Dim cmd As SqlCommand = conn.CreateCommand

'Specify that a stored procedure is to be executed
cmd.CommandType = CommandType.StoredProcedure

'Deliberately fail to specify the procedure
'cmd.CommandText = "sp_Select_All_Employees"

Try
    'Open connection
    conn.Open()
```

```vbnet
        'Create data reader
        Dim dr As SqlDataReader = cmd.ExecuteReader

        'Close reader
        dr.Close()

    Catch ex As System.Data.SqlClient.SqlException
        Dim str As String
        str = "Source: " + ex.Source.ToString
        str += ControlChars.NewLine + "Exception Message: " + ex.Message
        MessageBox.Show(str, "Database Exception")

    Catch ex As Exception
        Dim str As String
        str = "Source: " + ex.Source.ToString
        str += ControlChars.NewLine + "Exception Message: " + ex.Message
        MessageBox.Show(str, "non-Database Exception")

    Finally
        If conn.State = ConnectionState.Open Then
            MessageBox.Show("Finally block Closing the connection", ➥
"Finally ")
            conn.Close()
        End If
    End Try
```

11. Run the program by pressing Ctrl+F5. Click the ADO.NET Exception-1 button, and you'll see the message box in Figure 16-3. Click OK.

Figure 16-3. *Handled exception message*

12. When the message box in Figure 16-4 appears, click OK, and then close the window.

Figure 16-4. *Message from* Finally *block*

How It Works

It would be highly unusual to miss setting the CommandText property. However, this is an expedient way to cause an ADO.NET exception. You specify the command is for a stored procedure call, but you don't specify the stored procedure to call:

```
'create command
Dim cmd As SqlCommand = conn.CreateCommand

'Specify that a stored procedure is to be executed
cmd.CommandType = CommandType.StoredProcedure
```

So when you call the ExecuteReader method, you get an exception, as shown in Figure 16-2 earlier. Though it is an unhandled exception, it still gives you an accurate diagnostic:

ExecuteReader: CommandText property has not been initialized.

and it even gives you the option to continue or quit, but leaving this decision to users isn't a good idea.

After seeing what happens without handling the exception, you place the call in a Try block:

```
Try
        'Open connection
        conn.Open()

        'Create data reader
        Dim dr As SqlDataReader = cmd.ExecuteReader

        'Close reader
        dr.Close()
```

and to handle the exception yourself, you code two Catch clauses:

```
Catch ex As System.Data.SqlClient.SqlException
        Dim str As String
        str = "Source: " + ex.Source.ToString
        str += ControlChars.NewLine + "Exception Message: " + ex.Message
        MessageBox.Show(str, "Database Exception")

    Catch ex As Exception
        Dim str As String
        str = "Source: " + ex.Source.ToString
        str += ControlChars.NewLine + "Exception Message: " + ex.Message
        MessageBox.Show(str, "non-Database Exception")
```

In the first Catch clause, you specify a database exception type. The second Catch clause, which produces the message box in Figure 16-3, is a generic block that catches all types of exceptions. Note the title of the message box in this Catch block: it says "Non-Database Exception." Although you may think that a failure to specify a command string is a database exception, it's actually an ADO.NET exception; in other words, this error is trapped before it gets to the database server.

So, when the button is clicked, since the CommandText property isn't specified, an exception is thrown and caught by the second Catch clause. Even though a Catch clause for SqlException is provided, the exception is a System.InvalidOperationException, a common exception thrown by the CLR, not a database exception.

The exception message indicates where the problem occurred: in the ExecuteReader method. The Finally block checks whether the connection is open and, if it is, closes it and gives a message to that effect. Note that in handling the exception you do not terminate the application.

```
Finally
    If conn.State = ConnectionState.Open Then
      MessageBox.Show("Finally block Closing the connection", "Finally ")
      conn.Close()
    End If
End Try
```

Try It Out: Handling an ADO.NET Exception (Part 2)

Let's try another example of an ADO.NET exception. You'll execute a stored procedure and then reference a nonexistent column in the returned dataset. This will throw an ADO.NET exception. This time, you'll code a specific Catch clause to handle the exception.

1. You'll use the sp_Select_All_Employees stored procedure you created in Chapter 6. If you haven't already created it, please go to Chapter 6 and follow the steps in "Try It Out: Working with a Stored Procedure in SQL Server."

2. Insert the code in Listing 16-3 into the body of the button2_Click method.

Listing 16-3. button2_Click()

```
Dim conn As SqlConnection = New SqlConnection _
("Data Source=.\sqlexpress;" & _
 "Integrated Security=True;" & _
 "database=northwind")

'create command
Dim cmd As SqlCommand = conn.CreateCommand

'Specify that a stored procedure is to be executed
cmd.CommandType = CommandType.StoredProcedure
cmd.CommandText = "sp_Select_All_Employees"

Try
    'Open connection
    conn.Open()
```

```
            'Create data reader
            Dim dr As SqlDataReader = cmd.ExecuteReader

            'Access nonexistent column
            Dim str As String = dr.GetValue(20).ToString

            'Close reader
            dr.Close()

        Catch ex As System.InvalidOperationException
            Dim str As String
            str = "Source: " + ex.Source.ToString
            str += ControlChars.NewLine + "Exception Message: " + ex.Message
            str += ControlChars.NewLine + ControlChars.NewLine
            str += "Stack Trace: " + ex.StackTrace
            MessageBox.Show(str, "Specific Exception")

        Catch ex As System.Data.SqlClient.SqlException
            Dim str As String
            str = "Source: " + ex.Source.ToString
            str += ControlChars.NewLine + "Exception Message: " + ex.Message
            MessageBox.Show(str, "Database Exception")

        Catch ex As Exception
            Dim str As String
            str = "Source: " + ex.Source.ToString
            str += ControlChars.NewLine + "Exception Message: " + ex.Message
            MessageBox.Show(str, "non-Database Exception")

        Finally
            If conn.State = ConnectionState.Open Then
                MessageBox.Show("Closing the connection")
                conn.Close()
            End If
        End Try
```

■**Tip** Testing whether a connection is open before attempting to close it isn't actually necessary. The Close method doesn't throw any exceptions, and calling it multiple times on the same connection, even if it's already closed, causes no errors.

---

3. Run the program by pressing Ctrl+F5. Click the ADO.NET Exception-2 button, and you'll see the message box in Figure 16-5. Click OK. When the Finally block message appears, click OK, and then close the window.

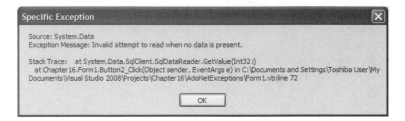

Figure 16-5. *Handling a specific ADO.NET exception*

4. For a quick comparison, you'll now generate a SQL Server exception, an error that occurs within the database. Alter the name of the stored procedure in the code to a name that doesn't exist at all within the Northwind database. For example:

```
cmd.CommandText = "sp_Select_No_Employees";
```

5. Run the program by pressing Ctrl+F5. Click the ADO.NET Exception-2 button, and you'll see the message box in Figure 16-6. Click OK. When the `Finally` block message appears, click OK, and then close the window.

Figure 16-6. *Handling a specific ADO.NET exception*

How It Works

First you create the data reader and try to access an invalid column:

```
'Create data reader
Dim dr As SqlDataReader = cmd.ExecuteReader

'Access nonexistent column
Dim str As String = dr.GetValue(20).ToString
```

so an exception is thrown because column 20, the value of which you try to get, doesn't exist. You add a new `Catch` clause to handle this kind of ADO.NET error:

```
Catch ex As System.InvalidOperationException
        Dim str As String
        str = "Source: " + ex.Source.ToString
        str += ControlChars.NewLine + "Exception Message: " + ex.Message
        str += ControlChars.NewLine + ControlChars.NewLine
        str += "Stack Trace: " + ex.StackTrace
        MessageBox.Show(str, "Specific Exception")
```

When an exception of type System.InvalidOperationException is thrown, this Catch clause executes, displaying the source, message, and stack trace for the exception. Without this specific Catch clause, the generic Catch clause will handle the exception. (Try commenting out this Catch clause and reexecuting the code to see which Catch clause handles the exception.)

Next, you run the program for a nonexistent stored procedure:

```
'Specify that a stored procedure is to be executed
cmd.CommandType = CommandType.StoredProcedure
cmd.CommandText = "sp_Select_No_Employees"
```

You catch your (first) database exception with

```
Catch ex As System.Data.SqlClient.SqlException
```

leading into the next topic: handling exceptions thrown by the database manager.

Handling Database Exceptions

An exception of type System.Data.SqlClient.SqlException is thrown when SQL Server returns a warning or error. This class is derived from System.SystemException and is sealed so it can't be inherited, but it has several useful members that can be interrogated to obtain valuable information about the exception.

An instance of SqlException is thrown whenever the .NET data provider for SQL Server encounters an error or warning from the database. Table 16-1 describes the properties of this class that provide information about the exception.

Table 16-1. SqlException *Properties*

Property Name	Description
Class	Gets the severity level of the error returned from the SqlClient data provider. The severity level is a numeric code that's used to indicate the nature of the error. Levels 1 to 10 are informational errors; 11 to 16 are user-level errors; and 17 to 25 are software or hardware errors. At level 20 or greater, the connection is usually closed.
Data	Gets a collection of key-value pairs that contain user-defined information.
ErrorCode	Specifies the HRESULT of the error.
Errors	Contains one or more SqlError objects that have detailed information about the exception. This is a collection that can be iterated through.
HelpLink	Specifies the help file associated with this exception.
InnerException	Gets the exception instance that caused the current exception.
LineNumber	Gets the line number within the Transact-SQL command batch or stored procedure that generated the exception.
Message	Defines the text describing the exception.
Number	Specifies the number that identifies the type of exception.
Procedure	Specifies the name of the stored procedure that generated the exception.

Continued

Table 16-1. *Continued*

Property Name	Description
Server	Specifies the name of the computer running the instance of SQL Server that generated the exception.
Source	Specifies the name of the provider that generated the exception.
StackTrace	Defines a string representation of the call stack when the exception was thrown.
State	Specifies a numeric error code from SQL Server that represents an exception, warning, or "no data found" message. For more information, see SQL Server Books Online.
TargetSite	Represents the method that throws the current exception.

When an error occurs within SQL Server, it uses a T-SQL RAISERROR statement to raise an error and send it back to the calling program. A typical error message looks like this:

```
Server: Msg 2812, Level 16, State 62, Line 1
Could not find stored procedure 'sp_DoesNotExist'
```

In this message, 2812 represents the error number, 16 represents the severity level, and 62 represents the state of the error.

You can also use the RAISERROR statement to display specific messages within a stored procedure. The RAISERROR statement in its simplest form takes three parameters. The first parameter is the message itself that needs to be shown. The second parameter is the severity level of the error. Any user can use severity levels 11 through 16. They represent messages that can be categorized as information, software, or hardware problems. The third parameter is an arbitrary integer from 1 through 127 that represents information about the state or source of the error.

Let's see how a SQL error, raised by a stored procedure, is handled in VB .NET. You'll create a stored procedure and use the following T-SQL to raise an error when the number of orders in the Orders table exceeds 10:

```
if @orderscount > 10
    raiserror (
        'Orders Count is greater than 10 - Notify the Business Manager',
        16,
        1
    )
```

Note that in this RAISERROR statement, you specify a message string, a severity level of 16, and an arbitrary state number of 1. When a RAISERROR statement that you write contains a message string, the error number is given automatically as 50000. When SQL Server raises errors using RAISERROR, it uses a predefined dictionary of messages to give out the corresponding error numbers.

Try It Out: Handling a Database Exception (Part 1): RAISERROR

Here, you'll see how to raise a database error and handle the exception.

1. Add a button to the Database tab page and change its Text property to Database Exception-1. Add a label to the right of this button, and for its Text property type **Calls a stored procedure that uses RAISERROR**.

2. Add a second button to the tab page, and change its Text property to Database Exception-2. Add a label to the right of this button, and for its Text property type **Calls a stored procedure that encounters an error**.

3. Add a third button to the tab page, and change its Text property to Database Exception-3. Add a label to the right of this button, and for its Text property type **Creates multiple SqlError objects**. The layout should look like Figure 16-7.

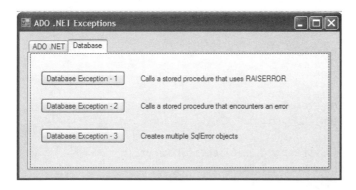

Figure 16-7. *Database tab page*

4. Using SSMSE, create a stored procedure in Northwind named sp_DbException_1, as follows:

```
create procedure sp_DbException_1
as
    set nocount on
    declare @ordercount int

    Select
        @ordercount = count(*)
    From
        Orders

    if @ordercount > 10
        raiserror (
            'Orders Count is greater than 10 - Notify the Business ➥
            Manager',
            16,
            1
        )
```

5. Add the code in Listing 16-4 to the button3_Click method.

Listing 16-4. button3_Click()

```vb
Dim conn As SqlConnection = New SqlConnection _
        ("Data Source=.\sqlexpress;" & _
         "Integrated Security=True;" & _
         "database=northwind")

'create command
Dim cmd As SqlCommand = conn.CreateCommand

'Specify that a stored procedure is to be executed
cmd.CommandType = CommandType.StoredProcedure
cmd.CommandText = "sp_DbException_1"

Try
    'Open connection
    conn.Open()

    'Execute stored procedure
    cmd.ExecuteNonQuery()

Catch ex As System.Data.SqlClient.SqlException
    Dim str As String
    str = "Source: " + ex.Source.ToString
    str += ControlChars.NewLine + "Number: " + ex.Number.ToString
    str += ControlChars.NewLine + "Message: " + ex.Message
    str += ControlChars.NewLine + "Class: " + ex.Class.ToString
    str += ControlChars.NewLine + "Procedure: " + ex.Procedure
    str += ControlChars.NewLine + "Line Number: " + ex.LineNumber.➡
ToString
    str += ControlChars.NewLine + "Server: " + ex.Server
    MessageBox.Show(str, "Database Exception")

Catch ex As System.Exception
    Dim str As String
    str = "Source: " + ex.Source.ToString
    str += ControlChars.NewLine + "Exception Message: " + ex.Message
    MessageBox.Show(str, "General Exception")

Finally
    If conn.State = ConnectionState.Open Then
        MessageBox.Show("Finally block Closing the connection", ➡
"Finally")
        conn.Close()
    End If
End Try
```

6. Run the program by pressing Ctrl+F5, and then click the Database Exception-1 button. You'll see the message box in Figure 16-8. Click OK to close the message box, click OK to close the next one, and then close the window.

Figure 16-8. RAISERROR *database exception message*

Observe the caption and contents of the message box. The source, message, name of the stored procedure, exact line number where the error was found, and name of the server are all displayed. You obtain this detailed information about the exception from the SqlException object.

How It Works

In the sp_DBException_1 stored procedure, you first find the number of orders in the Orders table and store the number in a variable called @ordercount:

```
select
    @ordercount = count(*)
from
    orders
```

If @ordercount is greater than ten, you raise an error using the RAISERROR statement:

```
if @ordercount > 10
    raiserror (
        'Orders Count is greater than 10 - Notify the Business Manager',
        16,
        1
    )
```

Then, in the button3_Click method, you execute the stored procedure using the ExecuteNonQuery method within a Try block:

```
    Try
            'Open connection
            conn.Open()

            'Execute stored procedure
            cmd.ExecuteNonQuery()
```

When the stored procedure executes, the RAISERROR statement raises an error, which is converted to an exception by ADO.NET. The exception is handled by

```
Catch ex As System.Data.SqlClient.SqlException
        Dim str As String
        str = "Source: " + ex.Source.ToString
        str += ControlChars.NewLine + "Number: " + ex.Number.ToString
        str += ControlChars.NewLine + "Message: " + ex.Message
        str += ControlChars.NewLine + "Class: " + ex.Class.ToString
        str += ControlChars.NewLine + "Procedure: " + ex.Procedure
        str += ControlChars.NewLine + "Line Number: " + ex.LineNumber.ToString
        str += ControlChars.NewLine + "Server: " + ex.Server
        MessageBox.Show(str, "Database Exception")
```

Try It Out: Handling a Database Exception (Part 2): Stored Procedure Error

Now you'll see what happens when a statement in a stored procedure encounters an error. You'll create a stored procedure that attempts an illegal INSERT, and then you'll extract information from the SqlException object.

1. Using SSMSE, create a stored procedure in Northwind named sp_DbException_2, as follows:

```
create procedure sp_DBException_2
as
    set nocount on
    insert into employees
    (
        employeeid,
        Firstname
    )
    values (50, 'Cinderella')
```

2. Insert the code in Listing 16-5 into the button4_Click method.

Listing 16-5. button4_Click()

```
Dim conn As SqlConnection = New SqlConnection _
  ("Data Source=.\sqlexpress;" & _
   "Integrated Security=True;" & _
   "database=northwind")

    'create command
    Dim cmd As SqlCommand = conn.CreateCommand

    'Specify that a stored procedure is to be executed
    cmd.CommandType = CommandType.StoredProcedure
    cmd.CommandText = "sp_DbException_2"
```

```vb
Try
 'Open connection
 conn.Open()

  'Execute stored procedure
  cmd.ExecuteNonQuery()

  Catch ex As System.Data.SqlClient.SqlException
  Dim str As String
  str = "Source: " + ex.Source.ToString
  str += ControlChars.NewLine + "Number: " +
  ex.Number.ToString
  str += ControlChars.NewLine + "Message: " + ex.Message
  str += ControlChars.NewLine + "Class: " + ex.Class.ToString
  str += ControlChars.NewLine + "Procedure: " + ex.Procedure
  str += ControlChars.NewLine + "Line Number: " +
  ex.LineNumber.ToString
  str += ControlChars.NewLine + "Server: " + ex.Server
  MessageBox.Show(str, "Database Exception")

    Catch ex As System.Exception
        Dim str As String
        str = "Source: " + ex.Source.ToString
        str += ControlChars.NewLine + "Exception Message: " +
        ex.Message
        MessageBox.Show(str, "General Exception")

    Finally
        If conn.State = ConnectionState.Open Then
            MessageBox.Show("Finally block Closing the
            connection", "Finally")
            conn.Close()
        End If
End Try
```

3. Run the program by pressing Ctrl+F5, and then click the Database Exception-2 button. You'll see the message box in Figure 16-9. Click OK to close the message box, click OK to close the next one, and then close the window.

Figure 16-9. *Stored procedure database exception message*

How It Works

The stored procedure tries to insert a new employee into the Employees table:

```
insert into employees
(
    employeeid,
    firstname
)
values (50, 'Cinderella')
```

However, since the EmployeeID column in the Employees table is an IDENTITY column, you can't explicitly assign a value to it.

■**Tip** Actually, you can—as the message indicates—if you use SET IDENTITY_INSERT employees OFF in the stored procedure before you attempt the INSERT. This would allow you to insert explicit EmployeeID values, but this seldom is, or should be, done.

When this SQL error occurs, the specific SqlException Catch clause traps it and displays the information. The Finally block then closes the connection.

It's possible for stored procedures to encounter several errors. You can trap and debug these using the SqlException object, as you'll see next.

Try It Out: Handling a Database Exception (Part 3): Errors Collection

The SqlException class SqlException class has an Errors collection property. Each item in the Errors collection is an object of type SqlError. When a database exception occurs, the Errors collection is populated. For the example, you'll try to establish a connection to a nonexistent database and investigate the SqlException's Errors collection.

1. Insert the code in Listing 16-6 into the button5_Click method. Note that you're intentionally misspelling the database name.

   Listing 16-6. button5_Click()

   ```
   Dim conn As SqlConnection = New SqlConnection _
               ("Data Source=.\sqlexpress;" & _
                "Integrated Security=True;" & _
                "database=northwnd")

           'create command
           Dim cmd As SqlCommand = conn.CreateCommand
   ```

```
            'Specify that a stored procedure is to be executed
            cmd.CommandType = CommandType.StoredProcedure
            cmd.CommandText = "sp_DbException_2"

            Try
                'Open connection
                conn.Open()

                'Execute stored procedure
                cmd.ExecuteNonQuery()

            Catch ex As System.Data.SqlClient.SqlException
                Dim str As String
                Dim i As Integer
                For i = 0 To ex.Errors.Count - 1 Step i + 1
                    str += ControlChars.NewLine & "Index #".ToString & _
                     i & ControlChars.NewLine & _
                    "Exception: " & ex.Errors(i).ToString() & ControlChars.New➥
Line & _
                    "Number: " & ex.Errors(i).Number.ToString() & ControlChars.➥
NewLine
                Next

                MessageBox.Show(str, "Database Exception")

            Catch ex As System.Exception
                Dim str As String
                str = "Source: " + ex.Source.ToString
                str += ControlChars.NewLine + "Exception Message: " + ex.Message
                MessageBox.Show(str, "ADO.NET Exception")

            Finally
                If conn.State = ConnectionState.Open Then
                    MessageBox.Show("Finally block Closing the connection", ➥
"Finally")
                End If
                conn.Close()
            End Try
        End Sub
```

2. Run the program by pressing Ctrl+F5, and then click the Database Exception-2 button. You'll see the message box in Figure 16-10.

Figure 16-10. *Handling multiple database errors*

Observe that two items are found in the Errors collection, and their error numbers are different.

How It Works

In the connection string, you specify a database that doesn't exist on the server; here you misspell Northwind as Northwnd:

```
Dim conn As SqlConnection = New SqlConnection _
("Data Source=.\sqlexpress;" & _
"Integrated Security=True;" & _
"database=northwnd")
```

When you try to open the connection, an exception of type SqlException is thrown and you loop through the items of the Errors collection and get each Error object using its indexer:

```
Catch ex As System.Data.SqlClient.SqlException
   Dim str As String
   Dim i As Integer
    For i = 0 To ex.Errors.Count - 1 Step i + 1
      str += ControlChars.NewLine & "Index #".ToString & i & _
      ControlChars.NewLine & _
      "Exception: " & ex.Errors(i).ToString() & ControlChars.NewLine & _
      "Number: " & ex.Errors(i).Number.ToString() & ControlChars.NewLine
    Next
         MessageBox.Show(str, "Database Exception")
```

This example shows that the SqlException object carries detailed information about every SQL error in its Errors collection.

Summary

In this chapter, you saw how to handle exceptions thrown by ADO.NET and by the SQL Server database. In particular, you learned how to handle both single and multiple database errors with the System.Data.SqlClient.SqlException class.

In the next chapter, you'll look at transactions and how to work with events.

■ ■ ■

Working with Events

Any type of application, either window based or web based, is designed and developed to help users achieve functionality and run their businesses. Users interact with applications by using input devices such as the keyboard or the mouse to provide input to these applications. Whatever users do using input devices gets translated into events that are recognized and thus cause certain actions to occur. Clicking by using a mouse is the most common task we computer users all do, and whenever we click, what should happen is recorded in the form of an event or an action.

In this chapter, we'll cover the following:

- Understanding events

- Properties of events

- Design of events

- Common events raised by controls

- Event generator and consumer

Understanding Events

An event can be defined as an action that a user can respond to or that can be handled in the form of code. Usually events are generated by a user action, such as clicking the mouse or pressing a key.

Events are associated with the controls you put in Windows Forms or web forms, and whenever you code any functionality behind a control's behavior, for example, a click of a mouse, then that associated event will be raised and the application will respond to that event.

No application can be written without events. *Event-driven applications* execute code in response to events. Each form and control exposes a predefined set of events that you can program against. If one of these events occurs and there is code in the associated event handler, that code is invoked.

Events enable a class or object to notify other classes or objects when something of interest occurs. The entire event system works in the form of the *publisher and subscriber model*. The class that sends or raises the event is known as the *publisher*, and the class that receives (or handles) that event is known as the *subscriber*.

In a typical Visual Basic Windows Forms Application or web application, you subscribe to events raised by controls such as Buttons, ListBoxes, LinkLabels, and so forth. The Visual Studio 2008 integrated development environment (IDE) allows you to browse the events that a control publishes and select the ones that you want it to handle. The IDE automatically adds an empty event handler method and the code to subscribe to the event.

Properties of Events

The events associated with any class or object work in some predefined manner. Here, we describe the properties of events and the way the publisher and subscriber works to achieve functionality:

- The publisher determines when an event is raised; the subscriber determines what action is taken in response to the event.

- An event can have multiple subscribers. A subscriber can handle multiple events from multiple publishers.

- Events that have no subscribers are never called.

- Events are typically used to signal user actions such as button clicks or menu selections in graphical user interfaces.

- When an event has multiple subscribers, the event handlers are invoked synchronously when an event is raised.

- Events can be used to synchronize threads.

- In the .NET Framework class library, events are based on the EventHandler delegate and the EventArgs base class.

Design of Events

Events happen either before their associated action occurs (*pre-events*) or after that action occurs (*post-events*). For example, when a user clicks a button in a window, a post-event is raised, allowing application-specific methods to execute. An event handler delegate is bound to the method to be executed when the system raises an event. The event handler is added to the event so that it is able to invoke its method when the event is raised. Events can have event-specific data (for example, a mouse-down event can include data about the screen cursor's location).

The event handler signature observes the following conventions:

- The return type is Void.

- The first parameter is named sender and is of type Object. This represents the object that raised the event.

- The second parameter is named e and is of type EventArgs or a derived class of EventArgs. This represents the event-specific data.

- The event takes only these two parameters.

Common Events Raised by Controls

Various controls come with Visual Studio 2008, and they are built to achieve different functionality from one another. However, the industry has identified a few events that are common among many controls, and most applications use only these types of controls.

Table 17-1 describes the common events among various controls.

Table 17-1. *Common Events*

Event Name	Description
Click	Usually occurs on left mouse click. This event can also occur with keyboard input in the situation when the control is selected and the Enter key is pressed.
DoubleClick	Occurs when the left mouse button is clicked twice rapidly.
KeyDown	Occurs when a key is pressed and a control has the focus.
KeyPress	Occurs when a key is pressed and a control has the focus.
KeyUp	Occurs when a key is released and a control has the focus.
MouseClick	Occurs only when a control is being clicked by the mouse.
MouseDoubleClick	Occurs when a control gets double-clicked by the mouse.
MouseDown	Occurs when the mouse pointer is located over a control and the mouse button is being clicked.
MouseUp	Occurs when a mouse button is released over a control.
MouseEnter	Occurs when the mouse pointer enters a control.
MouseHover	Occurs when the mouse pointer is positioned over a control.
MouseLeave	Occurs when the mouse pointer rests on a control.
MouseMove	Occurs when the mouse rotates or moves over a control.
MouseWheel	Occurs when the user revolves the mouse wheel and a control has the focus.

Event Generator and Consumer

Another way of thinking of an event is as a mechanism that notifies the Windows operating system or the .NET Framework that something has happened in the application, and so the functionality takes place once it receives a response back from the .NET Framework or Windows platform.

The application, which has the controls with functionality associated with them in the form of events, is known as the *consumer*, and the .NET Framework or Windows platform, which receives the request for the event to take place, is known as the *event generator*.

As you know, controls come with various types of events to serve particular functionality. The code segment known as the event handler notifies the application once an event has occurred so the proper actions can be implemented behind that event handler.

Try It Out: Creating an Event Handler

In this exercise, you will see how to add an event handler for a control that you have on a Windows Form.

1. Open a new Windows Forms Application project, and rename the solution and project as Chapter17. Rename Form1.vb to Events.vb, and also modify the Text property of the form to Events.

2. Open the Toolbox and drag a Button control over to the form. Select the Button control, navigate to the Properties window, and for the control's Text property type **Click Me**. Then click the lightning bolt button located on the toolbar shown in the Properties window, and you will see the entire list of events that the Button control supports; event handlers could be written for all these events (see Figure 17-1). Also notice the tooltip titled "Events" under the lightning bolt button.

3. By default, the Click event comes preselected, and the text area beside the event is blank. Double-click in this blank area, and you will see that an event handler named button1_Click has been created, as shown in Figure 17-2.

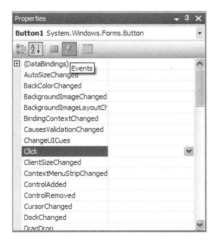

Figure 17-1. *The events list in Designer mode*

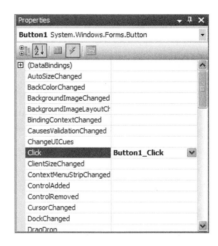

Figure 17-2. *Event handler creation in Designer mode*

4. Since the button1_Click event handler has been generated, its template will be available in Code view. Switch to Code view of the Windows Form, named Events.cs, to view the event handler and to prepare to write the functionality for the Click event (see Figure 17-3).

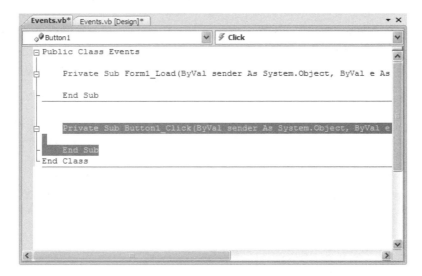

Figure 17-3. *Event handler in Code view*

5. Inside the button1_Click() event handler, write the following line of code:

```
MessageBox.Show("I have been clicked")
```

6. Build and run the application, click button1, and you will see a dialog box appear due to the event that is raised when the button is clicked.

How It Works

The most common event that a button handles, which also happens to be the default, is the Click event. In this example, you write code to flash a message box whenever a user clicks the button on the form:

```
MessageBox.Show("I have been clicked")
```

Try It Out: Working with Mouse Movement Events

In this exercise, you will see the events that are associated with movements of the mouse. To try them, follow these steps:

1. Navigate to Solution Explorer and open the Events form in Design view.

2. Drag a TextBox control onto the Windows Form just under the button1 control. Select the TextBox control, and you will see an arrow on the top-right border of the control; this arrow is called a *Smart Tag*.

■**Note** The Smart Tag feature is available with some controls. The main purpose of this feature is to provide a generalized way for developers to specify a set of actions for a control at design time. Clicking a component's Smart Tag icon allows you to select from a list of available actions offered from the Smart Tag panel.

---

3. Click the Smart Tag, and a small panel will appear showing a check box for the Multi-Line property to be enabled (see Figure 17-4).

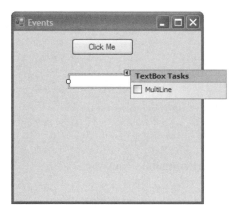

Figure 17-4. *Smart Tag for the TextBox control*

4. Click the MultiLine check box shown in the Smart Tag pop-up, and you will see the height of the TextBox increase, as shown in Figure 17-5.

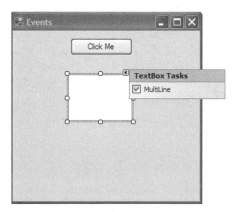

Figure 17-5. *Setting the MultiLine property using the Smart Tag of the TextBox control*

5. Now click outside the TextBox on the form itself to retain the new size the MultiLine property has given to the TextBox by default. If you want, you can also use the handles (the small three rectangles on each border line) to resize the TextBox control.

■**Tip** The MultiLine property of a TextBox can also be set without using the Smart Tag feature. You can directly set the MultiLine property to True, which is set to False by default.

6. Drag a Label control from the Toolbox to below the TextBox and set its AutoSize property to False. Also, set the Label's Font Size property to 12 and TextAlign property to MiddleCenter. Now your Events form will look like the one shown in Figure 17-6.

Figure 17-6. *The Events Windows Form with controls*

7. Select the TextBox, open the Properties window, and click the Events button. In the events list, double-click in the text area of the MouseEnter and MouseLeave events. This will simply create the event handlers for these two mouse movement events.

8. Switch to Code view and add the following code to the MouseEnter and MouseLeave event handlers:

```
Private Sub TextBox1_MouseEnter(ByVal sender As System.Object, _
 ByVal e As System.EventArgs) Handles TextBox1.MouseEnter
        Label1.Text = "Mouse Enters into the TextBox"
End Sub

Private Sub TextBox1_MouseLeave(ByVal sender As System.Object, _
 ByVal e As System.EventArgs) Handles TextBox1.MouseLeave
        Label1.Text = "Mouse Leaves the TextBox"
End Sub
```

9. Go to the Build menu and click Build Solution; you should receive a message indicating a successful build.

10. Press F5 to run the application. You will now see a message in the Label control depending on the action you perform with your mouse. Move the mouse pointer over the text box, and you'll see the message shown in Figure 17-7.

Figure 17-7. *Demonstrating the* MouseEnter *event*

11. Now move the pointer outside of the text box, and you will see the message shown in the Label control change (see Figure 17-8).

Figure 17-8. *Demonstrating the* MouseLeave *event*

How It Works

The MouseEnter event will occur when you take the mouse pointer into the text box having the focus, and this will be recognized by the MouseEnter event handler, resulting in the appropriate message being displayed in the Label control.

In the same way, when you move the mouse pointer away from the focus of the text box, the MouseLeave event gets into the action, and again the appropriate message is displayed in the Label control.

Try It Out: Working with the Keyboard's KeyDown and KeyUp Events

In this exercise, you will work with the KeyDown and KeyUp events, which are associated with controls that can receive input from the keyboard whenever a user presses or releases the Alt, Ctrl, or Shift key. To try these events, follow these steps:

1. Navigate to Solution Explorer and open the Events.vb form in Design view.

2. Select the TextBox control, open the Properties window, and click the Events button. In the events list, double-click in the text area of KeyDown event. This will simply create an event handler for the KeyDown event.

3. Switch to Code view and add the following code to the KeyDown event handler:

```
Private Sub TextBox1_KeyDown(ByVal sender As System.Object, _
ByVal e As System.Windows.Forms.KeyEventArgs) Handles TextBox1.KeyDown
        If e.Alt = True Then
            Label1.Text = "The Alt key has been pressed"
        Else
            If e.Control = True Then
                Label1.Text = "The Ctrl key has been pressed"
            Else
                If e.Shift = True Then
                    Label1.Text = "The Shift key has been pressed"
                End If
            End If
        End If
    End Sub
```

4. Switch back to Design view again. Select the TextBox control, open the Properties window, and click the Events button. In the events list, double-click in the text area of the KeyUp event. This will simply create an event handler for the keyboard's KeyUp event.

5. Switch to Code view and add the following code to the KeyUp event handler:

```
Private Sub TextBox1_KeyUp(ByVal sender As System.Object, _
ByVal e As System.Windows.Forms.KeyEventArgs) Handles TextBox1.KeyUp
    If e.Alt = False Or e.Control = False Or e.Shift = False Then
        Label1.Text = "The Key has been released"
    End If
End Sub
```

6. Go to the Build menu and click Build Solution; you should see a message indicating a successful build.

7. Press F5 to run the application. Move the mouse pointer over the text box, click once, and then press and release the Alt, Ctrl, or Shift key; you will see a message displayed in the Label control indicating which key you pressed.

How It Works

With the KeyDown event, you recognize which key is pressed at a particular point in time. The conditional if statement helps you trace which key has been pressed and will display the message in the Label control:

```
        If e.Alt = True Then
            Label1.Text = "The Alt key has been pressed"
        Else

    If e.Control = True Then
                Label1.Text = "The Ctrl key has been pressed"
            Else

                If e.Shift = True Then
                    Label1.Text = "The Shift key has been pressed"
                End If
```

The KeyUp event recognizes whenever the key that was pressed has been released, and as a result displays the appropriate message in the Label control:

```
If e.Alt = False Or e.Control = False Or e.Shift = False Then
        Label1.Text = "The Key has been released"
End If
```

Try It Out: Working with the Keyboard's KeyPress Event

In this exercise, you will work with the KeyPress event. The KeyPress event gets into the action whenever the associated control receives input in the form of a keypress; if that key has an ASCII value, the KeyPress event is raised. To try this event, follow these steps:

1. Navigate to Solution Explorer and open the Events.vb form in Design view.

2. Select the TextBox control, open the Properties window, and click the Events button. In the events list, double-click in the text area of the KeyPress event. This will simply create an event handler for the KeyPress event.

3. Switch to Code view and add the following code to the KeyPress event handler:

```
Private Sub TextBox1_KeyPress(ByVal sender As System.Object, ByVal e As _
                        System.Windows.Forms.KeyPressEventArgs) _
                        Handles TextBox1.KeyPress
        If Char.IsDigit(e.KeyChar) = True Then
            Label1.Text = "You have pressed a Numeric key"
        Else
            If Char.IsLetter(e.KeyChar) = True Then
                Label1.Text = "You have pressed a Letter key"
            End If
        End If
    End Sub
```

4. Now go to the Build menu and click Build Solution; you should see a message indicating a successful build.

5. Press F5 to run the application. Click inside the text box and then press a number or letter key on the keyboard. You will see a message is displayed in the Label control indicating which type of key you pressed.

How It Works

With the KeyPress event, you recognize whether a numeric or alphabetic key has been pressed at a particular point in time. The conditional if statement helps you trace which key has been pressed and displays the appropriate message in the Label control:

```
If Char.IsDigit(e.KeyChar) = True Then
        Label1.Text = "You have pressed a Numeric key"
    Else
        If Char.IsLetter(e.KeyChar) = True Then
            Label1.Text = "You have pressed a Letter key"
        End If
    End If
```

Summary

In this chapter, you saw how to handle events with respect to the mouse and keyboard. In particular, you learned how events are handled when a mouse enters and leaves a control. You also learned how to trap an event whenever an Alt, Ctrl, or Shift key is pressed.

In the next chapter, you'll look at how to work with text and binary data.

CHAPTER 18

■■■

Working with Text and Binary Data

Some kinds of data have special formats, are very large, or vary greatly in size. Here, we'll show you techniques for working with text and binary data.

In this chapter, we'll cover the following:

- Understanding SQL Server text and binary data types

- Storing images in a database

- Retrieving images from a database

- Working with text data

We'll also present the T-SQL for creating tables in the tempdb database, which is intended to hold any temporary table. We'll start by covering what data types support these kinds of data.

Understanding SQL Server Text and Binary Data Types

SQL Server provides the types CHAR, NCHAR, VARCHAR, NVARCHAR, BINARY, and VARBINARY for working with reasonably small text and binary data. You can use these with text (character) data up to a maximum of 8,000 bytes (4,000 bytes for Unicode data, NCHAR, and NVARCHAR, which use 2 bytes per character).

For larger data, which SQL Server 2005 calls *large-value data types*, you should use the VARCHAR(MAX), NVARCHAR(MAX), and VARBINARY(MAX) data types. VARCHAR(MAX) is for non-Unicode text, NVARCHAR(MAX) is for Unicode text, and VARBINARY(MAX) is for images and other binary data.

■**Warning** In SQL Server 2000, large data was stored using NTEXT, TEXT, and IMAGE data types. These data types are deprecated and will likely be removed in the future. If you work with legacy applications, you should consider converting NTEXT, TEXT, and IMAGE to NVARCHAR(MAX), VARCHAR(MAX), and VARBINARY(MAX), respectively. However, the System.Data.SqlDbType enumeration does not yet include members for these data types, so we use VARCHAR(MAX) and VARBINARY(MAX) for column data types, but Text and Image when specifying data types for command parameters.

An alternative to using these data types is to not store the data itself in the database but instead define a column containing a path that points to where the data is actually stored. This can be more efficient for accessing large amounts of data, and it can save resources on the database server by transferring the demand to a file server. It does require more complicated coordination and has the potential for database and data files to get out of sync. We won't use this technique in this chapter.

■**Tip** Since SSE databases cannot exceed 4GB, this technique may be your only alternative for very large text and image data.

Within a Visual Basic program, binary data types map to an array of bytes (byte[ ]), and character data types map to strings or character arrays (char[ ]).

■**Note** DB2, MySQL, Oracle, and the SQL standard call such data types *large objects* (LOBs); specifically, they're binary large objects (BLOBs) and character large objects (CLOBs). But, as with many database terms, whether BLOB was originally an acronym for anything is debatable. Needless to say, it's always implied a data type that can handle large amounts of (amorphous) data, and SQL Server documentation uses BLOB as a generic term for large data and data types.

Storing Images in a Database

Let's start by creating a database table for storing images and then loading some images into it. We'll use small images but use VARBINARY(MAX) to store them. In the examples, we'll demonstrate using images in C:\Documents and Settings\Toshiba User\My Documents\Visual Studio 2008\Projects\Chapter18\Image; you can use the path of the location where you have some images in your PC.

Try It Out: Loading Image Binary Data from Files

In this example, you'll write a program that creates a database table and then stores images in it.

1. Create a new Console Application project named Chapter18. When Solution Explorer opens, save the solution.

2. Rename the Chapter18 project to LoadImages. Rename `Module1.vb` to `LoadImages.vb`, and replace its code with the code in Listing 18-1.

Listing 18-1. `LoadImages.vb`

```vb
Imports System
Imports System.Data
Imports System.Data.SqlClient
Imports System.IO
Namespace LoadImages
    Friend Class LoadImages

        Private imageFileLocation As String = _
        "C:\Documents and Settings\Toshiba User" & _
        "\My Documents\Visual Studio 2008\Projects\Chapter18\Image\"
        Private imageFilePrefix As String = "painting-almirah"
        Private numberImageFiles As Integer = 1
        Private imageFileType As String = ".jpg"
        Private maxImageSize As Integer = 10000
        Private conn As SqlConnection = Nothing
        Private cmd As SqlCommand = Nothing
        Shared Sub Main()
            Dim loader As New LoadImages()

            Try
                ' Open connection
                loader.OpenConnection()
                ' Create command
                loader.CreateCommand()
                ' Create table
                loader.CreateImageTable()
                ' Prepare insert
                loader.PrepareInsertImages()
                ' Insert images
                Dim i As Integer
                For i = 1 To loader.numberImageFiles
                    loader.ExecuteInsertImages(i)
                Next i
```

```
            Catch ex As Exception
                Console.WriteLine(ex.ToString())
            Finally
                loader.CloseConnection()
                Console.WriteLine("Press any key to continue......")
                Console.ReadLine()
            End Try
        End Sub
        Private Sub OpenConnection()
            ' Create connection
            conn = New SqlConnection("Server=.\sqlexpress;" & _
                    "Integrated Security=True;Database=tempdb")
            ' Open connection
            conn.Open()
        End Sub
        Private Sub CloseConnection()
            ' close connection
            conn.Close()
            Console.WriteLine("Connection Closed.")
        End Sub
        Private Sub CreateCommand()
            cmd = New SqlCommand()
            cmd.Connection = conn
        End Sub
        Private Sub ExecuteCommand(ByVal cmdText As String)
            Dim cmdResult As Integer
            cmd.CommandText = cmdText
            Console.WriteLine("Executing command:")
            Console.WriteLine(cmd.CommandText)
            cmdResult = cmd.ExecuteNonQuery()
        End Sub

        Private Sub CreateImageTable()
            ExecuteCommand("CREATE Table imagetable" & _
                        "(imagefile nvarchar(20)," & _
                        "imagedata varbinary(max))")
        End Sub
        Private Sub PrepareInsertImages()
            cmd.CommandText = "" & ControlChars.CrLf & _
            "insert into imagetable" & ControlChars.CrLf & _
            "values (@imagefile, @imagedata)" & ControlChars.CrLf _
            ""
            cmd.Parameters.Add("@imagefile", SqlDbType.NVarChar, 20)
            cmd.Parameters.Add("@imagedata", SqlDbType.Image, 1000000)
```

```vb
            cmd.Prepare()
        End Sub

        Private Sub ExecuteInsertImages(ByVal _
        imageFileNumber As Integer)
            Dim imageFileName As String = Nothing
            Dim imageImageData() As Byte = Nothing

            imageFileName = imageFilePrefix + _
            imageFileNumber.ToString() _
            & imageFileType
            imageImageData = LoadImageFile _
            (imageFileName, imageFileLocation, maxImageSize)

            cmd.Parameters("@imagefile").Value = imageFileName
            cmd.Parameters("@imagedata").Value = imageImageData

            ExecuteCommand(cmd.CommandText)
            Console.WriteLine(ControlChars.NewLine)
        End Sub
        Private Function LoadImageFile(ByVal fileName As String, _
        ByVal fileLocation As String, ByVal maxImageSize _
        As Integer) As Byte()
            Dim imagebytes() As Byte = Nothing
            Dim fullpath As String = fileLocation & fileName
            Console.WriteLine(ControlChars.NewLine)
            Console.WriteLine("Loading File:")
            Console.WriteLine(fullpath)
            Dim fs As New FileStream(fullpath, _
            FileMode.Open, FileAccess.Read)
            Dim br As New BinaryReader(fs)
            imagebytes = br.ReadBytes(maxImageSize)

            Console.WriteLine("Imagebytes has length {0} bytes.", _
                            imagebytes.GetLength(0))
            Console.WriteLine(ControlChars.NewLine)
            Return imagebytes
        End Function
    End Class
End Namespace
```

■**Note** If you want to run the LoadImages program again, you must ensure that you drop/delete the imagetable from the SQL Server tempdb database; it is already present and your program will try to re-create it, which means you will receive an exception.

3. Run the program by pressing Ctrl+F5. You should see output similar to that in Figure 18-1. It shows the information for loading an image we have on our PC at the specified location, the operations performed, and the size of each of the image.

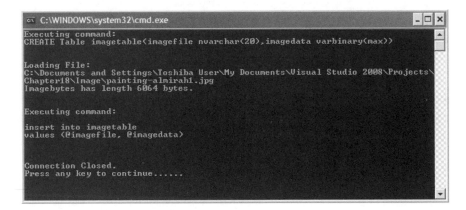

Figure 18-1. *Loading image data*

4. To see the image you have inserted into the database, open SQL Server Management Studio Express (SSMSE) and run a SELECT query on the image table you have created in the tempdb database (see Figure 18-2).

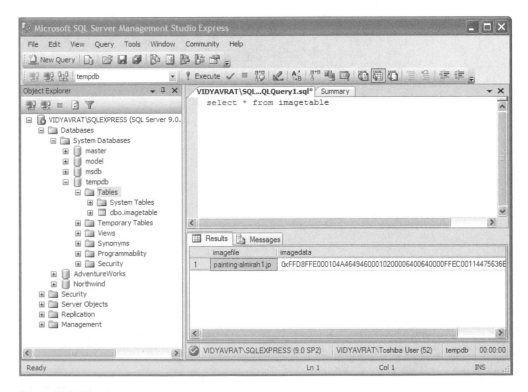

Figure 18-2. *Viewing image data*

How It Works

In the Main method, you do three major things. You call an instance method to create a table to hold images:

```
' Create table
loader.CreateImageTable()
```

You call an instance method to prepare a command (yes, you finally prepare a command, since you expect to run it multiple times) to insert images:

```
' Prepare insert
loader.PrepareInsertImages()
```

You then loop through the image files and insert them:

```
' Insert images
Dim i As Integer
For i = 1 To loader.numberImageFiles
loader.ExecuteInsertImages(i)
Next i
```

Note that you connect to tempdb, the temporary database that's re-created when SQL Server starts:

```
' Create connection
conn = New SqlConnection("Server=.\sqlexpress;" & _
"Integrated Security=True;Database=tempdb")
' Open connection
conn.Open()
```

The tables in this database are temporary; that is, they're always deleted when SQL Server stops. This is ideal for these examples and many other situations, but don't use tempdb for any data that needs to persist permanently.

When you create the table, a simple one containing the image file name and the image, you use the VARBINARY(MAX) data type for the imagedata column:

```
Private Sub CreateImageTable()
ExecuteCommand("CREATE Table imagetable" & _
"(imagefile nvarchar(20)," & _
"imagedata varbinary(max))")
End Sub
```

But when you configure the INSERT command, you use the Image member of the SqlDbType enumeration, since there is no member for the VARBINARY(MAX) data type. You specify lengths for both variable-length data types, because you can't prepare a command unless you do.

```
Private Sub PrepareInsertImages()
cmd.CommandText = "" & ControlChars.CrLf & _
"insert into imagetable" & ControlChars.CrLf & _
"values (@imagefile, @imagedata)" & ControlChars.CrLf
```

```
cmd.Parameters.Add("@imagefile", _
SqlDbType.NVarChar, 20)
cmd.Parameters.Add("@imagedata", _
SqlDbType.Image, 1000000)

cmd.Prepare()
End Sub
```

The ExecuteInsertImages method accepts an integer to use as a suffix for the image file name, calls LoadImageFile to get a byte array containing the image, assigns the file name and image to their corresponding command parameters, and then executes the command to insert the image:

```
Private Sub ExecuteInsertImages(ByVal _
        imageFileNumber As Integer)
            Dim imageFileName As String = Nothing
            Dim imageImageData() As Byte = Nothing

            imageFileName = imageFilePrefix + _
            imageFileNumber.ToString() _
            & imageFileType
            imageImageData = LoadImageFile _
            (imageFileName, imageFileLocation, maxImageSize)

            cmd.Parameters("@imagefile").Value = imageFileName
            cmd.Parameters("@imagedata").Value = imageImageData

            ExecuteCommand(cmd.CommandText)
            Console.WriteLine(ControlChars.NewLine)
    End Sub
```

The LoadImageFile function reads the image file, displays the file name and number of bytes in the file, and returns the image as a byte array:

```
Private Function LoadImageFile(ByVal fileName As String, _
        ByVal fileLocation As String, ByVal maxImageSize _
        As Integer) As Byte()
            Dim imagebytes() As Byte = Nothing
            Dim fullpath As String = fileLocation & fileName
            Console.WriteLine(ControlChars.NewLine)
            Console.WriteLine("Loading File:")
            Console.WriteLine(fullpath)
            Dim fs As New FileStream(fullpath, _
            FileMode.Open, FileAccess.Read)
            Dim br As New BinaryReader(fs)
            imagebytes = br.ReadBytes(maxImageSize)
```

```
            Console.WriteLine("Imagebytes has length {0} bytes.", _
                             imagebytes.GetLength(0))
            Console.WriteLine(ControlChars.NewLine)
            Return imagebytes
End Function
```

Rerunning the Program

Since the program always creates the imagetable table, you must cycle (stop and restart) SSE before rerunning the program, to remove the table by re-creating an empty tempdb database. You'll see how to avoid this problem in "Working with Text Data" later in this chapter.

Retrieving Images from a Database

Now that you've stored some images, you'll see how to retrieve and display them with a Windows application.

Try It Out: Displaying Stored Images

To display your stored images, follow these steps:

1. Add a Windows Forms Application project named DisplayImages to your solution. Rename Form1.vb to DisplayImages.vb.

2. Add a text box, a button, and a picture box to the form and set the button's Text property to Show Image and the form's Text property to Display Images, as in Figure 18-3.

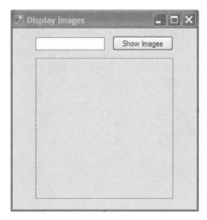

Figure 18-3. *Design view of Display Images form*

3. Add a new class named Images to this Windows Form project. Replace the code in Images.vb with the code in Listing 18-2.

Listing 18-2. `Images.vb`

```vb
Imports Microsoft.VisualBasic
Imports System
Imports System.Data
Imports System.Data.SqlClient
Imports System.Drawing
Imports System.IO


Namespace DisplayImage
    Public Class Images
        Private imageFilename As String = Nothing
        Private imageBytes() As Byte = Nothing

        Private imageConnection As SqlConnection = Nothing
        Private imageCommand As SqlCommand = Nothing
        Private imageReader As SqlDataReader = Nothing

        ' Constructor
        Public Sub New()
            imageConnection = New SqlConnection("Server=.\sqlexpress;" & _
            "Integrated Security=True;Database=tempdb")
            imageCommand = New SqlCommand("" & ControlChars.CrLf & _
            "select" & ControlChars.CrLf & "imagefile," & _
            ControlChars.CrLf & "imagedata" & ControlChars.CrLf & _
            "from" & ControlChars.CrLf & "imagetable" & _
            ControlChars.CrLf & "", imageConnection)

            ' Open connection and create data reader
            imageConnection.Open()
            imageReader = imageCommand.ExecuteReader()
        End Sub

        Public Function GetImage() As Bitmap
            Dim ms As New MemoryStream(imageBytes)
            Dim bmap As New Bitmap(ms)

            Return bmap
        End Function

        Public Function GetFilename() As String
            Return imageFilename
        End Function
```

```
        Public Function GetRow() As Boolean
            If imageReader.Read() Then
                imageFilename = CStr(imageReader.GetValue(0))
                imageBytes = CType(imageReader.GetValue(1), Byte())

                Return True
            Else
                Return False
            End If
        End Function

        Public Sub EndImages()
            ' Close the reader and the connection.
            imageReader.Close()
            imageConnection.Close()
        End Sub
    End Class
End Namespace
```

4. Insert the code in Listing 18-3 into DisplayImages.vb before the call to
   InitializeComponent(). You can access DisplayImages.vb by right-clicking
   DisplayImages.vb and selecting View Code, which will take you to Code view.

Listing 18-3. *Initializing Image Display in the* DisplayImages *class*

```
images = New DisplayImage.Images()

        If images.GetRow() Then
            Me.TextBox1.Text = images.GetFilename()
            Me.PictureBox1.Image = CType(images.GetImage(), Image)
        Else
            Me.TextBox1.Text = "DONE"
            Me.PictureBox1.Image = Nothing
        End If
```

5. Insert the code in Listing 18-3 into the button1_Click event handler. You can access the
   button1_click event handler by navigating to Design view of the DisplayImages form
   and double-clicking the Button control.

6. Insert the highlighted line that follows into the Dispose method (above components.
   Dispose()) of DisplayImages in DisplayImages.Designer.vb:

```
            images.EndImages();
            If disposing AndAlso components IsNot Nothing Then
              components.Dispose()
            End If
              MyBase.Dispose(disposing)
```

7. Make DisplayImages the startup project and run it by pressing Ctrl+F5. You should see the output shown in Figure 18-4.

Figure 18-4. *Displaying images*

How It Works

You declare a type, Images, to access the database and provide methods for the form components to easily get and display images. In its constructor, you connect to the database and create a data reader to handle the result set of a query that retrieves all the images you stored earlier:

```
' Constructor
Public Sub New()
    imageConnection = New SqlConnection("Server=.\sqlexpress;" & _
    "Integrated Security=True;Database=tempdb")
    imageCommand = New SqlCommand("" & ControlChars.CrLf & _
    "select" & ControlChars.CrLf & "imagefile," & _
    ControlChars.CrLf & "imagedata" & ControlChars.CrLf & _
    "from" & ControlChars.CrLf & "imagetable" & _
    ControlChars.CrLf & "", imageConnection)

    ' Open connection and create data reader
    imageConnection.Open()
    imageReader = imageCommand.ExecuteReader()
End Sub
```

When the form is initialized, the new code creates an instance of Images, looks for an image with GetRow(), and, if it finds one, assigns the file name and image to the text box and picture box with the GetFilename and GetImage methods, respectively:

```
images = New DisplayImage.Images()

        If images.GetRow() Then
            Me.TextBox1.Text = images.GetFilename()
            Me.PictureBox1.Image = CType(images.GetImage(), Image)
        Else
            Me.TextBox1.Text = "DONE"
            Me.PictureBox1.Image = Nothing
End If
```

You call the endImages method when the form terminates to close the connection. (Were you to use a dataset instead of a data reader, you could close the connection in the Images instance immediately after the images are retrieved, which would be a good exercise for you to attempt.)

```
Protected Overrides Sub Dispose(ByVal disposing As Boolean)
        images.EndImages()
        If disposing AndAlso components IsNot Nothing Then
            components.Dispose()
        End If
        MyBase.Dispose(disposing)
End Sub
```

The image is returned from the database as an array of bytes. The PictureBox control Image property can be a Bitmap, Icon, or Metafile (all derived classes of Image). Bitmap supports a variety of formats, including BMP, GIF, and JPG. The GetImage function, shown here, returns a Bitmap object:

```
Public Function GetImage() As Bitmap
Dim ms As New MemoryStream(imageBytes)
Dim bmap As New Bitmap(ms)

Return bmap
End Function
```

Bitmap's constructor doesn't accept a byte array, but it will accept a MemoryStream (which is effectively an in-memory representation of a file), and MemoryStream has a constructor that accepts a byte array. So, you create a memory stream from the byte array and then create a bitmap from the memory stream.

Working with Text Data

Handling text is similar to handling images except for the data type used for the database column.

Try It Out: Loading Text Data from a File

To load text data from a file, follow these steps:

1. Add a Visual Basic Console Application project named LoadText to the solution.

2. Rename Module1.vb to LoadText.vb, and replace the code with that in Listing 18-4.

Listing 18-4. LoadText.vb

```vbnet
Imports System
Imports System.Data
Imports System.Data.SqlClient
Imports System.Data.SqlTypes
Imports System.IO
Namespace LoadText
    Friend Class LoadText

        Private Shared fileName As String = "C:\Documents and Settings" & _
        "\Toshiba User\My Documents\Visual Studio 2008" & _
        "\Projects\Chapter18\LoadText\LoadText.vb"

        Private conn As SqlConnection = Nothing
        Private cmd As SqlCommand = Nothing

        Shared Sub Main()
            Dim loader As New LoadText()
            Try
                ' Get text file
                loader.GetTextFile(fileName)
                ' Open connection
                loader.OpenConnection()
                ' Create command
                loader.CreateCommand()
                ' Create table
                loader.CreateTextTable()
                ' Prepare insert command
                loader.PrepareInsertTextFile()
                ' Load text file
                loader.ExecuteInsertTextFile(fileName)
                Console.WriteLine("Loaded {0} into texttable.", fileName)
            Catch ex As SqlException
                Console.WriteLine(ex.ToString())
```

```vb
            Finally
                loader.CloseConnection()
                Console.WriteLine("Press any key to continue........")
                Console.ReadLine()
            End Try
        End Sub

    Private Sub CreateTextTable()
            ExecuteCommand("IF EXISTS" & ControlChars.CrLf & _
            "(" & ControlChars.CrLf & "SELECT" & ControlChars.CrLf & _
            "*" & ControlChars.CrLf & "FROM" & ControlChars.CrLf & _
            "INFORMATION_SCHEMA.TABLES" & ControlChars.CrLf & _
            "WHERE" & ControlChars.CrLf & "TABLE_NAME='TEXTTABLE'" & _
            ControlChars.CrLf & ")" & ControlChars.CrLf & _
            "DROP TABLE TEXTTABLE")

            ExecuteCommand("CREATE TABLE TEXTTABLE" & _
            ControlChars.CrLf & "(" & ControlChars.CrLf & _
            "textfile varchar(255)," & ControlChars.CrLf & _
            "textdata varchar(max))" & ControlChars.CrLf)
        End Sub

        Private Sub OpenConnection()
            ' Create connection
            conn = New SqlConnection("Server=.\sqlexpress;" & _
                    "Integrated Security=True;Database=tempdb")
            ' Open connection
            conn.Open()
        End Sub

        Private Sub CloseConnection()
            ' Close connection
            conn.Close()
        End Sub


        Private Sub CreateCommand()
            cmd = New SqlCommand()
            cmd.Connection = conn
        End Sub
```

```vbnet
    Private Sub ExecuteCommand(ByVal commandText As String)
            Dim commandResult As Integer
            cmd.CommandText = commandText
            Console.WriteLine("Executing command:")
            Console.WriteLine(cmd.CommandText)
            commandResult = cmd.ExecuteNonQuery()
            Console.WriteLine("ExecuteNonQuery returns {0}.", commandResult)
        End Sub

  Private Sub PrepareInsertTextFile()
            cmd.CommandText = "" & ControlChars.CrLf & _
            "insert into texttable" & ControlChars.CrLf & _
            "values (@textfile, @textdata)" & ControlChars.CrLf

            cmd.Parameters.Add("@textfile", SqlDbType.NVarChar, 30)
            cmd.Parameters.Add("@textdata", SqlDbType.Text, 1000000)
        End Sub

        Private Sub ExecuteInsertTextFile(ByVal textFile As String)
            Dim textData As String = GetTextFile(textFile)
            cmd.Parameters("@textfile").Value = textFile
            cmd.Parameters("@textdata").Value = textData
            ExecuteCommand(cmd.CommandText)
        End Sub

        Private Function GetTextFile(ByVal textFile As String) As String
            Dim textBytes As String = Nothing
            Console.WriteLine("Loading File: " & textFile)

            Dim fs As New FileStream(textFile, FileMode.Open, FileAccess.Read)
            Dim sr As New StreamReader(fs)
            textBytes = sr.ReadToEnd()

            Console.WriteLine("TextBytes has length {0} bytes.", ➥
    textBytes.Length)

            Return textBytes
        End Function
    End Class
End Namespace
```

3. Make LoadText the startup project, and run it by pressing Ctrl+F5. You should see the results in Figure 18-5.

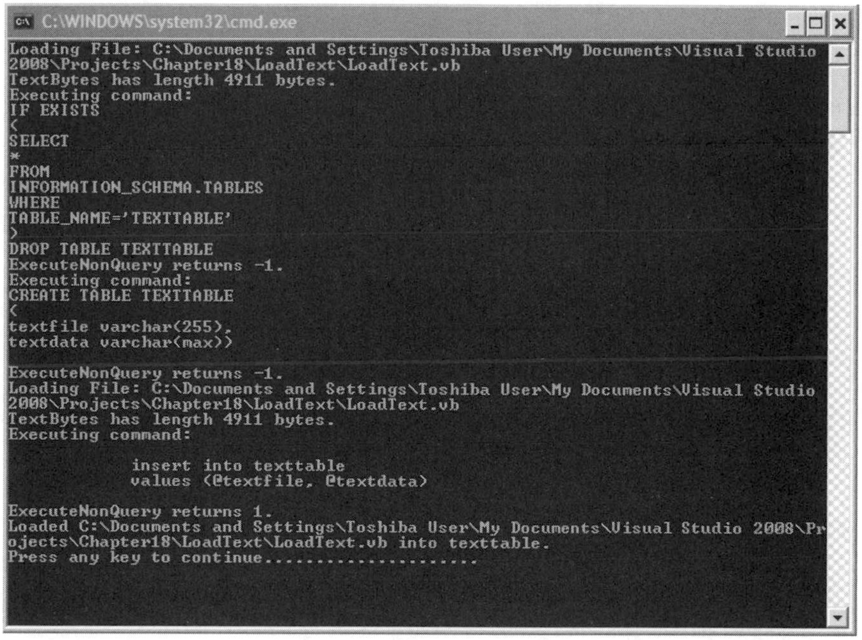

Figure 18-5. *Loading a text file into a table*

How It Works

You simply load the source code for the LoadText program:

```
Private Shared fileName As String = "C:\Documents and Settings" & _
"\Toshiba User\My Documents\Visual Studio 2008" & _
        "\Projects\Chapter18\LoadText\LoadText.vb"
```

into a table:

```
cmd.CommandText = "" & ControlChars.CrLf & _
"insert into texttable" & ControlChars.CrLf & _
"values (@textfile, @textdata)" & ControlChars.CrLf

cmd.Parameters.Add("@textfile", SqlDbType.NVarChar, 30)
'the image gets stored in the form of of an Image string.
' figure 1000000 specifies the bytes for the amount to
' specify the size of the Image string.

   cmd.Parameters.Add("@textdata", SqlDbType.Text, 1000000)
```

that you created in the temporary database:

```
ExecuteCommand("IF EXISTS" & ControlChars.CrLf & _
"(" & ControlChars.CrLf & "SELECT" & ControlChars.CrLf & _
"*" & ControlChars.CrLf & "FROM" & ControlChars.CrLf & _
"INFORMATION_SCHEMA.TABLES" & ControlChars.CrLf & _
"WHERE" & ControlChars.CrLf & "TABLE_NAME='TEXTTABLE'" & _
ControlChars.CrLf & ")" & ControlChars.CrLf & _
"DROP TABLE TEXTTABLE")

ExecuteCommand("CREATE TABLE TEXTTABLE" & _
ControlChars.CrLf & "(" & ControlChars.CrLf & _
"textfile varchar(255)," & ControlChars.CrLf & _
"textdata varchar(max))" & ControlChars.CrLf)
```

Note that you first check to see whether the table exists. If it does, you drop it so you can re-create it.

■**Note** The `information_schema.tables` *view* (a named query) is compatible with the SQL standard `INFORMATION_SCHEMA` view of the same name. It limits the tables you can see to the ones you can access. Microsoft recommends you use the new *catalog views* to get database metadata in SQL Server 2005, and SQL Server itself uses them internally. The catalog view for this query would be `sys.tables`, and the column name would be `name`. We've used the `INFORMATION SCHEMA` view here because you may still see it often.

Instead of the `BinaryReader` you use for images, `GetTextFile` uses a `StreamReader` (derived from `System.IO.TextReader`) to read the contents of the file into a `string`:

```
Private Function GetTextFile(ByVal textFile As String) As String
        Dim textBytes As String = Nothing
        Console.WriteLine("Loading File: " & textFile)

        Dim fs As New FileStream(textFile, FileMode.Open, FileAccess.Read)
        Dim sr As New StreamReader(fs)
        textBytes = sr.ReadToEnd()

        Console.WriteLine("TextBytes has length {0} bytes.", textBytes.Length)

        Return textBytes
    End Function
```

Otherwise, the processing logic is basically the same as you've seen many times throughout the book: open a connection, access a database, and then close the connection.

Now let's retrieve the text you just stored.

Retrieving Data from Text Columns

Retrieving data from text columns is just like retrieving it from the smaller character data types. You'll now write a simple console program to see how this works.

Try It Out: Retrieving Text Data

To retrieve data from text columns, follow these steps:

1. Add a Visual Basic Console Application project named RetrieveText to the solution.

2. Rename Module1.vb to RetrieveText.vb, and replace the code with that in Listing 18-5.

Listing 18-5. RetrieveText.vb

```vb
Imports Microsoft.VisualBasic
Imports System
Imports System.Data
Imports System.Data.SqlClient

Namespace RetrieveText
    Public Class RetrieveText
        Private textFile As String = Nothing
        Private textChars() As Char = Nothing
        Private conn As SqlConnection = Nothing
        Private cmd As SqlCommand = Nothing
        Private dr As SqlDataReader = Nothing

        Public Sub New()
            ' Create connection
            conn = New SqlConnection("Server=.\sqlexpress;" & _
                    "Integrated Security=True;Database=tempdb")

            ' Create command
            cmd = New SqlCommand("" & ControlChars.CrLf & _
            "select" & ControlChars.CrLf & "textfile," & _
            ControlChars.CrLf & "textdata" & _
            ControlChars.CrLf & "from" & _
            ControlChars.CrLf & "texttable" & _
            ControlChars.CrLf & "", conn)

            ' Open connection
            conn.Open()
```

```vb
    ' Create data reader
    dr = cmd.ExecuteReader()
End Sub
Public Function GetRow() As Boolean
    Dim textSize As Long
    Dim bufferSize As Integer = 100
    Dim charsRead As Long
    textChars = New Char(bufferSize - 1) {}

    If dr.Read() Then
        ' Get file name
        textFile = dr.GetString(0)
        Console.WriteLine("------ start of file:")
        Console.WriteLine(textFile)
        textSize = dr.GetChars(1, 0, Nothing, 0, 0)
        Console.WriteLine("--- size of text: {0} characters -----", _
        textSize)
        Console.WriteLine("--- first 100 characters in text -----")
        charsRead = dr.GetChars(1, 0, textChars, 0, 100)
        Console.WriteLine(New String(textChars))
        Console.WriteLine("--- last 100 characters in text -----")
        charsRead = dr.GetChars(1, textSize - 100, textChars, 0, 100)
        Console.WriteLine(New String(textChars))

        Return True
    Else
        Return False
    End If
End Function

Public Sub endRetrieval()
    ' Close the reader and the connection.
    dr.Close()
    conn.Close()
    Console.WriteLine("Press Any Key to Continue...........")
    Console.ReadLine()

End Sub
Shared Sub Main()
    Dim rt As RetrieveText = Nothing
    Try
        rt = New RetrieveText()
```

```
                 Do While rt.GetRow() = True
                     Console.WriteLine("----- end of file:")
                     Console.WriteLine(rt.textFile)
                     Console.WriteLine("==========================")
                 Loop
            Catch ex As SqlException
                 Console.WriteLine(ex.ToString())
            Finally
                 rt.endRetrieval()
            End Try
        End Sub
    End Class
End Namespace
```

3. Make RetrieveText the startup project and run it by pressing Ctrl+F5. You should see the results in Figure 18-6.

Figure 18-6. *Retrieving text from a table*

How It Works

After querying the database:

```
' Create command
cmd = New SqlCommand("" & ControlChars.CrLf & _
"select" & ControlChars.CrLf & "textfile," & _
ControlChars.CrLf & "textdata" & _
ControlChars.CrLf & "from" & _
ControlChars.CrLf & "texttable" & _
ControlChars.CrLf & "", conn)
```

```
' Open connection
conn.Open()

' Create data reader
dr = cmd.ExecuteReader()
```

you loop through the result set (but here there is only one row), get the file name from the table with GetString(), and print it to show which file is displayed. You then call GetChars() with a null character array to get the size of the VARCHAR(MAX) column:

```
If dr.Read() Then
                ' Get file name
                textFile = dr.GetString(0)
                Console.WriteLine("------ start of file:")
                Console.WriteLine(textFile)
                textSize = dr.GetChars(1, 0, Nothing, 0, 0)
                Console.WriteLine("--- size of text: {0} characters -----", _
                textSize)
                Console.WriteLine("--- first 100 characters in text -----")
                charsRead = dr.GetChars(1, 0, textChars, 0, 100)
                Console.WriteLine(New String(textChars))
                Console.WriteLine("--- last 100 characters in text -----")
                charsRead = dr.GetChars(1, textSize - 100, textChars, 0, 100)
                Console.WriteLine(New String(textChars))

                Return True
        Else
                Return False
```

Rather than print the whole file, you display the first 100 bytes, using GetChars() to extract a substring. You do the same thing with the last 100 characters.

Otherwise, this program is like any other that retrieves and displays database character data.

Summary

In this chapter, you explored SQL Server's text and binary data types. You also practiced storing and retrieving binary and text data using data types for SQL Server large objects and ADO.NET.

In the next chapter, you will learn about the most exciting feature of .NET 3.5: Language Integrated Query (LINQ).

■ ■ ■

Using LINQ

Writing software means that you have to have a database sitting at the back end, and most of the time goes into writing queries to retrieve and manipulate data. Whenever someone talks about data, we tend to only think of the information that is contained in a relational database or in an XML document.

The kind of data access that we had prior to the release of .NET 3.5 was only meant for or limited to accessing data that resides in traditional data sources as the two just mentioned. But with the release of .NET 3.5, which has Language Integrated Query (LINQ) incorporated into it, it is now possible to deal with data residing beyond the traditional homes of information storage. For instance, you can query a generic `List()` type containing a few hundred integer values and write a LINQ expression to retrieve the subset that meets your criterion— for example, either even or odd.

The LINQ feature, as you may have gathered, is one of the major differences between .NET 3.0 and .NET 3.5. LINQ is a set of features in Visual Studio 2008 that extends powerful query capabilities into the language syntax of C# and VB .NET.

LINQ introduces a standard, unified, easy-to-learn approach for querying and modifying data, and can be extended to support potentially any type of data store. Visual Studio 2008 includes LINQ provider assemblies that enable the use of LINQ queries with various types of data sources including relational data, XML, and in-memory data structures.

In this chapter, we'll cover the following:

- Introduction to LINQ

- Architecture of LINQ

- LINQ project structure

- Using LINQ to Objects

- Using LINQ to SQL

- Using LINQ to XML

Introduction to LINQ

LINQ is an innovation that Microsoft made with the release of Visual Studio 2008 and .NET Framework version 3.5 that promises to revolutionize the way that developers have been working with data before the release of .NET 3.5. As we mentioned previously, LINQ introduces the standard and unified concept of querying various types of data sources falling in the range of relational databases, XML documents, and even in-memory data structures. LINQ supports all these types of data stores with the help of LINQ query expressions of first-class language constructs in Visual Basic 2008.

LINQ offers the following advantages:

- LINQ offers common syntax for querying any type of data source; for example, you can query an XML document in the same way as you query a SQL database, an ADO.NET dataset, an in-memory collection, or any other remote or local data source that you have chosen to connect to and access by using LINQ.

- LINQ bridges the gap and strengthens the connection between relational data and the object-oriented world.

- LINQ speeds development time by catching many errors at compile time and including IntelliSense and debugging support.

- LINQ query expressions (unlike traditional SQL statements) are strongly typed.

■**Note** Strongly typed expressions ensure access to values as the correct type at compile time and so prevent type mismatch errors being caught when the code is compiled rather than at runtime.

As discussed in Chapter 2 as well, .NET 3.5 assemblies are green bit assemblies and can be found in the C:\Program Files\Reference Assemblies\Microsoft\Framework\v3.5 folder. The LINQ assemblies provide all the functionality of accessing various types of data stores under one umbrella. The core LINQ assemblies are listed in Table 19-1.

Table 19-1. *Core LINQ Assemblies*

Assembly Name	Description
System.LINQ	Provides classes and interfaces that support LINQ queries
System.Collections.Generic	Allows users to create strongly typed collections that provide better type safety and performance than nongeneric strongly typed collections (LINQ to Objects)
System.Data.LINQ	Provides the functionality to use LINQ to access relational databases (LINQ to SQL)
System.XML.LINQ	Provides functionality for accessing XML documents using LINQ (LINQ to XML)
System.Data.Linq.Mapping	Designates a class as an entity class associated with a database

---

■**Note** Though it's called Language Integrated *Query*, LINQ can be used to update database data. We'll only cover simple queries here to give you your first taste of LINQ, but LINQ is a general-purpose facility for accessing data. In many respects, it's the future of ADO.NET. For a concise but comprehensive introduction to LINQ, see Fabio Claudio Ferracchiati's *LINQ for Visual BASIC 2005* (Apress, 2006) or have a look at the LINQ Project site at http://msdn2.microsoft.com/en-us/netframework/aa904594.aspx.

Architecture of LINQ

LINQ consists of three major components:

- LINQ to Objects

- LINQ to ADO.NET, which includes

  - LINQ to SQL (formerly called DLinq)

  - LINQ to DataSets (formerly called LINQ over DataSets)

  - LINQ to Entities

- LINQ to XML (formerly called XLinq)

Figure 19-1 depicts the LINQ architecture, which clearly shows the various components of LINQ and their related data stores.

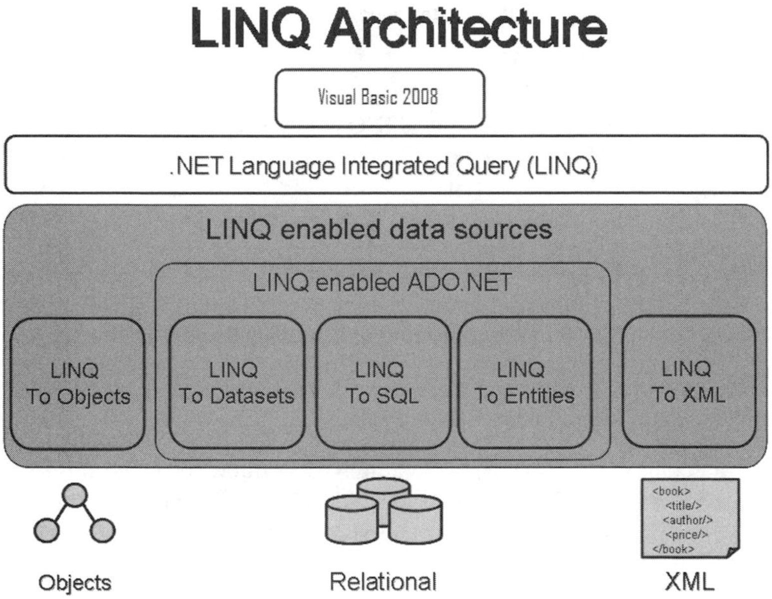

Figure 19-1. *LINQ architecture*

LINQ to Objects deals with in-memory data. Any class that implements the IEnumerable(Of T) interface (in the System.Collections.Generic namespace) can be queried with Standard Query Operators (SQOs).

■**Note** SQOs are a collection of methods that form the LINQ pattern. SQO methods operate on sequences, where a *sequence* represents an object whose type implements the interface IEnumerable(Of T) or the interface IQueryable(Of T). The SQO provides query capabilities including filtering, projection, aggregation, sorting, and so forth.

LINQ to ADO.NET (also known as LINQ-enabled ADO .NET) deals with data from external sources, basically anything ADO.NET can connect to. Any class that implements IEnumerable(Of T) or IQueryable(Of T) (in the System.Linq namespace) can be queried with SQOs. The LINQ to ADO.NET functionality can be achieved by using the System.Data.Linq namespace.

LINQ to XML is a comprehensive API for in-memory XML programming. Like the rest of LINQ, it includes SQOs, and it can also be used in concert with LINQ to ADO.NET, but its primary purpose is to unify and simplify the kinds of things that disparate XML tools, such as XQuery, XPath, and XSLT, are typically used to do. The LINQ to XML functionality can be achieved by using the System.Xml.Linq namespace.

■Note LINQ on the .NET Compact Framework includes a subset of the desktop LINQ features. One of the differences between LINQ on the .NET Framework and LINQ on the .NET Compact Framework is that on the .NET Compact Framework, only SQOs are supported. LINQ to DataSets and LINQ to DataTables are supported, and LINQ to XML is also supported except for XPath extensions.

In this chapter, we'll work with the three techniques LINQ to Objects, LINQ to SQL, and LINQ to DataSets, since they're most closely related to the Visual Basic 2008 database programming we've covered in this book.

LINQ Project Structure

Visual Studio 2008 allows you to use LINQ queries, and to create a LINQ project, follow these steps:

1. Open Visual Studio 2008 and select File ➤ New ➤ Project.

2. In the New Project dialog box that appears, by default .NET Framework 3.5 is chosen in the list of available .NET Framework versions supported by Visual Studio 2008. Select the type of project you would like the LINQ feature to be part of. For example, we will be using a Console Application project (see Figure 19-2).

3. Type the name **Chapter19** for the chosen project and click OK. The new Console Application project named Chapter19 will appear. In a Visual Basic Console Application, the LINQ namespaces are added under the References folder in Solution Explorer, as shown in Figure 19-3.

Now you are ready to work with a LINQ project, and all you need to do is add the code functionality and required namespaces to the project and test the application. Let's begin using LINQ.

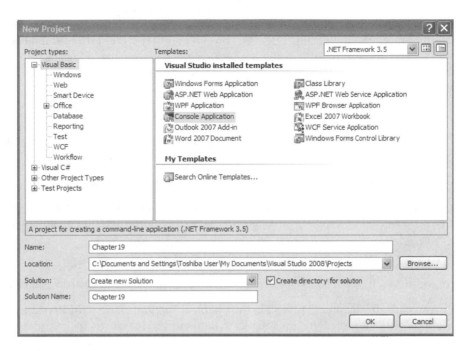

Figure 19-2. *Choosing a LINQ-enabled Console Application project*

Figure 19-3. *LINQ references*

Using LINQ to Objects

The term LINQ to Objects refers to the use of LINQ queries to access in-memory data structures. You can query any type that supports IEnumerable(Of T). This means that you can use LINQ queries not only with user-defined lists, arrays, dictionaries, and so on, but also in conjunction with .NET Framework APIs that return collections. For example, you can use the

System.Reflection classes to return information about types stored in a specified assembly, and then filter those results by using LINQ. Or you can import text files into enumerable data structures and compare the contents to other files, extract lines or parts of lines, group matching lines from several files into a new collection, and so on.

LINQ queries offer three main advantages over traditional For Each loops:

- They are more concise and readable, especially when filtering multiple conditions.

- They provide powerful filtering, ordering, and grouping capabilities with a minimum of application code.

- They can be ported to other data sources with little or no modification.

In general, the more complex the operation you want to perform on the data, the greater the benefit you will realize by using LINQ as opposed to traditional iteration techniques.

Try It Out: Coding a Simple LINQ to Objects Query

In this exercise, you'll use LINQ to Objects to retrieve some names from an array of strings.

1. Right-click the Chapter19 project in the Chapter19 solution, select the Rename option, and rename the project to LinqToObjects. Rename Module1.vb to LinqToObjects.vb. Replace the code in LinqToObjects.vb with the code in Listing 19-1.

Listing 19-1. LinqToObjects.vb

```
Imports System
Imports System.Text
Imports System.Linq
Imports System.Collections.Generic

Namespace Chapter19
    Class LinqToObjects
        Shared Sub Main(ByVal args As String())

            Dim names As String() = {"James Huddleston", "Pearly", _
            "Rupali Agarwal", "Fabio Claudio", "Vamika Agarwal", _
            "Sofia Merchant", "Vidya Vrat Agarwal"}
                'Dim name As String
                Dim namesOfPeople As IEnumerable(Of String) = _
                From name In names _
                Where (name.Length <= 16) _
                Select name
```

```
                    For Each name In namesOfPeople
                        Console.WriteLine(name)
                    Next
                End Sub
            End Class
        End Namespace
```

2. Run the program by pressing Ctrl+F5, and you should see the results shown in Figure 19-4.

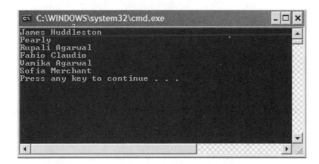

Figure 19-4. *Retrieving names from a string array using LINQ to Objects*

How It Works

You declare a string array called names:

```
Dim names As String() = {"James Huddleston", "Pearly", _
"Rupali Agarwal", "Fabio Claudio", "Vamika Agarwal", _
"Sofia Merchant", "Vidya Vrat Agarwal"}
```

In order to retrieve names from the string array, you query the string array using IEnumerable(Of String) and also loop through the names array with the help of For Each using the LINQ to Objects query syntax:

```
Dim namesOfPeople As IEnumerable(Of String) = _
From name In names _
Where (name.Length <= 16) _
Select name

For Each name In namesOfPeople
Console.WriteLine(name)
Next
```

Using LINQ to SQL

LINQ to SQL is a facility for managing and accessing relational data as objects. It's logically similar to ADO.NET in some ways, but it views data from a more abstract perspective that simplifies many operations. It connects to a database, converts LINQ constructs into SQL, submits the SQL, transforms results into objects, and even tracks changes and automatically requests database updates.

A simple LINQ query requires three things:

- Entity classes

- A data context

- A LINQ query

Try It Out: Coding a Simple LINQ to SQL Query

In this exercise, you'll use LINQ to SQL to retrieve all customers from the Northwind Customers table.

1. Navigate to Solution Explorer, right-click the Chapter19 solution, and select Add ➤ New Project. From the provided list of Visual Studio installed templates, choose Console Application and name the newly added project **LinqToSql**. Click OK.

2. Rename Module1.vb to LinqToSql.vb. Replace the code in LinqToSql.vb with the code in Listing 19-2.

Listing 19-2. LinqToSql.vb

```vb
Imports System
Imports System.Linq
Imports System.Data.Linq
Imports System.Data.Linq.Mapping
Imports System.Data.Linq.DataContext

Namespace Chapter19
    Class LinqToSql
        <Table(Name:="Customers")> _
        Public Class Customer
        <Column()> _
        Public customerId As String
        <Column()> _
        Public companyName As String
        <Column()> _
        Public city As String
        <Column()> _
        Public counTry As String
    End Class
```

```vbnet
        Shared Sub Main(ByVal args() As String)
          ' connection string
          Dim connString As String = "server = .\sqlexpress;" & _
          "Integrated security = True;database = northwind"

          'create data context
          Dim db As DataContext = New DataContext(connString)

          'create typed table
          Dim Customers As Table(Of Customer) = _
          db.GetTable(Of Customer)()

          'query database
          Dim custs = From c In Customers _
          Select c

          'display customers
          For Each c In custs
          Console.WriteLine("{0}, {1}, {2}, {3}", _
          c.customerId, c.companyName, c.city, c.counTry)
          Next
        End Sub
      End Class
    End Namespace
```

3. Right-click the LinqToSql project and select the Set as StartUp Project option.

4. Run the program by pressing Ctrl+F5, and you should see the results shown in Figure 19-5.

Figure 19-5. *Retrieving customer data with LINQ to SQL*

How It Works

You define an *entity class*, Customer:

```
<Table(Name:="Customers")> _
Public Class Customer
<Column()> _
Public customerId As String
<Column()> _
Public companyName As String
<Column()> _
Public city As String
<Column()> _
Public counTry As String
```

Entity classes provide objects in which LINQ stores data from data sources. They're like any other Visual Basic class, but LINQ defines attributes that tell it how to use the class.

The <Table> attribute marks the class as an entity class and has an optional Name property that can be used to give the name of a table, which defaults to the class name. That's why you name the class Customers rather than Customer. A more typical approach would be

```
<Table(Name:="Customers")> _
Public Class Customer
```

and then you'd have to change the typed table definition to

```
Dim Customers As Table(Of Customer) = _
db.GetTable(Of Customer)()
```

to be consistent.

The <Column()> attribute marks a field as one that will hold data from a table. You can declare fields in an entity class that don't map to table columns, and LINQ will just ignore them, but those decorated with the <Column()> attribute must be of types compatible with the table columns they map to. (Note that since SQL Server table and column names aren't case sensitive, the default names do not have to be identical in case to the names used in the database.)

You create a *data context*:

```
'create data context
Dim db As DataContext = New DataContext(connString
```

A data context does what an ADO.NET connection does, but it also does things that a data provider handles. It not only manages the connection to a data source, but also translates LINQ requests (expressed in SQO) into SQL, passes the SQL to the database server, and creates objects from the result set.

You create a *typed table*:

```
'create typed table
Dim Customers As Table(Of Customer) = _
db.GetTable(Of Customer)()
```

A typed table is a collection (of type `System.Data.Linq.Table(Of T)` whose elements are of a specific type. The `GetTable` method of the `DataContext` class tells the data context to access the results and indicates where to put them. Here, you get all the rows (but only four columns) from the Customers table, and the data context creates an object for each row in the customers typed table.

You initialize the local variable with a *query expression*:

```
From c In Customers _
Select c
```

A query expression is composed of a `From` clause and a *query body*. You use the simplest form of the `From` clause and query body here. This `From` clause declares an iteration variable, `c`, to be used to iterate over the result of the expression, `customers`—that is, over the typed table you earlier created and loaded. A query body must include a `select` or `groupby` clause that may be preceded by `where` or `orderby` clauses.

Your `select` clause is the most primitive possible:

```
Select  c
```

and, like a SQL `SELECT *`, gets all columns, so the variable `custs` is implicitly typed to handle a collection of objects that contain all the fields in the `Customers` class.

Finally, you loop through the `custs` collection and display each customer. Except for the use of the var type, which is a new data type in Visual Basic 2008, in the `For Each` statement, this was just Visual Basic 2005.

```
'display customers
For Each c In custs
Console.WriteLine("{0}, {1}, {2}, {3}", _
c.customerId, c.companyName, c.city, c.counTry)
Next
```

Despite the new Visual Basic 2008 features and terminology, this should feel familiar. Once you get the hang of it, it's an appealing alternative for coding queries. You basically code a query expression instead of SQL to populate a collection that you can iterate through with a `For Each` statement. However, you provide a connection string, but don't explicitly open or close a connection. Further, no command, data reader, or indexer is required. You don't even need the `System.Data` or `System.Data.SqlClient` namespaces to access SQL Server.

Pretty cool, isn't it?

Try It Out: Using the where Clause

Here, you'll modify LinqToSql to retrieve only customers in the United States.

1. Add the following two bold lines to `LinqToSql.vb`:

```
'query database
Dim custs = From c In Customers _
where c.country = "USA"
select  c
;
```

2. Rerun the program by pressing Ctrl+F5, and you should see the results shown in Figure 19-6.

Figure 19-6. *Retrieving only U.S. customers with a* where *clause*

How It Works

You simply use a Visual Basic 2008 Where clause to limit the rows selected:

```
Where c.country = "USA"
```

It is just like a SQL WHERE clause, except for using "USA" instead of 'USA', since you code using Visual Basic 2008 here, not T-SQL.

Using LINQ to XML

LINQ to XML provides an in-memory XML programming API that integrates XML querying capabilities into Visual Basic 2008 to take advantage of the LINQ framework and add query extensions specific to XML. LINQ to XML provides the query and transformation power of XQuery and XPath integrated into .NET.

From another perspective, you can also think of LINQ to XML as a full-featured XML API comparable to a modernized, redesigned System.Xml API plus a few key features from XPath and XSLT. LINQ to XML provides facilities to edit XML documents and element trees in memory, as well as streaming facilities.

Try It Out: Coding a Simple LINQ to XML Query

In this exercise, you'll use LINQ to XML to retrieve element values from an XML document.

1. Navigate to Solution Explorer, right-click the Chapter19 solution, and select Add ➤ New Project. From the provided list of Visual Studio installed templates, choose Console Application and name the newly added project **LinqToXml**. Click OK.

2. Rename Module1.vb to LinqToXml.vb. Replace the code in LinqToXml.vb with the code in Listing 19-3.

Listing 19-3. LinqToXml.vb

```vb
Imports System
Imports System.Linq
Imports System.Xml.Linq


Namespace Chapter19
    Class LinqToXml
        Shared Sub Main(ByVal args() As String)
            'load the productstable.xml in memory
            Dim doc As XElement = XElement.Load _
            ("C:\Documents and Settings" & _
            "\Toshiba User\My Documents\Visual Studio 2008" & _
            "\Projects\Chapter19\productstable.xml")
            'Dim prodname As VariantType
            'query xml doc
            Dim products = From prodname In _
            doc.Descendants ("products") _
            Select prodname.Value

            'display details
            For Each prodname In products
            Console.WriteLine("Product's Detail = {0}", prodname)
            Next
        End Sub
    End Class
End Namespace
```

■**Note** We have specified the `productstable.xml` file, which is located in a specific location on my machine; you can use another XML file path based on your machine and XML file availability. The `product-stable.xml` is also available with the source code for this chapter.

3. Right-click the LinqToXml project and select the Set as StartUp Project option.

4. Run the program by pressing Ctrl+F5, and you should see the results shown in Figure 19-7.

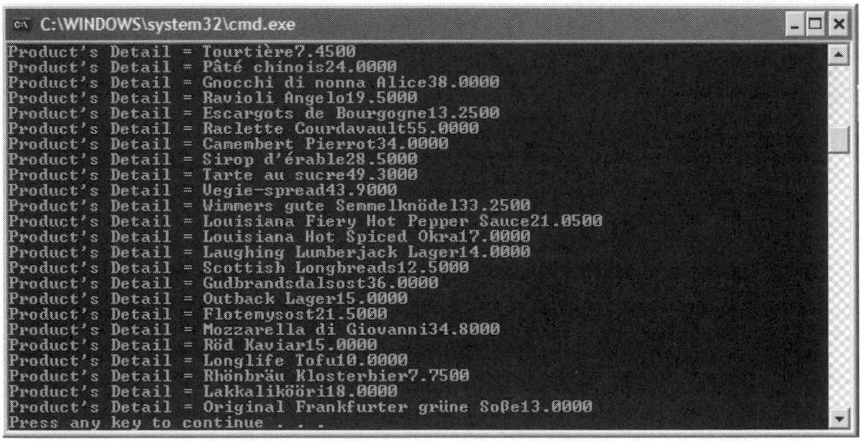

Figure 19-7. *Retrieving product details with LINQ to XML*

How It Works

You specify the following statement using the XElement of System.Linq.Xml to load the XML doc in memory:

```
Dim doc As XElement = XElement.Load _
("C:\Documents and Settings" & _
"\Toshiba User\My Documents\Visual Studio 2008" & _
"\Projects\Chapter19\productstable.xml")
```

You also write the following statement to query the XML doc, where the Descendants method will return the values of the descendant elements for the specified element of the XML document.

```
Dim products = From prodname In _
doc.Descendants ("products") _
Select prodname.Value
```

Summary

In this chapter, we covered the essentials of using LINQ for simple queries. We introduced you to the three flavors of LINQ, mainly LINQ to Objects, LINQ to SQL, and LINQ to XML. We discussed several new features of Visual Basic 2008 that support using LINQ queries.

In the next chapter, we will look at LINQ features for ADO.NET 3.5.

■■■

Using ADO.NET 3.5

The world thought that the database APIs were mature enough with the release of ADO.NET 2.0, but data access API–related innovations are still taking place and still growing. They are reasonably straightforward to use and let you simulate the same kinds of data structures and relationships that exist in relational databases.

However, you don't interact with data in datasets or data tables in the same way you do with data in database tables. The difference between the relational model of data and the object-oriented model of programming is considerable, and ADO.NET 2.0 does relatively little to reduce impedance between the two models.

With the release of .NET Framework 3.5 and the addition of Language Integrated Query (LINQ) to Visual Studio 2008, a new version of ADO.NET has also been introduced: ADO.NET 3.5. To work with ADO.NET 3.5 features, you need to have ADO.NET 3.5 Entity Framework (ADO.NET 3.5 EF) and ADO.NET 3.5 Entity Framework Tools. This chapter will introduce you to the ADO.NET 3.5 Entity Data Model (EDM).

In this chapter, we'll cover the following:

- Understanding ADO.NET 3.5 Entity Framework

- Understanding the Entity Data Model

- Working with the Entity Data Model

Understanding ADO.NET 3.5 Entity Framework

The vision behind ADO.NET 3.5, the latest version of ADO.NET, is to extend the level of abstraction for database programming, which completely removes the impedance mismatch between data models and development languages that programmers use to write software applications.

Two revolutionary innovations have made this entire mission successful: LINQ and ADO.NET 3.5 EF. ADO.NET 3.5 EF exists as a new part of the ADO.NET family of technologies.

With ADO.NET 3.5 EF, developers can focus on data through an object model instead of through the traditional logical/relational data model, helping to abstract the logical data schema into a conceptual model to allow interaction with that model through a new data provider called `EntityClient`. It abstracts the logical database structure using a conceptual layer, a mapping layer, and a logical layer. In this chapter, we review the purpose of each of these layers.

ADO.NET 3.5 EF allows developers to write less data access code, reduces maintenance, and abstracts the structure of the data into a more business-friendly manner. It can also help to reduce the number of compile-time errors since it generates strongly typed classes from the conceptual model.

ADO.NET 3.5 EF generates a conceptual model that developers can write code against using a new data provider called `EntityClient`, as mentioned previously. `EntityClient` follows a model similar to familiar ADO.NET objects, using `EntityConnection` and `EntityCommand` objects to return an `EntityDataReader`.

■**Note** You can download ADO.NET 3.5 EF and ADO.NET 3.5 Entity Framework Tools from `http://www.microsoft.com/downloads`.

Understanding the Entity Data Model

The core of ADO.NET 3.5 EF is in its Entity Data Model. ADO.NET 3.5 EF supports a logical store model that represents the relational schema from a database. A relational database often stores data in a different format from what the application can use. This typically forces developers to retrieve the data in the same structure as that contained in the database. Developers then often feed the data into business entities that are more suited for handling business rules. ADO.NET 3.5 EF bridges this gap between data models using mapping layers. There are three layers active in ADO.NET 3.5 EF's model:

- Conceptual layer

- Mapping layer

- Logical layer

These three layers allow data to be mapped from a relational database to a more object-oriented business model. ADO.NET 3.5 EF defines these layers using XML files. These XML files provide a level of abstraction so developers can program against the OO conceptual model instead of the traditional relational data model.

The conceptual model is defined in an XML file using Conceptual Schema Definition Language (CSDL). CSDL defines the entities and the relationships as the application's business layer knows them. The logical model, which represents the database schema, is defined in an XML file using Store Schema Definition Language (SSDL). The mapping layer, which is defined using Mapping Schema Language (MSL), maps the other two layers. This mapping is what allows developers to code against the conceptual model and have those instructions mapped into the logical model.

Working with the Entity Data Model

Most applications running today cannot exist without having a database at the back end. The application and the database are highly dependent on each other—that is, they are tightly coupled—and so it becomes so obvious that any change made either in the application or in the database will have a huge impact on the other end; tight coupling is always two-way, and altering one side will require changes to be in sync with the other side. If changes are not reflected properly, the application will not function in the desired manner, and the system will break down.

Let's have look at tight coupling by considering the following code segment, which we used in Chapter 11 as part of Listing 11-3:

```
'create connection
  Dim conn As SqlConnection = New SqlConnection _
  ("Data Source=.\sqlexpress;" & _
   "Integrated Security=True;" & _
   "database=northwind")

  'create command (with both text and connection)
  Dim sql As String = "select firstname,lastname from employees"

  Dim cmd As SqlCommand = New SqlCommand(sql, conn)
  Console.WriteLine("Command created and connected.")

  Try
      'Open connection
      conn.Open()

        'execute query
      Dim rdr As SqlDataReader = cmd.ExecuteReader
```

Assume you have deployed the preceding code into production along with the database, which has the column names as specified in the select query. Later, the database administrator (DBA) decides to change the column names in all the tables to implement new database policies: he modifies the employees table and changes the firstname column to EmployeeFirstName and the lastname column to EmployeeLastName.

After these database changes are made, the only way to prevent the application from breaking is by modifying all the code segments in source code that refers to the firstname and lastname columns, rebuild, retest, and deploy the whole application again. The modified code segment in the preceding code will appear as follows:

```
'create command
 Dim sql As String = "select EmployeeFirstName,EmployeeLastName from employees"
```

Though on the surface it doesn't seem difficult to make such changes, if you factor in the possibility that there might be many database-related code segments that require modification of the column names according to the new column naming scheme, this can end up being a tedious approach to upgrade an application so that it can work with the modified database.

With ADO.NET 3.5 EF's Entity Data Model, Microsoft has made entity-relationship modeling executable. Microsoft achieved this by a combination of XML schema files and ADO.NET 3.5 EF APIs. The schema files are used to define a conceptual layer to expose the data store's schema (for example, the schema for a SQL Server database) and to create a map between the two. ADO.NET 3.5 EF allows you to write your programs against classes that are generated from the conceptual schema. The EDM then takes care of all of the translations as you extract data from the database by allowing you to interact with that relational database in an object-oriented way.

The EDM makes it possible for the client application and the database schema to evolve independently in a loosely coupled fashion without affecting and breaking each other.

The EDM of ADO.NET 3.5 EF provides a conceptual view of the database schema that is used by the application. This conceptual view is described as an XML mapping file in the application. The XML mapping file maps the entity properties and associated relationships to the database tables.

This mapping is the magic wand that abstracts the application from the changes made to the relational database schema. So rather than modifying all the database-oriented code segments in an application to accommodate changes made in the database schema, you just need to modify the XML mapping file in such a way that it reflects all the changes made to the database schema. In other words, the solution offered by ADO.NET 3.5 EDM is to modify the XML mapping file to reflect the schema change without changing any source code.

Try It Out: Creating an Entity Data Model

In this exercise, you will see how to create an EDM.

1. Create a Windows Forms Application project named EntityDataModel.

2. Right-click the solution, choose the Rename option, and then name the solution Chapter20.

3. Right-click the project and select Add ➤ New Item. From the provided Visual Studio templates choose ADO.NET Entity Data Model and name it **NorthwindModel**; your screen should look like the one in Figure 20-1. Click Add.

4. The Entity Data Model Wizard will start, with the Choose Model Contents screen appearing first. Select the Generate From Database option, as shown in Figure 20-2. Click Next.

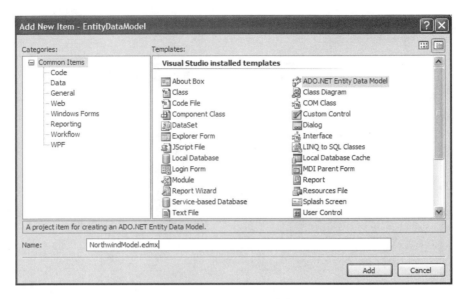

Figure 20-1. *Adding an ADO.NET Entity Data Model*

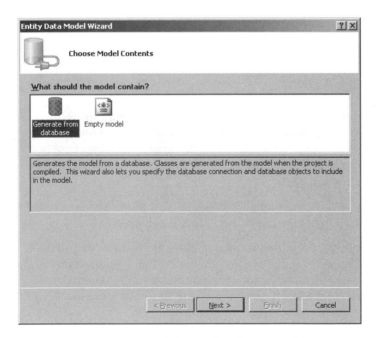

Figure 20-2. *Entity Data Model Wizard—Choose Model Contents screen*

5. The Choose Your Data Connection screen appears next, as shown in Figure 20-3. Click New Connection.

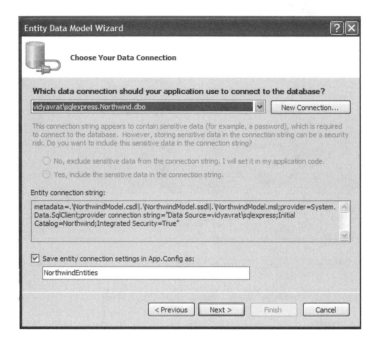

Figure 20-3. *Entity Data Model Wizard—Choose Your Data Connection screen*

6. Next, the Connection Properties dialog box appears. Enter **.\sqlexpress** in the Server name list box and ensure that the Use Windows Authentication radio button option is selected. From the list box provided below the Select or Enter a Database Name radio button, select Northwind. Your dialog box should appear as shown in Figure 20-4. Click Test Connection.

7. A message box should flash showing the message "Test connection succeeded." Click OK. Now click OK in the Connection Properties dialog box.

8. The Choose Your Data Connection window appears again, displaying all the settings you've made so far. Ensure the check box option Save Entity Connection Settings in App.Config As is checked and has NorthwindEntities as a value entered in it. Change the value to **NorthwindEntitiesConnectionString**, as shown in Figure 20-5. Click Next.

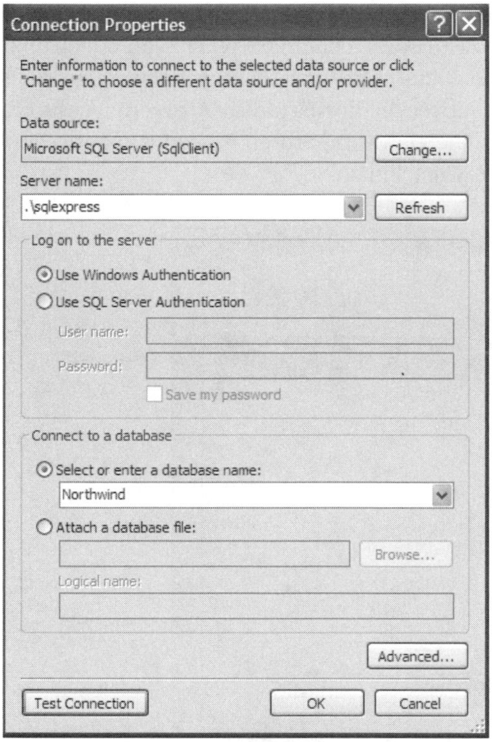

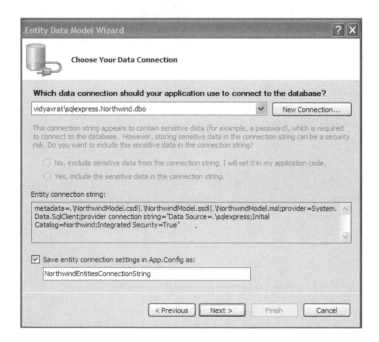

Figure 20-4. *Entity Data Model Wizard—Connection Properties dialog box*

Figure 20-5. *Entity Data Model Wizard—Choose Your Data Connection screen with settings displayed*

9. The Choose Your Database Objects screen now appears. Expand the Tables node. By default, all the tables in the selected Northwind database will have a check box with a check mark in it. Remove all the check marks from all the check boxes except for the ones beside the Employees and EmployeeTerritories tables. Also remove the check marks from the check boxes next to the Views and Stored Procedures node. You will see the screen shown in Figure 20-6. Click Finish.

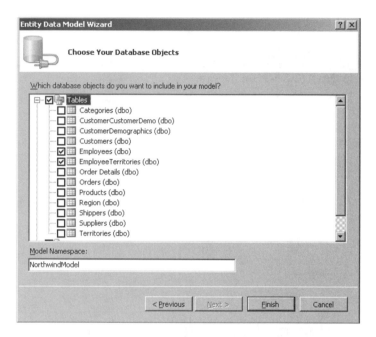

Figure 20-6. *Entity Data Model Wizard—Choose Your Database Objects screen*

10. Navigate to Solution Explorer, and you will see that a new `NorthwindModel.edmx` object has been added to the project, as shown in Figure 20-7.

Figure 20-7. *Solution Explorer displaying the generated Entity Data Model*

11. Double-click NorthwindModel.edmx to view the generated Entity Data Model in Design view. It should appear as shown in Figure 20-8.

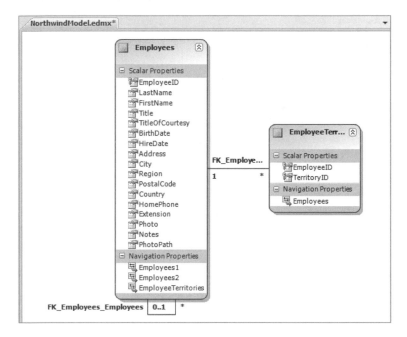

Figure 20-8. *Entity Data Model in Design view*

12. The generated Entity Data Model also has an XML mapping associated with it. To view the XML mapping, navigate to Solution Explorer, right-click NorthwindModel.edmx, and choose the Open With option. From the dialog box that appears, select XML Editor and click OK. You should see the XML mapping as shown in Figure 20-9.

13. Switch to the Design view of Form1. For the Name property of the form, type **Employees**, and for the Text property, type **Employees Detail**.

14. Drag a Button control onto the form For the Name property, type **btnEmployees**, and for the Text property, type **Get Employees**.

15. Drag a ListBox control onto the form below the Button control, and for its Name property type **lstEmployees**. The form should appear as shown in Figure 20-10.

```
NorthwindModeLedmx                                                    ▼ ✕
  <?xml version="1.0" encoding="utf-8"?>
 <edmx:Edmx Version="1.0" xmlns:edmx="http://schemas.microsoft.com/ado/2007/06/edm
   <edmx:Designer xmlns="http://schemas.microsoft.com/ado/2007/06/edmx">
     <edmx:Connection>
       <DesignerInfoPropertySet>
         <DesignerProperty Name="MetadataArtifactProcessing" Value="CopyToOutputDi
       </DesignerInfoPropertySet>
     </edmx:Connection>
     <edmx:Options>
       <DesignerInfoPropertySet>
         <DesignerProperty Name="ValidateOnBuild" Value="true" />
       </DesignerInfoPropertySet>
     </edmx:Options>
     <edmx:ReverseEngineer />
     <edmx:Diagrams ><Diagram Name="NorthwindModel"><EntityTypeShape EntityType="N
   </edmx:Designer>
   <edmx:Runtime>
     <!-- CSDL content -->
     <edmx:ConceptualModels>
       <Schema Namespace="NorthwindModel" Alias="Self" xmlns="http://schemas.micro
         <EntityContainer Name="NorthwindEntitiesConnectionString">
           <EntitySet Name="Employees" EntityType="NorthwindModel.Employees" />
           <EntitySet Name="EmployeeTerritories" EntityType="NorthwindModel.Employ
           <AssociationSet Name="FK_Employees_Employees" Association="NorthwindMode
             <End Role="Employees" EntitySet="Employees" />
             <End Role="Employees1" EntitySet="Employees" />
           </AssociationSet>
           <AssociationSet Name="FK_EmployeeTerritories_Employees" Association="No
             <End Role="Employees" EntitySet="Employees" />
             <End Role="EmployeeTerritories" EntitySet="EmployeeTerritories" />
```

Figure 20-9. *XML mapping associated with the Entity Data Model*

Figure 20-10. *Design view of the form*

16. Double-click the Button control to go to Code view. Before proceeding with adding the code for the button's click event, add the following namespace to the project:

```
Imports System.Data.EntityClient
```

17. Switch back to the click event of the button and add the code shown in Listing 20-1.

Listing 20-1. *Creating a Connection Using the Entity Data Model*

```
Dim connection As EntityConnection = New EntityConnection _
"name=NorthwindEntitiesConnectionString")
        connection.Open()
        Dim command As EntityCommand = connection.CreateCommand()
        command.CommandText = "select E.FirstName,E.LastName " & _
        "from NorthwindEntitiesConnectionString.Employees as E"
        Dim reader As EntityDataReader = _
        command.ExecuteReader(CommandBehavior.SequentialAccess)
        lstEmployees.Items.Clear()
        While reader.Read()
            lstEmployees.Items.Add(reader("FirstName") + _
            " " + reader("LastName"))
        End While
```

18. Build the solution and run the project. When the Employees Detail form appears, click the Get Employees button. The screen shown in Figure 20-11 should display.

Figure 20-11. *Displaying the Employees Detail form*

How It Works

Because you are working with an Entity Data Model, you don't have to deal with SqlConnection, SqlCommand, and so forth. Here you create a connection object referencing the EntityConnection, pass the entire connection string that is stored with the name NorthwindEntitiesConnectionString in the App.config file, and then open the connection:

```
Dim connection As EntityConnection = New EntityConnection _
"name=NorthwindEntitiesConnectionString")
connection.Open()
```

After specifying opening the connection, it's time to create the Command object using EntityCommand, and then specify the query to the CommandText property. Notice that the From clause of the query is composed of EntityContainer.EntitySet, thus including the name of the connection string, which represents the EntityContainer, suffixed with the table name, which is actually an EntitySet:

```
Dim command As EntityCommand = connection.CreateCommand()
command.CommandText = "select E.FirstName,E.LastName " & _
"from NorthwindEntitiesConnectionString.Employees as E"
```

■**Note** The EntityContainer element is named after the database schema, and all "Entity sets" that should be logically grouped together are contained within an EntityContainer element. An EntitySet represents the corresponding table in the database.

Now you have to specify the reader object, which will read the data stream from the database and populate the ListBox control. You do so by using the EntityDataReader object, and then you also specify the ExecuteReader method to return the results. The ExecuteReader method also requires an enumeration value to be specified; for this example, you use the CommandBehavior.SequentialAccess enumeration value to tell the ADO.NET 3.5 runtime to retrieve and load the data sequentially and receive it in the form of a stream:

```
Dim reader As EntityDataReader = _
command.ExecuteReader(CommandBehavior.SequentialAccess)
```

Next, you specify the code to tell the reader that it has to add the data values in the ListBox until the reader is able to read the data:

```
lstEmployees.Items.Clear()
While reader.Read()
    lstEmployees.Items.Add(reader("FirstName") + _
    " " + reader("LastName"))
 End While
```

Try It Out: Schema Abstraction Using an Entity Data Model

In the previous exercise, you created an Entity Data Model named NorthwindModel; in this exercise, you will see how this Entity Data Model will help developers achieve schema abstraction and modify the database without touching the data access code throughout the project or in the Data Access Layer (DAL).

1. Start SQL Server Management Studio Express, expand the Database node, expand the Northwind database node, and then expand the Tables node. In the list of tables, expand the dbo.Employees node and then expand the Columns folder.

2. Select the LastName column, right-click, and select the Rename option. Rename the LastName column to EmployeesLastName.

3. Select the FirstName column, right-click, and select the Rename option. Rename the FirstName column to EmployeesFirstName.

4. Now exit from SQL Server Management Studio Express by selecting File ➤ Exit.

5. Switch to the Chapter20 solution and then run the EntityModel project. The Employees Detail form should load. Click the Get Employees button; this raises an exception window with the message "CommandExecutionException was unhandled." Click View Detail located under Actions.

6. The View Detail dialog box opens. Expand the exception to see the exception details. If you look at InnerException, you will see a message that indicates the cause of this exception, and that is because you have just renamed the FirstName and LastName database columns. The exception details should appear as shown in Figure 20-12.

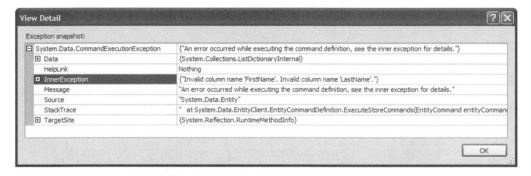

Figure 20-12. *Exception details*

7. Click OK to close the exception's View Detail window, and choose Debug ➤ Stop Debugging.

8. To fix this application, you have to modify the XML mapping file created by the Entity Data Model, the NorthwindModel.edmx file you created earlier in the chapter and shown previously in Figures 20-7 and 20-8. To view the XML mapping, navigate to Solution Explorer, right-click NorthwindModel.edmx, and choose the Open With option. From the provided dialog box, select XML Editor and click OK. You will see the XML mapping as shown previously in Figure 20-9.

9. In the opened XML mapping file, navigate to the `<!-- SSDL content -->` section and modify LastName in the `<Property Name="LastName" Type="nvarchar" Nullable="false" MaxLength="20" />` XML tag to EmployeesLastName; the tag should appear as `<Property Name="EmployeesLastName" Type="nvarchar" Nullable="false" MaxLength="20" />` after the modification.

Note The logical model, which represents the database schema, is defined in an XML file using SSDL. This is why you need to modify the column names to map with the database schema.

---

10. Now you need to modify the <Property Name="FirstName" Type="nvarchar" Nullable="false" MaxLength="10" /> XML tag to appear as <Property Name="EmployeesFirstName" Type="nvarchar" Nullable="false" MaxLength="10" />. The modified SSDL content section having FirstName and LastName values will appear as shown in Figure 20-13.

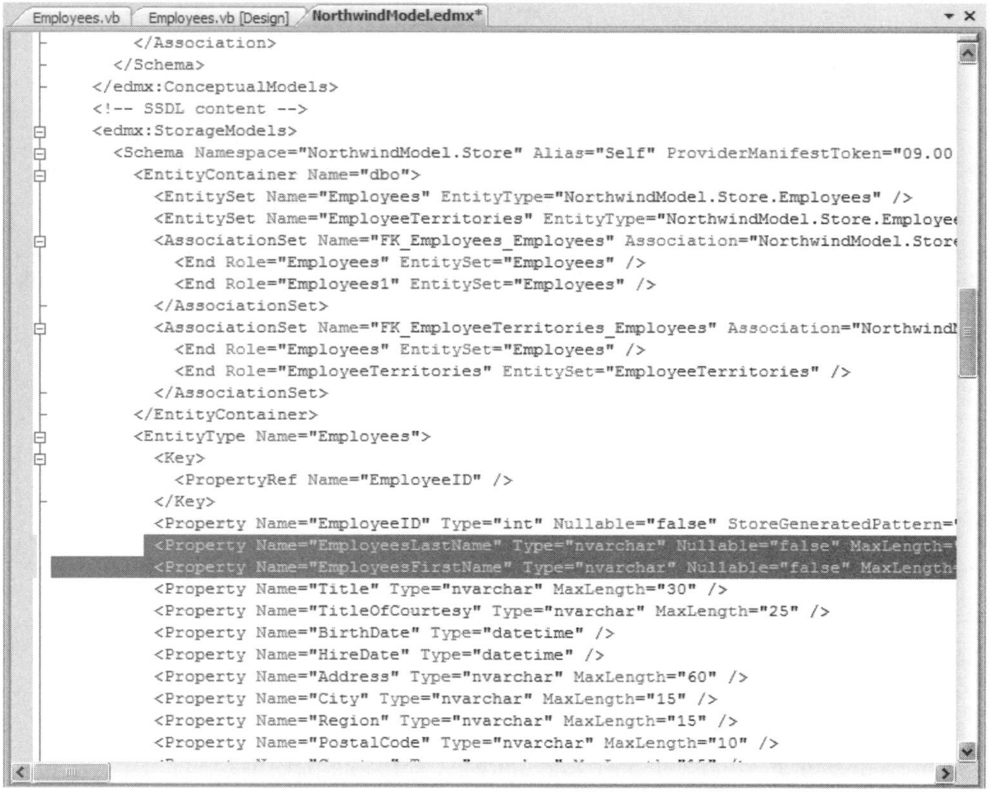

```
Employees.vb    Employees.vb [Design]    NorthwindModel.edmx*                                    ▾ ×
                  </Association>
              </Schema>
          </edmx:ConceptualModels>
      <!-- SSDL content -->
      <edmx:StorageModels>
          <Schema Namespace="NorthwindModel.Store" Alias="Self" ProviderManifestToken="09.00
              <EntityContainer Name="dbo">
                  <EntitySet Name="Employees" EntityType="NorthwindModel.Store.Employees" />
                  <EntitySet Name="EmployeeTerritories" EntityType="NorthwindModel.Store.Employee
                  <AssociationSet Name="FK_Employees_Employees" Association="NorthwindModel.Store
                      <End Role="Employees" EntitySet="Employees" />
                      <End Role="Employees1" EntitySet="Employees" />
                  </AssociationSet>
                  <AssociationSet Name="FK_EmployeeTerritories_Employees" Association="Northwind
                      <End Role="Employees" EntitySet="Employees" />
                      <End Role="EmployeeTerritories" EntitySet="EmployeeTerritories" />
                  </AssociationSet>
              </EntityContainer>
              <EntityType Name="Employees">
                  <Key>
                      <PropertyRef Name="EmployeeID" />
                  </Key>
                  <Property Name="EmployeeID" Type="int" Nullable="false" StoreGeneratedPattern="
                  <Property Name="EmployeesLastName" Type="nvarchar" Nullable="false" MaxLength=
                  <Property Name="EmployeesFirstName" Type="nvarchar" Nullable="false" MaxLength
                  <Property Name="Title" Type="nvarchar" MaxLength="30" />
                  <Property Name="TitleOfCourtesy" Type="nvarchar" MaxLength="25" />
                  <Property Name="BirthDate" Type="datetime" />
                  <Property Name="HireDate" Type="datetime" />
                  <Property Name="Address" Type="nvarchar" MaxLength="60" />
                  <Property Name="City" Type="nvarchar" MaxLength="15" />
                  <Property Name="Region" Type="nvarchar" MaxLength="15" />
                  <Property Name="PostalCode" Type="nvarchar" MaxLength="10" />
```

Figure 20-13. *Modifying the SSDL content section*

11. Now look for the <!-- C-S mapping content --> section and modify the <ScalarProperty Name="LastName" ColumnName="LastName" /> tag to appear as <ScalarProperty Name="LastName" ColumnName="EmployeesLastName" />.

■**Note** The conceptual model is defined in an XML file using CSDL. CSDL defines the entities and the relationships as the application's business layer knows them. This is why you need to modify the column names to be readable and easy to find by the entity.

12. Next, modify the <ScalarProperty Name="FirstName" ColumnName="FirstName" /> tag to appear as <ScalarProperty Name="FirstName" ColumnName="EmployeesFirstName" />. The modified C-S mapping content section having FirstName and LastName values will appear as shown in Figure 20-14.

Figure 20-14. *Modifying the C-S mapping content section*

13. Now build the Chapter20 solution and run the application. When the Employees Detail form is open, click the Get Employees button. This should populate the list box with the employees' FirstName and LastName values, as shown earlier in Figure 20-11.

14. Switch back to the Form1.vb. You should still see the same SELECT query with FirstName and LastName column names, even though you have modified the column names in the Northwind database's Employees table. But by taking advantage of the schema abstraction feature of the Entity Data Model, you only have to specify the updated column names in the XML mapping file under the SSDL content and C-S mapping content sections.

Summary

In this chapter, you looked at ADO.NET 3.5 and its Entity Data Model feature. You also looked at the prerequisites you need to take full advantage of ADO.NET 3.5.

You also learned how schema abstraction works and how it will help you to achieve loose coupling between a database and the data access code or DAL.

Index

You Need the Companion eBook

Your purchase of this book entitles you to buy the companion PDF-version eBook for only $10. Take the weightless companion with you anywhere.

We believe this Apress title will prove so indispensable that you'll want to carry it with you everywhere, which is why we are offering the companion eBook (in PDF format) for $10 to customers who purchase this book now. Convenient and fully searchable, the PDF version of any content-rich, page-heavy Apress book makes a valuable addition to your programming library. You can easily find and copy code—or perform examples by quickly toggling between instructions and the application. Even simultaneously tackling a donut, diet soda, and complex code becomes simplified with hands-free eBooks!

Once you purchase your book, getting the $10 companion eBook is simple:

❶ Visit **www.apress.com/promo/tendollars/**.

❷ Complete a basic registration form to receive a randomly generated question about this title.

❸ Answer the question correctly in 60 seconds, and you will receive a promotional code to redeem for the $10.00 eBook.

THE EXPERT'S VOICE™

Offer valid through 10/08.